Mental Health and Mental Illness:
Policies, Programs, and Services

MENTAL HEALTH
and
MENTAL ILLNESS

POLICIES, PROGRAMS, AND SERVICES

Phillip Fellin

The University of Michigan
School of Social Work

F. E. PEACOCK PUBLISHERS, INC.   *Itasca, Illinois*

Advisory Editor in Social Work:

Donald Brieland
Jane Addams College of Social Work
University of Illinois at Chicago

Library of Congress Catalog Card No. 95-71667

ISBN 0-87581-398-4

Printed in the United States of America

Printing: 10 9 8 7 6 5 4 3 2 1

Year: 01 00 99 98 97 96

1.
Mental Health Policies and Services

Public mental health policies and services represent a collective response to mental illness, which is one of the most perplexing personal and social problems affecting American society. This response involves both the promotion of mental health and the treatment of mental illness. It acknowledges that "Mental disorders are a major source of suffering and disability, cause havoc in families and the community, and account for a large load on medical care institutions, social agencies, and sheltered facilities" (Mechanic, 1986, p. 190). The magnitude of the problem of mental illness in America has been documented through the Epidemiological Catchment Area program sponsored by the federal government. These studies indicate that approximately 28 percent of American adults are affected annually by mental and addictive disorders. However, fewer than one in three of the ill report seeking help for these problems during a one-year period (Regier et al., 1993). A second national study, the National Comorbidity Survey, shows similar results: 29.5% of the respondents reported having had a mental disorder in the past 12 months, but only one in five indicated that they had sought professional help during this time period (Kessler et al., 1994).

Epidemiological studies provide ample evidence that large numbers of Americans are affected by mental disorders, a sizable proportion of whom are left unserved by the mental health system. Consequently, it is not surprising to find vast negative personal, social, and economic impacts of mental illness on American society, including the costs of mental health care, loss of productivity in the workplace, family problems, and community disorganization (Rochefort, 1989; Taube, 1990; Rice, Kelman, & Miller, 1992). For example, estimates of the costs of addictive and mental disorders range from 273 billion dollars in 1990 to 370.4 billion dollars in 1992, with more than half of these costs related to mental disorders (SAMHSA, 1994c). The effects—financial, personal, family, and community—can be characterized as the social problem of mental illness.

Society's response to this problem consists of mental health policies developed at various levels of government and implemented through public and private treatment and service programs. The history of public mental health policy making and service delivery in the United States has been recorded by a number of authors (Dorwart & Epstein, 1993; Grob, 1987, 1992, 1994; Kiesler & Sibulkin, 1987; Mechanic, 1989; Rochefort, 1993). Becoming familiar with this history is a useful exercise for mental health professionals, as it provides a context for understanding current policies, programs, and services. History confirms that "The inescapable presence of the mentally ill has always raised important issues. What is society's obligation toward them? What is the most effective way of meeting their varied needs? Should the protection of the public take precedence over the human needs of the mentally ill? The responses to these and other questions have varied sharply over time. Public policies have often blended such contradictory elements as compassion, sympathy, rejection, and stigmatization" (Grob, 1994, p. 3).

References to the history of mental health policy making and responses to the above questions appear throughout this book. The purpose of this text is to create a foundation for thinking about the major mental health issues of today and the future. Both the historical and current literature in this area reveal what Bachrach (1985) has called the semantic habits of discussing mental health and mental illness. The reader should realize that some of the terminology used in relation to mental health and mental illness is viewed by consumers and their family members as inappropriate and stigmatizing (Rochefort, 1993). In this regard, there is considerable variation and lack of agreement in the acceptance and currency of language in the mental health/mental illness literature, in professional groups, and in client/patient/advocacy groups. We have tried to use concepts that are not pejorative and to avoid terms that are objectionable to consumers of mental health services (Caras, 1994; Hatfield & Lefley, 1993).

SOCIAL WORK AND MENTAL HEALTH

Social workers have long been involved in mental health programs, with current social work practice well established in the delivery of mental health services. Clinical social workers are major providers of treatment, as well as related social services, for people with emotional problems and mental disorders. Social workers have interdisciplinary relationships with other mental health personnel, especially psychiatrists, psychologists, nurses, and substance abuse counselors. Social workers often participate in multidisciplinary teams working in locations such as community mental health centers, hospitals, and managed care organizations.

A number of books on social work practice focus on the skills necessary for working with mentally ill people. In their book, *Involuntary Clients in Social Work Practice*, Ivanoff, Blythe, and Tripodi (1994) illustrate phases of research-based practice with a focus on mental health clients. Gerhart (1990), in *Caring for the Chronically Mentally Ill*, discusses practice policies, principles, and diagnostic processes involved in serving this population. Reid (1992), in *Task Strategies*, discusses the assessment and treatment of clients with chronic mental illness and people under emotional distress, such as depression and anxiety. Allen-Meares (1995), in *Social Work with Children and Adolescents*, examines public policies and other factors affecting the mental health needs of children and adolescents; she also presents practice strategies for work with children and adolescents at risk. Each of these books includes case histories illustrating the application of practice principles to clients and their problems. The reader can benefit from examining case examples from this literature and relating them to policy and service issues presented in this book. Of special interest are books that examine the role of social workers in case management, since this practice mode is especially useful in the delivery of services for mentally ill persons (Allen-Meares, 1995; Rothman, 1992, 1994; Rose, 1992). Excellent case studies on ethnic minority groups are presented in Gaw (1993), *Culture, Ethnicity, and Mental Illness*. For vignettes on homeless persons with mental illness, the reader may consult Kuhlman's (1994) *Psychology on the Streets: Mental Health Practice with Homeless Persons*.

Social workers serve clients of the mental health system at both "micro" and "macro" levels of practice. Social work interventions occur at the interpersonal level, including individual, family, and small group treatment, as well as through organizational and community activities, such as community organization, social planning, administration, and policy development. Social workers in various fields of service, such as public welfare, criminal and juvenile justice, families and children, health, education, and employment services are very likely to have interactions with the mental health system and/or deliver mental health services. Knowledge and skills related to these fields of service are a part of the education of social workers for roles in both "micro" and "macro" practice. The goal of this book is to provide an understanding of mental health policies and services that goes beyond foundation content on mental health included in beginning social work courses on social welfare policies and services (Johnson, 1995; Popple & Leighninger, 1993). This book is intended to complement the knowledge social work students gain through courses on social work methods, human behavior and the social environment, fields of service, and field practice education.

PREVIEW

The material in this chapter provides a context for studying mental health policy, programs, services, and service systems. First, we examine the process and politics of mental health policy making and policy analysis, looking at examples of mental health policies. This presentation provides direction for the succeeding chapters of the book, in which we explore the meaning of mental health and illness, epidemiological knowledge about the nature and prevalence of mental illness, and the historical development of mental health policies, services, and financing patterns in the United States. Once this knowledge base is established, we turn our attention to the rights of consumers of mental health services. Exploration of this topic is followed by a discussion of issues related to special population groups, including ethnic minority groups; women, children, and adolescents; homeless mentally ill persons; and older adults. In each chapter we highlight controversial issues relative to mental health policy development and program implementation. A summary chapter identifies key issues to assist the reader in evaluating the present field of mental health and to stimulate thought about mental health systems for the future.

Our focus in this book is on *public* mental health policies and services, while recognizing significant interrelationships with the private mental health sector. The emphasis on public policies allows us to examine the mental health area as an example of governmental social policy, defined as "action to influence the course of societal change and to allot societal resources among various groups" (Martin, 1990, p. 1). Because they are public, these resources become social entitlements "intended to meet social needs—to help people" (p. 8).

The choice of chapter topics and the organizational structure of the book are in large part patterned after the works of Mechanic (1989), *Mental Health and Social Policy*, and Rochefort (1989), *Handbook on Mental Health Policy in the United States*. Additional references that have significantly influenced the contents of the book include Grob (1994), *The Mad Among Us*; Grob (1991), *From Asylum to Community: Mental Health Policy in Modern America*; Rochefort (1993), *From Poorhouses to Homelessness: Policy Analysis and Mental Health Care*; and Robins and Regier (1991), *Psychiatric Disorders in America*. Throughout this book, especially in the final chapter on Future Mental Health Policies and Services, we identify significant issues and controversies in the field of mental health and mental illness. This focus draws upon the model of discussion presented by Kirk and Einbinder (1994) in *Controversial Issues in Mental Health*.

DEFINING POLICY

Our framework for examining mental health policies, programs, and services is drawn from definitions established by Mayer and Greenwood (1980), Mayer (1985), and Gilbert and Specht (1986). A *policy* is viewed as a statement of a goal, or a set of goals, with *goals* defined as "the expression of a value in terms of an idealized future state of affairs,…as broad, general statements that create a sense of common purpose" (Mayer, 1985, p. 114). Policy statements usually focus on conditions or behaviors of individuals, systemic properties of communities or societies, and/or properties of an institution or organization (Mayer, 1985). Mental health policies usually focus on one or more goals related to these conditions.

Objectives are closely related to policy, as they provide operational definitions of goals. According to Mayer (1985), "Objectives represent a measurable expression of the results that are desired in a given policy or plan" (p. 137). Objectives should be stated so as to meet four criteria: "(1) an observable condition that is to be attained or changed; (2) a finite population of which that condition is a characteristic; (3) an amount of change which the policy maker seeks to attain with respect to that condition; and (4) a time period in which the change is to take place" (p. 139). A program "consists of a set of objectives, a set of activities by which those objectives are to be achieved, and a set of administrative procedures by which those activities are to be carried out" (p. 19). The components of a program are usually referred to as services. These definitions of policies, objectives, and programs guide our exploration of the process of mental health policy making and the development of mental health programs and services.

THE PROCESS OF POLICY MAKING

Policies may be generated at several levels: legislative, judicial, administrative, executive, and direct professional practice (Dobelstein, 1990; Flynn, 1992). Policy making involves the recognition of interrelationships between policies and programs. Thus, the policy-making process includes policy formulation, social program development, implementation of policies through social programs, and social policy evaluation. Strictly speaking, one might argue that policy making is concerned only with policy formulation—that is, activities related to the determination of goals, needs assessment, and specification of objectives. However, a broader and more customary interpretation of policy making also includes the development of programs, delivery of services, and program evaluation. Following evaluation, the process involves a feedback loop back to the original policy, a view which allows for changes in goals, objectives, and social programs.

This broad framework involves a number of stages in the policy-making process, specified by Mayer and Greenwood (1980) and Mayer (1985) as follows:

1. Determination of goals
2. Needs assessment
3. Specification of objectives
4. Design of alternative courses of action
5. Estimation of consequences of alternative actions
6. Selection of course(s) of action
7. Implementation
8. Evaluation
9. Feedback

While this model might suggest that policy making and program implementation follow a rational process, in actual practice there is likely to be overlap between the various stages. For example, program evaluation is not reserved for the conclusion of program implementation, but occurs at at all stages of the process.

Policy analysis is an important activity within the policy-making process. Policy analysis is "a multi-faceted process of ascertaining, measuring, and evaluating the ends and means of a policy, as well as their interrelationship" (Mayer & Greenwood, 1980, p. 13). Policy analysis usually deals with one or the other of these questions: "Does the policy or program work?" and "How does the policy or program work?" (p. 13). To answer these questions, policy analysts use various methodologies to ascertain the efficiency, effectiveness, feasibility, and ethics of policies and programs (Mayer & Greenwood, 1980). An analysis of efficiency deals with the benefits of a program in relation to costs, usually measured by benefit-cost and cost-effectiveness ratios. An effectiveness model focuses on the extent to which the program produces the desired objectives. A feasibility approach emphasizes the "political" nature of implementing programs, asking whether the program has the political support of some constituency, such as a state legislature or county government. Finally, the policy analyst may wish to evaluate policies in terms of ethics: that is, the extent to which the goals and objectives established by the policy makers are consistent with the values of their constituencies.

Another useful conceptualization of the policy-making process has been developed by Gilbert and Specht (1986). Their view of the policy process is very much like the political perspective of Lasswell (1936), looking at who gets what, when, and how. Policy design is viewed in terms of dimensions of choice, and policy making is seen as a benefit allocation mechanism. Emphasis is placed on the "product or set of policy choices that evolve from the planning process" (Gilbert & Specht, 1986, p. 26). Four major dimensions of policy choice are the following (p. 37):

- What are the bases of social allocations?
- What are the types of social provisions to be allocated?
- What are the strategies for the delivery of these provisions?
- What are the methods of financing these provisions?

The idea of the bases of social allocations refers to the "who" in "who gets what." This represents a way of examining the eligibility criteria for individuals who are to receive the social benefits. The "what" and "how" questions refer to the programs, services, delivery systems, organizational arrangements, and/or delivery strategies. Finally, there are policy choices related to the financing of mental health services through public and private sectors. All of these policy questions may be examined along three axes (Gilbert & Specht, p. 37):

- the range of alternatives within each dimension (who, what, how);

- the social values that lend support to these alternatives;
- the theories or assumptions implicit in these alternatives.

There is some correspondence between the process of policy making described by Mayer and Greenwood (1980) and Mayer (1985) in relation to the Gilbert and Specht (1986) model. The steps in the Mayer and Greenwood/Mayer framework that involve establishment of goals, needs assessment, and the specification of objectives are similar to Gilbert and Specht's focus on who will be offered benefits. The steps of considering alternatives and selection of courses of action are related to what benefits are to be provided, with the implementation phase related to how benefits are financed and delivered.

MENTAL HEALTH POLICY

Our discussion of policy making and policy analysis provides a foundation for the examination of mental health policies, programs, and services (Armour, 1989). At this point, it is useful to ask, "What are mental health policies?" Rochefort (1993) proposes a definition "that considers mental health policies to be all governmental activities specifically concerned with the prevention and treatment of mental disorders as well as with the living situations of mentally ill persons" (p. 5). Put in somewhat different terms, "Improvements in the mental health status of the population are the ultimate objective of mental health policy" (p. 9). Public mental health policies come under the general term of social policy or public policy and may be viewed as a collection of governmental goals established to meet social objectives. The boundaries of social policy are unclear, but this category certainly includes mental health policies. Still another way of locating mental health policies is to include them under the general area of health policy.

One of the difficulties in understanding mental health policies is the fact that these policies may not fit our conceptual definitions of policy very well. This is a particular problem at the federal level of government, since national mental health policy seems to be a collection of fragmented policies and programs rather than a unified, overall set of goals. This feature is illustrated by Kiesler's (1980) definition of national mental health policy as "the *de facto* or *de jure* aggregate of laws, practices, social structures, or actions occurring within our society, the intent of which is improved mental health of individuals or groups" (p. 1066). An important aspect of this definition is the inclusion of *de facto* and *de jure* policies. *De jure* policies are stated in documents, laws, and mission statements. They constitute the written and intended goals of a governmental or organizational unit. *De facto* policies are those policies that emerge out of actual practices, both by administrative personnel and by professionals at a direct service level (Kiesler & Sibulkin, 1987). Our review of the history of mental health policy development in Chapter 4 indicates that *de facto* policies frequently guide the provision of mental health services. *De facto* policies are not always intentional and may even have negative or contradictory consequences in relation to *de jure* policies.

POLITICS OF MENTAL HEALTH POLICY MAKING

Public mental health policies are generated by the executive, judicial, and legislative branches of government through a process Rochefort (1993) has called "the politics of mental health policy formulation" (p. 123). Policy makers within these governmental units have an "assigned interest" in mental health policies, programs, and services (Rochefort, 1989; Marmor & Gill, 1989). State government policies exist within the context of federal policies, with communities operating within these higher levels of government. There is a considerable amount of variation in state mental health policies and in the extent to which they allocate resources to policy implementation (Torrey, 1990). "Because resources designated for mental health are limited, different subgroups compete vigorously to achieve their priorities" (Mechanic, 1994, p. 501). Along with governmental policy makers, three other groups with political interests are community service providers, consumer advocacy groups, and the general public (Rochefort, 1989, 1993). Providers may influence policy in their day-to-day activities but are most likely to affect policy through membership in organizations such as unions and professional and service delivery organizations such as the American Psychiatric Association, National Association of Social Workers, American Psychological Association, and the National Council of Community Mental Health Centers.

Consumers of mental health services have an interest in mental health policies but usually find it difficult to directly influence these policies. When consumers are able to combine with family members and other advocates, however, they can exert a greater influence on policy makers. The major avenues for influence are through membership in local mental health boards, through organizations such as the Alliance for the Mentally Ill, mental health associations, and self-help groups with advocacy goals. Finally, the general public may influence mental health policies through public opinion, voting, membership in voluntary organizations, and contacts with political representatives.

FEDERAL AGENCIES AND MENTAL HEALTH

At the federal level, the major governmental unit granted responsibility for mental health policies is the National Institute of Mental Health, established with the passage of the National Mental Health Act of 1946 (P.L. 79-487). This legislation has served as a basis for the creation of mental health policies and provision of mental health services funded at the federal level. In 1974, Congress established the Alcohol, Drug Abuse, and Mental Health Administration (ADAMHA), which included the National Institute of Mental Health, the National Institute on Drug Abuse, and the National Institute on Alcohol Abuse and Alcoholism. By 1990, two offices had been added to ADAMHA, the Office for Substance Abuse Prevention and the Office for Treatment Improvement. In 1992, ADAMHA was reorganized by the ADAMHA Reorganization Act of 1992 (P.L. 102-321). Under this reorganization, the three research institutes within ADAMHA were transferred to the National Institutes of Health. ADAMHA then became the Substance Abuse and Mental Health Services Administration (SAMHSA).

The new SAMHSA was "designed to intensify and improve services for alcohol, drug abuse, and mental health problems nationwide, in large part by assisting state and local agencies to expand capacity and access to these services, to improve the quality of services, and to develop community-wide approaches to addressing these problems" (ADAMHA, 1992, p. 1). There are three centers within SAMHSA: the Center for Substance Abuse Treatment, the Center for Substance Abuse Prevention, and the Center for Mental Health Services. In addition to these centers, there are three other organizational units. The Office of Applied Studies is involved in data gathering, analysis, program evaluations, and dissemination. The Office for Women's Services focuses on "issues involved in providing substance abuse and mental health services for women...medical care, psychological treatment, social services, and establishment of necessary links to jobs, housing and transportation" (ADAMHA, 1992, p. 7). The Office for Women's Services gives special attention to primary care of substance-abusing mothers and their children and to the needs of minority women. The Office on AIDS "addresses the critical public health problems posed by HIV disease among substance abusers and persons with mental illness" (SAMHSA, 1994c, p. 4). Special attention to alcohol prevention and treatment policies and to minority concerns is provided by two associate administrators. Despite the presence of federal offices focused on mental health, there remains a concern on the part of mental health professionals that there is no national mental health policy—that is, "no coherent policy direction and no clear, understandable mission agreed on by even a simple majority of professionals" (Marshall, 1992, p. 1065).

POLICY MAKING AT FEDERAL AND STATE LEVELS

Mental health policies at the federal level appear to be highly influenced by the presidency and the Congress. This influence is illustrated by Andrulis and Mazade (1983) in their analysis of the impact of changes in the national political environment on mental health policies and services from 1946 to the beginning of the Reagan administration. These authors contrast the policies of the Carter administration, incorporated into the Mental Health Systems Act of 1980, with the policies established with the rescision of the Act by the Reagan administration. Under the Reagan administration, the federal role in mental health policies and programs was diminished through a funding mechanism of block grants to the states, resulting in changes in service programs, preventive services, research and training, and reimbursement and insurance policies. These national policy changes can be viewed as the politics of policy making, especially since they involve features such as

- fragmented and dispersed decision making that "impedes speedy and coordinated policy choice";
- ambivalence about the extent of public responsibility that produces "stop-and-go" periods of policy-making activity;
- confused lines of authority across different branches of government and federal, state, and local levels;
- national fiscal restraint that inhibits new federal policy commitments (Rochefort, 1993, p. 8).

Given increased state discretion in allocation of funds through block grants, it is useful to identify the principal actors in relation to mental health policies and services at the state and local levels:

- state administration, including state mental health director, the staff of state mental health system, the staff of community-based services, and the governor's office;

- state legislators and staff;
- constituencies of the mental health system, community mental health directors, CMHC board members, client/consumer groups, and unions (Andrulis & Mazade, 1983).

At the local community level, community mental health boards usually operate under the jurisdiction of county boards of commissioners or mental health authorities, entities that have political jurisdiction over policies and funding allocations. In carrying out these policies, mental health professionals may in fact make policy; that is, their day-to-day practice activities and decisions become *de facto* policy (Flynn, 1992).

The clear trend in mental health policy and services in the 1980s and 1990s has been a movement of responsibilities from the federal government to the state and local levels. This is evidenced by the rescision of the Mental Health Systems Act of 1980 and the subsequent introduction of block grant funding to states for mental health programs. At the same time, there has been an increase in the privatization of public services through the granting of contracts for services to private caregivers. In addition, business and industry have increased their involvement in the provision of mental health services. Issues related to these trends are discussed in later chapters, especially in our examination of the organization of mental health services in Chapter 5 and our focus on the financing of mental health services in Chapter 6.

Four major variables appear to have significant impact on the politics of mental health policy making and the allocation of resources: political idealism, political pragmatism, implementation expertise, and research data base (Regier, 1986). Political idealism is represented by the idea that "policy decisions are based not so much upon the needs of policy recipients as they are upon a philosophy of the proper role of government in our society" (p. 322). This principle is illustrated by "the movement of responsibilities to state and local levels and the encouragement of much greater investment in private mental health services" (p. 330). The second factor is political pragmatism, with resource allocation influenced by pragmatic political considerations. This results in "a targeting of existing resources to increase the effectiveness of treatment for specific types of disorders...rather than large service delivery system programs" (p. 330). The third factor determining health services policies is implementation expertise: that is, the skills and operations of the care providers. This is likely to involve management information systems and managed care through development of approaches such as diagnosis-related groups (DRGs). Finally, health policies may be influenced by data from studies on psychopathology, epidemiology, and services research. These types of studies are expected to produce a policy-relevant research data base.

EXAMPLES OF MENTAL HEALTH POLICIES

The most often cited mental health policy in recent decades is deinstitutionalization, a social movement discussed in Chapter 4. Deinstitutionalization has been of great concern to mental health policy makers because of its effects on severely mentally ill persons whose service needs are not always met upon discharge from institutions and return to the community. The State Comprehensive Mental Health Services Plans Act of 1986 (P.L. 99-660) is an example of a federal mental health policy designed to assist states in serving this population. This Act requires states to submit comprehensive plans in order to receive special funding. Two requirements for the plans serve as examples of policy statements:

"The State plan shall provide for the establishment and implementation of an organized community-based system of care for chronically mentally ill individuals" (Sec. 1920C);
"The State shall provide for the establishment and implementation of a program of outreach to, and services for, chronically mentally ill individuals who are homeless" (Sec. 1920C).

Some of the other requirements in regard to a State Comprehensive Mental Health Services Plan illustrate the various parts of the policy-making process identified by Mayer and Greenwood (1980). These include requirements for needs assessment and quantitative program targets, as well as descriptions of services, such as rehabilitation, employment, housing, medical and dental care, other support services, and case management services.

Another example of a federal mental health policy is the Americans with Disabilities Act of 1990 (P.L. 101-336). The purpose of this Act is "to provide a clear and comprehensive national mandate for the elimination of discrimination against individuals with disabilities" (Sec. 2). Disability is defined "with respect to an individual, (a) a physical or mental impairment that substantially limits one or more of the major life activities of such individual; (b) a record of such an impairment; or (c) being regarded as having such an impairment" (Sec. 3). This Act provides a legal recourse against discrimination on the basis of disabilities—discrimination that the Act describes as a serious and pervasive social problem. Of particular significance for people with mental disabilities is the section of the Act prohibiting discrimination with regard to a number of aspects of employment, such as hiring, advancement, discharge, compensation, and job training (Haimowitz, 1991).

The statement of the mission of the public mental health system in the State of Michigan is an example of a state mental health policy. A 1990 mission statement reads: "The mission of the mental health system is to restore, improve, enhance, develop and maintain the abilities of people who are or who may become developmentally disabled, emotionally disturbed or mentally ill and to ensure that they have the opportunity for maximum participation in the life and resources of the community" (State of Michigan, 1990, p. 3). With a new political administration in Michigan in 1991, a revised mission statement was created, stating that "The mission of the Department of Mental Health is to ensure that appropriate mental health services are accessible to Michigan citizens" (State of Michigan, 1991, p. 3). Under this policy, the State Department of Mental Health is not responsible for providing services but rather for ensuring their provision. A somewhat different type of policy was established for the state mental health system: "Michigan's public mental health system will serve citizens by diminishing the impact and incidence of developmental disability, organic brain and other neurological impairment or disease, emotional disturbance and mental illness" (State of Michigan, 1992, p. 24). A policy for community-level public mental health agencies states that they will plan and manage public systems of service in relation to the goals stated for the mental health system (p. 26). As is the case with Michigan state policy, this community-level policy does not require that community mental health agencies deliver services but that they assure that such services are provided.

MENTAL HEALTH PROGRAMS AND SERVICES

The development of mental health programs and services focuses on what benefits are to be offered and how they are to be delivered. Usually there is no clear distinction between programs and services. In the policy-making framework of Mayer and Greenwood (1980), a program is a sequence of activities or services developed through consideration of alternative courses of action and selection of a mode of service delivery. Programs and services involve what benefits are to be offered and how they are to be delivered. The program implementation phase of policy making is closely connected to the development of programs and services and strategies for delivering them. Program and services development and implementation are discussed in Chapter 5. At this point it is useful to identify some of the issues surrounding these phases of policy making.

An important issue in program development involves how mental health services are defined. George (1989) maintains that mental health services should be distinguished from other health and human services. She suggests that "mental health services be defined as any and all services provided for the purpose of the identification, diagnosis, and treatment of mental health problems" (p. 306). As she notes, this definition is not based on who provides the service or where it is provided. A central question concerns whether or not supportive services, such as financial assistance, congregate housing, and sheltered workshops to augment job skills, should be classified as mental health services. George (1989) contends that these services should not be defined as mental health services, since they are not treatment services, even though they function to "minimize the negative consequences of the disabilities or functional impairments experienced by the mentally ill" (p. 307). In contrast to this position, in this book we define mental health programs broadly, including a range of social services as well as clinical mental health treatments.

In keeping with this definition of mental health programs, the major types of mental health services include emergency services, hospitalization, partial hospitalization, residential treatment and supportive services, and psychosocial rehabilitation services. Entry into some of these services comes from an assessment of the individual by personnel in hospital emergency rooms, in community mental health centers, in clinics and offices of private physicians and psychiatrists, and by mental health professionals. Chapter 5 includes descriptions of the major types of mental health programs and services and how they are organized within a mental health service delivery system.

The diversity of types and severity of mental health disorders creates a number of issues related to mental health services and service delivery. Morrissey (1989) recommends that mental health services be viewed differently for persons with chronic, severe mental illness. He argues that a somewhat broader definition of services be used with this population, in contrast to defining services for non-chronic persons. This is an important issue for mental health service providers, as it has an impact on whether or not housing and other supportive services are offered by mental health agencies. Another issue concerns whether there should be one or two service delivery systems: that is, should there be one system for chronically mentally ill persons and another for non-chronic persons? These issues are of special relevance with regard to the functions of hospitals in contrast to community mental health centers.

MENTAL HEALTH SYSTEMS

The combination of mental health policies, programs, and services may be regarded as a mental health system. The term *mental health system* is used to describe a national, state, or local community system. Public mental health systems at these different levels are often intertwined with private mental health services, blurring the distinction between public and private service systems. Also, public mental health systems must interact with other major service systems, such as health care and social services. These features of mental health systems are complicated by the fact that the system parts have multiple goals and "are many and varied, including hospitals, clinics, nursing homes, jails and prisons, shelters for the homeless, hospital emergency rooms, health maintenance organizations, youth service agencies, and private practitioners" (NIMH, 1991, p. 36). This has led some observers to conclude that mental health policies and practices are a part of a "non-system," since service planning and delivery often seems to be fragmented and uncoordinated within mental health systems and with other care systems (Schulberg & Manderscheid, 1989). The idea of a national mental health system is complicated by the fact that the 50 states display considerable variation in the form and function of their policies and programs for mentally ill persons. A mental health system may operate as a subsystem of a general health system and/or a social services system. The consequence may be that such a system is unable to develop its own policies and services or to create a suitable level of integration with the organizations of the dominant systems (Dorwart & Epstein, 1993).

While the organizational and service delivery arrangments for mental health care may lack some of the ideal properties of systems at local community, state, and federal levels, it remains appropriate to view the organization of services and treatment related to mentally ill persons as a mental health system. Our focus is on efforts to improve the system's care of persons with mental illness and to promote mental health for all citizens. In this light, we discuss attempts to develop coordination and integration within mental health care systems and in relation to other external systems. Examples include the local community support systems sponsored by NIMH's Community Support Program, the mental health plans required in the states through the State Comprehensive Mental Health Services Plan of 1986 (P.L. 99-660), and the Stewart B. McKinney Homeless Assistance Act of 1987 (P.L. 100-77). The various strategies for attaining coordination and thereby improving systems of care have been developed at client, organization, and system levels. These include case management, multidisciplinary teams, community support systems, integrated services, mental health authorities, and innovative funding arrangements (Rochefort, 1993).

REVIEW

Conceptual frameworks for understanding the processes of making and analyzing mental health policies have been presented in this chapter. The process of policy making involves determination of goals, assessment of needs, specification of objectives, design of alternative actions, estimation of consequences of alternative actions, selection of courses of action, implementation, and evaluation (Mayer & Greenwood, 1980; Mayer, 1985). These components of policy making may be viewed in terms of policy choices or policy questions—that is, who gets benefits, what are the benefits, and how are benefits financed and delivered (Gilbert & Specht, 1986). Mental health policy making can be defined in terms of *de facto* and *de jure* policies developed and implemented at various governmental levels. Examples of mental health policies within federal, state, and community-level political structures are cited in this chapter, followed by a discussion of the nature of mental health services and mental health systems.

2.
Defining Mental Health and Mental Illness

$\mathbf{M}$ental health policy making and policy analysis require a basic understanding of the social problem to which policies are directed. As Mechanic (1989) has observed, "If our goal is to develop policies to deal with the prevention and treatment of mental illness and the facilitation of mental health, then we must clearly outline the dimensions of these concepts" (p. 16). This activity involves the definition, classification, and measurement of the concepts of health, illness, mental health, and mental illness. Before policies can be designed concerning who receives benefits, what the benefits are to be, and how they are to be delivered and financed, policy makers must answer the fundamental questions "What is mental health?" and "What is mental illness?"

Mental health professionals, consumers, and the general public may answer these questions in different ways and use different terminology. For example, discussions of mental illness employ concepts such as mental disease, mental disorders, diseases of the brain, mental disabilities, emotional problems, developmental disorders, personality disorders, psychological or psychiatric disabilities, and psychiatric problems. Consumers of mental health services may find these terms stigmatizing (Hatfield & Lefley, 1993). These concepts are related to a range of philosophical, ideological, and theoretical positions about health, illness, and disability. For example, "Medical sociologists have long pointed out that there is a distinction between 'disease,' which involves bodily dysfunction, and 'illness,' which is the patient's experience of the disease" (Hatfield & Lefley, 1993, p. 11). Mental illness, mental disorder, and mental disability appear to be the most commonly used generic concepts in the mental health field, especially with regard to diagnostic labels employed by mental health professionals. The terms "severe," "serious," and "persistent" mental illness are used as labels for people once referred to as having a chronic mental illness. Francell (1994) has suggested that these individuals "should not be described as 'mentally ill' but as having a neurobiological disorder" (p. 409). At the same time, some professionals question the use of the term *mentally ill* for individuals of less severe illness, disorder, or disability. Some of these persons with emotional or personality problems have come to be called the "worried well."

DEFINING HEALTH

Questions about the nature of mental health and mental illness can be framed within the broader concept of health. The World Health Organization defines health as "a state of complete physical, mental, and social well-being and not merely the absence of disease or infirmity" (WHO, 1948; Ware, 1989, p. 290). In keeping with this definition, Ware (1989) has identified several generic dimensions of health, including physical health, mental health, social functioning, role functioning, and general well-being. Within this framework, health is viewed in terms of a "full range of health states...from disease and infirmity to well-being...within each dimension" (p. 290). According to Ware (1989), five dimensions of health can be measured as follows:

- *physical health:* physical limitations, physical abilities, days in bed, and physical well-being;
- *mental health:* anxiety/depression, psychological well-being behavioral/emotional control, and cognitive functioning;
- *social functioning:* social contacts and other activities, and social ties or resources;
- *role functioning:* performance or capacity to perform usual role activities;
- *general health perceptions:* self-ratings of health, such as current health, health outlook, and pain.

While there are physical and mental dimensions of health, it is important to recognize the interdependence of these five aspects of health, especially the impact of the health of the body and the health of the mind on each other in relation to social and role functioning (Praeger & Scallet, 1992). Physical health usually refers to "the body and bodily needs," and mental health to "the mind and the emotional and intellectual status of the individual" (Ware, 1989, p. 290). The classification framework of *The Diagnostic and Statistical Manual of Mental Disorders,* Fourth Edition (DSM-IV) recognizes the importance and interrelationship of the five dimensions of health cited above. The manual notes that distinctions between mental and physical disorders may promote a false mind/body dualism and that "a compelling literature documents that there is much 'physical' in 'mental' disorders and much 'mental' in 'physical' disorders" (APA, 1994, p. xxi). The significance of various dimensions of health is apparent in the multiaxial system of DSM-IV, which includes the classification of clinical disorders, personality disorders, mental retardation, general medical conditions, psychosocial and environmental problems, and global assessment of functioning.

DEFINING MENTAL HEALTH AND MENTAL ILLNESS

According to Blumberg (1988), "...at any given phase of the life cycle, mental health generally may be defined as a state in which the individual is in proximate balance with the environment and reasonably able to cope with life's goals, activities, and vicissitudes" (p. 239). The measurement of mental health involves ascertaining an individual's level of behavioral functioning or dysfunction, and determining the frequency and intensity of psychological distress or psychological well-being (Ware, 1989). The question arises as to whether a person should be categorized as either mentally well or mentally ill, or whether mental health and mental illness should be viewed on a continuum of well-being. Praeger and Scallet (1992) argue against defining health and illness in either/or terms, claiming that "in reality, one's mental well-being cannot be neatly assigned into one of two mutually exclusive categories—mentally well or mentally ill—any more than one can be described as either physically well or sick" (p. 119). The concept of mental illness is problematic because it suggests that mental disorders are "permanent, unchanging, and hopeless" (p. 120). Yet, even severely mentally ill persons can, "with appropriate treatment and support, maintain a relative level of well-being most of the time" (p. 120). For other persons, mental disorders are often "transitory, treatable, and compatible with a normal, productive existence" (p. 120).

Two major ways of defining mental illness are through general conceptualizations and through specific disorders. Examples of general definitions can be found in documents of advocacy groups, in state mental health codes, and in professional manuals such as DSM-IV. An example of a definition by an advocacy group appears in an Alliance for the Mentally Ill chapter brochure, stating that mental illness is "a group of disorders causing severe disturbances in thinking, feeling, and relating which result in substantially diminished capacity for coping with the ordinary demands of life" (AMI, 1993). The Michigan Mental Health Code (State of Michigan, l990a) defines mental illness as a "substantial disorder of thought or mood which significantly impairs judgment, behavior, capacity to recognize reality, or ability to cope with the ordinary demands of life" (p. 29). The general definition of mental illness in DSM-IV focuses on disorders, as "each of the mental disorders is conceptualized as a clinically significant behavioral or psychological syndrome or pattern that occurs in an individual and that is associated with present distress (e.g., a painful symptom) or disability (i.e., impairment in one or more important areas of functioning) or with a significantly increased risk of suffering death, pain, disability, or an important loss of freedom" (p. xxi). Within this context, specific mental disorders are described in DSM-IV. We turn now to a discussion of the essential features of this manual, since it is the guide commonly used by professionals for the definition, classification, and diagnosis of psychiatric disorders.

DSM: CLASSIFICATION AND DIAGNOSIS

As a descriptive approach to the classification of mental disorders, DSM-IV identifies the clinical features of specific disorders pertaining to adults and children. The development of classification systems in psychiatry has an interesting history. Two useful references on this history are Kirk and Kutchins (1992), *The Selling of DSM*, and Wilson (1993), "DSM-III and the Transformation of American Psychiatry: A History." Kirk and Kutchins note that early efforts to classify mental disorders were made by the federal government for the U.S. census in the middle 1800s. The 1840 census used one category of mental disorder, idiocy; by 1880 seven categories were used (mania, melancholia, monomania, peresis, dementia, dipsomania, and epilepsy). In 1918 a manual developed by a committee of the American Medico-Psychological Association included 22 categories describing patients in mental institutions. Several editions of the manual appeared in the

years following, with the contents incorporated into a 1935 publication of the American Medical Association, *Standard Classified Nomen-
clature of Disease*. A new manual of psychiatric disorders was published
in 1952 by the American Psychiatric Association, *The Diagnostic and
Statistical Manual: Mental Diseases*. This manual included 106 categories
of disorders, moving away from a focus on somatic illness in earlier
classification systems to an inclusion of psychodynamic and psychoanalytic perspectives. The number of mental disorders listed in the
manual increased through succeeding editions to more than 350 categories in the current edition.

Among critics of the DSM system of classification are Kirk and
Kutchins (1992), who have challenged the validity and reliability of
the DSM. With the publication of DSM-IV, they continue to raise questions about the scientific foundation of the manual's disorders, based
on problems with reliability and validity. These authors claim, "The
psychiatrist's bible is filled with nonsense," and state that "it applies no
coherent standard of what constitutes a mental disorder" (Kirk &
Kutchins, 1994).

A different, more positive, perspective on the development of the
DSM system is presented by Wilson (1993), with particular attention to
DSM-III. Wilson characterizes the changes in classification systems of
the various editions of DSM in terms of psychosocial/biopsychosocial
and medical models of psychiatry. The psychosocial/biopsychosocial
model that influenced the development of the first DSM was based on
several assumptions: "1) that the boundary between the mentally well
and the mentally ill is fluid because normal persons can become ill if
exposed to severe-enough trauma, 2) that mental illness is conceived
along a continuum of severity...from neurosis to borderline conditions to psychosis, 3) that an untoward mixture of noxious environment and psychic conflict causes mental illness, and 4) that the
mechanisms by which mental illness emerges in the individual are
psychologically mediated..." (p. 400). One of the principal criticisms
of this early DSM model was that it "did not demarcate clearly the
well from the sick," leaving psychiatric diagnoses arbitrary (p. 402).
There was also a growing concern that the diagnostic criteria did not
meet standards of reliability, thus not allowing for evaluation of treatment outcomes.

Concerns about the nature of DSM-I and DSM-II, especially in
relation to diagnostic reliability, led to an emphasis on the development of DSM-III as a system that would allow for "the assessment of
easily observable symptoms" (p. 405). The orientation of DSM-III
was influenced by medical researchers, with the hope of giving
psychiatry a common language and a basis for empirical study of

psychiatric illness. One consequence was the development of the Epidemiological Catchment Studies of NIMH, using DSM-III as the context for data to be collected on mental illness in America. The creation of new modifications of the manual, DSM-IIIR and DSM-IV, has increasingly been based on the presence of empirical data about mental disorders.

The identification of mental disorders within the DSM system has not been without controversy. As we discuss in Chapter 9, objections to the inclusion of new diagnostic categories pertaining mainly to women have emerged with regard to DSM-III and DSM-IV. As a result, the category of Self-Defeating Personality Disorder is not included in DSM-IV, and Premenstrual Dysphoric Disorder is listed in an appendix as a proposal for a newly defined disorder.

Another controversial area has been the classification of homosexuality with respect to mental illness. As Krajeski (1993) has noted, until the removal of homosexuality from DSM-II in 1968, most psychiatrists viewed homosexuality as a mental disorder. A residual category "that referred to homosexual individuals who were dissatisfied with their sexual orientation," that is, "ego-systonic homosexuality," remained until 1987, when it was eliminated from DSM-III (p. 556). Still, there remain inaccurate stereotypes about gay men and lesbians with regard to mental health and mental illness, influenced by heterosexual bias and homophobia. Research studies of gay men and lesbians compared to other groups show no support for the idea that homosexuality is pathological (Krajeski, 1993). At the same time, treatment of gay and lesbian clients must take into account the diversity of this group and the stigma and discrimination they experience from American society with regard to their sexual orientation.

BASIC FEATURES OF DSM-IV

DSM-IV is a categorical classification of mental disorders for use in clinical, educational, and research settings (APA, 1994). For each disorder, information is included on diagnostic features, specific culture, age and gender features, prevalence, course, familial pattern, and differential diagnosis. A principal feature of DSM-IV is its multiaxial system framework, with five axes that guide the collection of information for assessment and treatment planning. The five axes (pp. 26–32) are as follows:

Axis I:	Clinical Disorders
Axis II:	Personality Disorders/Mental Retardation
Axis III:	General Medical Conditions

Axis IV: Psychosocial and Environmental Problems
Axis V: Global Assessment of Functioning

Axis I: Clinical Disorders

Disorders usually first diagnosed in infancy, childhood, or adolescence
(exluding Mental Retardation, which is diagnosed on Axis II).
Delirium, Dementia, and Amnestic and Other Cognitive Disorders
Mental Disorders Due to a General Medical Condition
Substance-Related Disorders
Schizophrenia and Other Psychotic Disorders
Mood Disorders
Anxiety Disorders
Somatoform Disorders
Factitious Disorders
Dissociative Disorders
Sexual and Gender Identity Disorders
Eating Disorders
Impulse-Control Disorders Not Elsewhere Classified
Adjustment Disorders
Other Conditions That May Be a Focus of Clinical Attention

Axis II: Personality Disorders/Mental Retardation

Paranoid Personality Disorder
Schizoid Personality Disorder
Antisocial Personality Disorder
Histrionic Personality Disorder
Narcissistic Personality Disorder
Avoidant Personality Disorder
Dependent Personality Disorder
Obsessive-Compulsive Personality Disorder
Personality Disorder Not Otherwise Specified
Mental Retardation

Axis III: General Medical Conditions

This axis includes a number of general medical conditions that may be associated with mental disorders in such a way that they are "potentially relevant to the understanding or management of the individual's mental disorder" (p. 27). DSM-IV includes a listing of general medical conditions, along with codes from the International Classification of Diseases.

Axis IV: Psychosocial and Environmental Problems

Axis IV comprises a number of psychosocial and environmental problems that "may affect the diagnosis, treatment, and prognosis of mental disorders" (p. 29), including the following:

- problems with primary support group;
- problems related to the social environment;
- educational problems;
- occupational problems;
- housing problems;
- economic problems;
- problems with access to health care services;
- problems related to interaction with the legal system/crime;
- other psychosocial and environmental problems.

Axis V: Global Assessment of Functioning

The Global Assessment of Functioning scale is used to report "the clinician's judgment of the individual's overall level of functioning" (p. 30). This scale permits the clinician to assess "psychological, social, and occupational functioning on a hypothetical continuum of mental health-illness" on a scale of 0 to 100 (with 100 representing superior functioning) (p. 32). This scale appears in a DSM-IV chapter on multiaxial assessment.

PROFESSIONAL USE OF DSM-IV

The professional's understanding of the DSM-IV classification system can be enhanced by reading the *DSM-IV Case Book* (Spitzer et al., 1994). This book includes descriptions of cases, "accounts of real patients, edited to focus on information relevant to differential diagnosis. . ." (p. xi). For each case, there is a discussion of a diagnosis related to the criteria established in DSM-IV.

DSM-IV includes a number of caveats related to its use. For example, "There is no assumption that each category of mental disorder is a completely discrete entity with absolute boundaries dividing it from other mental disorders or from no mental disorder" (APA, 1994, p. xxii). Clinical judgment is essential in the use of the manual, as it is meant to be used by "individuals with appropriate clinical training and experience in diagnosis" (p. xxiii). The use of the manual for making a diagnosis is only "the first step in a comprehensive evaluation," a process which requires "additional information about the person being evaluated in order to create a comprehensive evaluation" (p. xxv). There is a recognition that special attention must be given to evaluations of persons from different ethnic groups and cultural backgrounds. Thus, DSM-IV includes a presentation of cultural variations in mental disorders, a description of culture-bound syndromes for disorders, and an outline "to assist the clinician in systematically evaluating and reporting the impact of the individual's cultural context" (p. xxiv).

An important feature of DSM involves the use of numbers linked to names of disorders (Cutler, 1991). Numerals are used to denote various dimensions of disorders, such as the age of onset, chronological length of symptoms, and numbers of symptoms. On the whole, this classification system assists the diagnostic process by taking the client "from subjective words to objective numerals as a first step toward treatment" (Cutler, 1991, p. 156). Codes for mental disorders assist in the collection of data on the incidence and prevalence of disorders and are consistent with the codes used in the International Classification of Diseases of the World Health Organization. Finally, DSM codes are used by the Health Care Financing Administration "for purposes of reimbursement under the Medicare system" and by the private sector for insurance purposes (APA, 1994, p. 1).

Mental health professionals need to be acquainted with some special categories that are used to group disorders for policy and practice purposes. We will look at four of these categories now to highlight some of the distinctive features of these disorders. These groups of disorders are disorders of children and adolescents, severe mental disorders (serious and persistent mental illness), substance-related disorders, and comorbid disorders (dual diagnosis).

DISORDERS OF CHILDREN AND ADOLESCENTS

The DSM classification system includes a number of disorders first diagnosed in infancy, childhood, or adolescence. All of these disorders except mental retardation are listed under Axis I, including learning disorders, motor skills disorders, communication disorders, pervasive developmental disabilities (e.g., autism), attention deficit and disruptive behavior disorders, feeding and eating disorders of infancy or early childhood, tic disorders, and elimination disorders. Mental retardation is classified on Axis II, defined in terms of sub-average intellectual functioning and impairments in social adaptation, with onset of the disorder before age 18 (APA, 1994).

There is considerable disagreement with regard to applying classification systems of mental disorders to mentally retarded persons. As Campbell and Malone (1991) note, "mentally retarded persons may be free of psychiatric problems" (p. 374). In fact, "In recent decades, mentally retarded persons have been considered separately from those with mental disorders in the psychiatric literature" (p. 374). However, increasing attention has been given to "dual diagnosis" and to the "difficulties in the diagnosis of mental disorders in persons with mental retardation" (Szymanski, 1994, p. 22). Some mentally retarded individuals are viewed as having a developmental disorder determined by biological conditions. Another category of mentally retarded individuals is viewed as a "cultural-familial or psychosocially disadvantaged type, with no identifiable physical cause and with apparent environmental and familial factors" (King & Noshpitz, 1991, p. 37). Within these types, which often overlap, there is a high degree of heterogeneity of persons with mental retardation.

Mental health professionals need to be sensitive to the policy and service implications of the ways disorders of young people are defined and classified. For example, mental disorders are usually included under the broad concept of developmental disabilities, referring to limitations of physical and/or mental abilities that affect one's daily life activities. The principal features of developmental disabilities have been defined as follows in the Rehabilitation and Comprehensive Services and Developmental Disabilities Amendment of 1978 (P.L. 95-602):

> Developmental disability means a severe, chronic disability of a person which is attributable to a mental or physical impairment or combination of mental and physical impairment and is manifest before twenty-two years of age; is likely to continue indefinitely; results in substantial functional limitations in three or more of the following areas of major life activity: self care, receptive and expressive language, learning, mobility, self-direction, capacity for independent living, economic self-sufficiency.

Federal and state policies, funding patterns, and services often distinguish between mental retardation and mental disorders, while recognizing the frequency and complexities of comorbidity (Campbell & Malone, 1991; Fletcher & Dosen, 1993; Matson & Barrett, 1993). This has led to a situation where "In most U.S. jurisdictions, agencies responsible for mental retardation services function independently and have different funding sources" (Patterson, Higgins, & Dyck, 1995, p. 243). The causes of disorders of children and adolescents are often defined in terms of developmental problems, each with its own etiology associated with special service needs. As a result, often there is a lack of coordination between service organizations so that "developmentally disabled clients with a concomitant mental illness are often under-served or inappropriately treated because of interorganizational barri-ers…" (p. 243). Still, deinstitutionalization of mentally retarded persons has been accomplished through development of "less restrictive or normalized conditions in private or public community-based residen-tial facilities" (Campbell & Malone, 1991, p. 375). Federal legislation, es-pecially the Education for All Handicapped Children Act of 1975 (P.L. 94-142) and succeeding legislation, has led to special services for inclusion of persons with developmental disabilities in the U.S. edu-cational system (Weisz, 1995). In Chapter 10 we explore some of the im-plications of these policies for services to young people.

SEVERE MENTAL ILLNESS

Some individuals diagnosed as mentally ill are labeled as having a chronic illness, currently referred to as severe/serious and persistent mental illness. The basic elements for defining *chronic mental illness* have been identified by Bachrach (1988) as diagnosis, duration, and disability. While the criteria for these three dimensions are not exact, there is some agreement that a diagnosis of serious/severe disorders includes illnesses such as schizophrenia and major depressive disorder. Duration of the illness is expected to be persistent—that is, long-term or indefinite. Disability usually involves "functional capacities in rela-tion to three or more primary aspects of daily life…personal hygiene and self-care, self-direction, interpersonal relationships, social trans-actions, learning, and recreation" (Tessler & Goldman, 1982, p. 5). The use of the term "chronic patient" has generated considerable contro-versy, especially among current and former patients who feel the term is stigmatizing. At the same time, Bachrach (1992) identifies a poten-tially positive feature of the term: it places an emphasis on duration of illness and therefore may help to establish entitlement rights.

The special recognition of persons with severe and persistent men-tal illness is considered essential for policy making and planning, since the individuals in this category appear to be the most disabled and also the most underserved (Gerhart, 1990; Hollingsworth, 1994). Some years ago Test (1981) identified some of the essential treatment and service needs of persons with chronic mental illness, including resi-dential services, financial assistance, psychiatric treatment, psychoso-cial treatments, and services to family and community. Of central importance was the idea that to be effective these services needed to be delivered from an individualized approach, made assertively available, and provided over an ongoing period of time.

Programs that follow some of the principles advanced by Test can be evaluated through a quality of life interview (Lehman, 1988). To assess the global well-being of severely mentally ill persons, Lehman conceived of "general well-being as a product of personal characteristics, objective life conditions in various life domains, and satisfaction with life conditions in these various domains" (p. 52). Evaluative instruments such as a quality of life interview provide information from the patient's point of view, data which can be used in the development and implementation of mental health policies and service programs for severely mentally ill persons.

From a medical perspective, the value of psychiatric treatment for people with severe mental disorders has been evaluated in a number of clinical studies (Keith & Matthews, 1993). These studies are reviewed in an issue of the *Psychopharmacology Bulletin* (1993) with regard to the treatment of schizophrenia, bipolar disorder, major depression, panic disorder, and obsessive-compulsive disorder, as well as treatment of geropsychiatric patients, children, and adolescents. Data are now available on the effectiveness of a number of different types of treatment for severe mental illness, including pharmacological treatments, psychosocial interventions and therapies, behavioral/cognitive treatments, and psychiatric rehabilitation.

Although these treatments have contributed to the health and well-being of severely mentally ill persons, care in the community has some limitations. Psychiatric rehabilitation for these individuals depends heavily on the social welfare system, a system which often fails to respond to housing, employment training, and financial needs (Aviram, 1990). Living in the community has special effects on this population in terms of "daily hassles—that is, the concerns, worries, or events that disrupt a person's well-being and daily life" (Segal & VanderVoort, 1993, p. 276). In a study of sheltered care residents in California, researchers found that persons with severe mental illness had a number of daily hassles, particularly loneliness, boredom, concerns about crime, declining physical abilities, and concerns about money. Young people were more likely than older adults to perceive the social environment as stressful. There were few gender differences in relation to hassles, with women more concerned about physical illness and effects of medication.

Many individuals with severe mental illness are cared for in the community by family members and/or friends. These caregivers experience a range of objective and subjective burdens, especially when the ill person lives with the caregiver. In a study of these burdens,

Jones et al. (1995) define objective burdens in terms of observable, tangible costs associated with mental illness, in contrast to subjective burdens perceived by the caregiver. These burdens were examined in relation to behaviors required of the caregiver (such as grooming, medication, housework, shopping, and cooking) as well as results of client behaviors (such as embarrassment, being kept up at night, and physical violence). The researchers found a higher level of objective burdens than subjective burdens. This study illustrates the impact of serious mental illness on client caregivers and suggests the need for mental health professionals to assist in reducing these burdens.

SUBSTANCE-RELATED DISORDERS

Substance-related disorders constitute one of sixteen major diagnostic classes of DSM-IV disorders. This group of disorders has been given special attention by both policy makers and service providers. As mentioned in Chapter 1, the federal agency established by Congress in 1974 originally was called the Alcohol, Drug Abuse, and Mental Health Administration (ADAMHA), and included three separate institutes: Mental Health, Drug Abuse, and Alcohol Abuse and Alcoholism. With the reorganization of this agency in 1992, ADAMHA became the Substance Abuse and Mental Health Services Administration (SAMHSA). The title of this agency served to give special and separate emphasis to services for alcohol and drug abuse problems on a par with mental health problems. The separation of alcohol and other substance-related problems is reflected in reports of Epidemiologic Catchment Area (ECA) data analyzed in terms of mental and addictive disorders. In addition, reports on comorbidity usually focus on mental disorders with alcohol and other drug abuse (Regier et al., 1990).

There is considerable disagreement among professionals with regard to classification of alcoholism and other substance use as disorders (Cocozzelli & Hudson, 1989; Helzer, Burnam, & McEvoy, 1991). The specific identification of these disorders as distinct from other mental disorders may convey the impression that alcoholism and substance use are not related to mental disorders but are simply physical disorders. DSM-IV clearly establishes alcohol and substance abuse/dependence within the classification of mental disorders, emphasizing the need to recognize possible overlap of physical, social, and psychological disabilities in these disorders. The Manual employs the term "substance" to refer to "a drug of abuse, a medication, or a toxin" (APA, 1994, p. 175). Substance-related disorders include substance use (dependence/abuse) and substance-induced disorders. Included within this framework are criteria for classifying alcohol-related disorders and other substance-related disorders. In addition, the Manual recognizes that substance-induced disorders and related disorders "cause a variety of symptoms that are characteristics of other mental disorders," such as psychotic disorders, mood disorders, and anxiety disorders (p. 192).

DUAL DIAGNOSIS

Dual diagnosis refers to "the concurrence of two separate diagnostic entities in one person" (Slaby, 1991, p. 3). The term *comorbidity* is used in epidemiological studies to describe this concurrence. While *dual diagnosis* may be used in reference to any two illnesses, the most frequent usage is in regard to a psychiatric disorder along with alcohol abuse/dependence and/or drug abuse/dependence (Lehman, Myers, & Corty, 1989; Minkoff & Drake, 1991). Among the most common of these concurrent illnesses are combinations of alcoholism or other substance abuse with affective disorders, schizophrenia, panic disorder, and antisocial personality (Coryell, 1991).

Because of recognition of high rates of comorbid disorders, increased attention has been given to the diagnostic process and the criteria for classifying these disorders (Lehman et al., 1989). There is usually some effort to identify one illness as "major" and the other as "minor," or as "primary" and "secondary" (Miller, 1993). There is also increased attention to treatment approaches with regard to patients with dual diagnosis (Sabshin, 1991; Osher & Kofoed, 1989). As Sabshin (1991) has noted, "For psychopharmacology, potential drug interactions will require special attention in the treatment of patients with comorbid disorders. Comorbidity will also accelerate the tendency for psychiatric practitioners to use combinations of psychotherapy and psychopharmacology, with greater attention to their therapeutic interactions" (p. 345).

There are numerous issues related to community treatment of patients with dual diagnoses. The literature suggests that patients with dual diagnoses of substance abuse and psychiatric disorders "are more problematic to work with, frequently use emergency services, are difficult to evaluate and often misdiagosed, are less responsive to treatment, frequently resist available services, and are at higher risk for suicide and violence" (Howland, 1990, p. 59). These individuals are believed to be "particularly vulnerable to infectious diseases such as HIV/AIDS, other sexually transmitted diseases, and tuberculosis" (SAMHSA, 1994a, p.18).

Persons with a dual diagnosis of substance abuse and other psychiatric illness are not a homogeneous group. They require special individual attention in assessment and classification, as well as in treatment planning (Lehman et al., 1994; Miller & Stimmel, 1993; Weiss, Mirin, & Frances, 1992). Those who are "dually diagnosed with severe mental illness and substance use disorders constitute a particularly vulnerable subgroup with complex service needs" (Drake, Osher, & Wallach, 1991, p. 1149).

ALTERNATIVE DEFINITIONS OF MENTAL ILLNESS

The DSM system represents a medical, disease-focused model of classification. An alternative perspective, sometimes labeled a social deviance model, defines illness in terms of failure to adjust to societal/ environmental/social group circumstances. A major development of this perspective came from the work of Thomas Szasz (1960, 1974). Szasz (1974) referred to "the myth of mental illness" to convey his idea that "there is no such thing as mental illness" (p. 1). Szasz objected to the application of the term *mental illness* to problems in living that display deviations in behavior, thinking, or affect. From this perspective, illness is biological, and other problems should be viewed, not as illness, but as deviant and nonconforming behavior. This argument by Szasz is based on the view that "the standards by which patients are defined as sick are psychosocial, ethical, and legal but not medical" (Mechanic, 1989, p. 26).

An alternative perspective on defining mental illness and mental disorders that does not depart so dramatically from the DSM system is found in Wakefield's (1992) work. Wakefield reviews the value and scientific components of alternative definitions in his comprehensive and insightful analysis of the concept of mental disorder. Wakefield defines this concept from a harmful dysfunction perspective. He presents the idea that harm to a person's well-being concerns social values and norms, with dysfunction viewed as a biological term referring to a failure in a person's physical and/or mental internal mechanisms. Thus, "A condition is a mental disorder if and only if (a) the condition causes some harm or deprivation of benefit to the person as judged by the standards of the person's culture (the value criterion), and (b) the condition results from the inability of some mental mechanism to perform as its natural function..." (p. 385). Wakefield acknowledges that the DSM definition of mental disorder is in part consistent with his, but he suggests that a more explicit application of the ideas of harm and dysfunction in DSM criteria would result in more appropriate differentiation of mental disorders.

CAUSES OF MENTAL ILLNESS AND MENTAL HEALTH

The fact that a rather sophisticated classification of mental disorders exists in DSM-IV does not mean that there is agreement about what causes mental health or mental illness. In fact, the Manual avoids linkages between specific disorders and their causes. Still, mental health professionals are concerned with the major explanations of health and illness. These are often characterized in relationship to the social environment, personality development, and/or biological/genetic factors. These explanations are grounded in knowledge from the biological sciences and the social and behavioral sciences, and are influenced by ideological stances of individuals and groups of professionals adhering to a given approach. These perspectives are elaborated upon in most psychology and abnormal psychology textbooks (Davidson & Neale, 1994; Nevid, Rathus, & Greene, 1994). Various conceptions of causes or etiology of illness are related to theories of interventions, treatment, and therapy for these disorders.

Mental health professionals often approach the question of causation by recognizing both environmental and biological factors, noting their interaction, and relating these factors differentially to certain mental disorders or emotional problems. Mechanic (1989) categorizes these perspectives under the theoretical labels of genetics (heredity), psychosocial development, learning, social stress, and societal reaction. Rosenfield (1989) describes causation in terms of theoretical models, such as the psychoanalytic model ("the dynamics of early childhood development underlie psychiatric symptomatology"); behavioral model ("reinforcements for maladaptive behavior and reward/punishment histories of individuals as producing disturbed behavior"); biological model ("physiological, biochemical, and genetic causes of psychopathology"); stressful events model (stressful life events cause psychiatric disorders) (pp. 55–56).

Some of these theories of causation have empirical foundation from research studies. For example, research on disorders such as schizophrenia, bipolar affective disorders, and severe alcoholism supports the role of genetic, biochemical, and physiological causes related to these illnesses (Johnson, 1989; Gerhart, 1990). Other explanations of illness have received less empirical support, such as psychosocial development perspectives that focus on the importance of childhood development and family interaction on personality, emotional problems, and mental disorders (Mechanic, 1989). Research on development has included study of the role of stressful life events on illness, and the ways in which social supports, social networks, and personal and social resources mediate these events. In recent years there has been an abundance of research on learning theory, the relationship between reinforcements and maladaptive behavior, and the application of behavioral orientations to treatment. Findings from these studies have led to claims of scientific validation of behavioral treatment approaches.

Discussions of the definition of mental disorder and the nature of causation are illustrated in debates over violence as an illness and as a public health problem (Wright, 1995). For example, controversies arose over a Violence Initiative by National Institutes of Health researchers that appeared to "define violence as a pathology, characteristic of inner-city kids who have something 'wrong' with them" (p. 71). In this debate, biological, genetic, and environmental theories of causes of behavior were advanced to explain inner-city violence. This has led to controversial views of violence as a response to the environment or as "a biochemical syndrome that may be remedied with drugs" (p. 68).

COMMUNITY REACTIONS TO MENTAL ILLNESS

Discussions of labeling include the use of the term *stigma* as a major way of depicting social conceptions of mental illness (Link, Cullen, Frank, & Wozniak, 1987). Stigmatization of mental illness has been defined as "the marginalization and ostracism of individuals because they are mentally ill" (Fink & Tasman, 1992, p. xi). Individuals sometimes define their own behavior as illness, while at other times these individuals are defined as ill by other people. Mechanic (1989) suggests that lay definitions are often based on a continuum of goodness-badness, rather than on a health-illness continuum. Thus, "unlike physical illness, mental illness is usually thought of by the public as characterizing the whole person rather than just one aspect of his functioning" (p. 37). Illness is placed on a goodness-badness continuum when individuals are viewed as being responsible for their own illness, such as a mental disorder. There is a stigma attached to the disorder, especially when the ill person's behaviors are viewed as potentially dangerous or socially destructive.

CAUSES OF STIGMA

The general public's perception that mentally ill people are likely to be dangerous has usually been viewed as a cause of stigma. Mental health advocates generally have contended that mental illness is not associated with violence—that is, mentally ill people are no more like-ly to be dangerous than the general population. However, recent re-search studies do not fully support this view (Torrey, 1994; Monahan, 1992; Mulvey, 1994). As Torrey (1994) has pointed out, "Although the vast majority of individuals with serious mental illness are not more dangerous than members of the general population, recent findings suggest the existence of a subgroup that is more dangerous" (p. 653). Members of this subgroup are likely to be currently ill and to have a history of violent behavior, substance abuse, and noncompliance with medications (Monahan, 1992).

One argument advanced to explain public attitudes toward the mentally ill is related to the stigmatized status of patients. Link (1987) suggests that official labeling of individuals as mentally ill "transforms a person's beliefs about the devaluation and discrimination of mental patients into an expectation of rejection" (p. 97). Thus, when individ-uals are labeled mentally ill, they believe they are now in a group of people viewed negatively by others. The consequences include expec-tations and fears of rejection, viewed by Link (1987) as "demoraliza-tion," and a lowering of capacities such as obtaining jobs and earning an income. Studies of community residents and psychiatric patients have supported this conceptualization of labeling effects, showing that "labeling and stigma are associated with important domains of pa-tients' lives" (p. 108). These studies suggest that labels have a strong in-fluence on the public and their attitudes and behaviors toward mental patients. Labels also affect patients in regard to their expectations of the reactions of the public to them, leading to a feeling of stigmatization.

MASS MEDIA AND STIGMA

Major souces of information about mental health and mental illness include the mass media: newspaper and television reporting, as well as movies. As Dubin and Fink (1992) have observed, "While less than 3% of mentally ill patients could be categorized as dangerous, 77% of mentally ill people depicted on prime-time television are presented as dangerous" (p. 3). In a 1989 survey of adults' perceptions of mental illness, the major sources of information about mental illness came from television (87% of respondents) and newspapers (76%) (Borin-stein, 1992). While these sources sometimes present illness in a positive light, there is a much greater promulgation of myths, stereotypes, and stigmatizing portrayals of people with mental illness and psychiatrists (Gabbard & Gabbard, 1992). Examples of ways in which movie stereo-types of mentally ill persons contribute to stigmatization are provided in the work of Hyler et al. (1991). Common stereotypes are described in terms of rebellious free spirit, homicidal maniac, seductress, enlightened member of society, narcissistic parasite, and zoo specimen.

Stereotypes of psychiatrists and other mental health professionals are also commonly held by the public and portrayed in films. Some types of psychiatrists found in movies are described by Gabbard and Gabbard (1992) as the libidinous lecher, the eccentric buffoon, the unempathic cold fish, the rationalist foil, the repressive agent of society, the unfulfilled woman, the evil mind doctor, the vindictive psychiatrist, the omniscient detective, and the dramatic healer. These representations exemplify a form of antipsychiatry and may serve to perpetuate stigmatization of mentally ill people (Dain, 1994).

Public education has been suggested as a way to combat negative portrayals of people with mental disorders (Mayer & Barry, 1992). Types of education include improved communications with the press, collaboration of mental health agencies in educational efforts, and participation with patient advocacy groups in protesting negative images and supporting positive images. An example of public education is found in the remarks of Barbara Bush presented before a symposium on the Decade of the Brain (Congressional Record, 1991). First Lady Bush commented in regard to brain research, "But your progress is doing something else vitally important: It's helping to demystify illnesses that have long been stigmatized....to understand rather than fear...to accept and appreciate, rather than avoid." She went on to say that "People with mental illness, and their families, are especially vulnerable to stigma. Parents often get the blame when children become mentally ill...and adults who develop mental disorders are sometimes thought to have flawed characters, or moral fiber, or will."

REVIEW

Concepts of mental health and mental illness are considered as a part of an overall definition of health. Mental health/illness is variously defined by professionals; by patients and their primary groups, such as families, neighbors, friends, and work acquaintances; and by the general public. The principal features of the DSM-IV classification system of the American Psychiatric Association have been presented, since it is the major framework professionals use to define and classify mental disorders. Traditional theories regarding causation of mental illness are identified. Attention is given to definitions of mental illness by members of the general community and to the effects of labeling and stigma on mental health consumers.

Definitions of mental health and mental illness influence policy makers in their deliberations about the allocation of scarce resources for services, for research into the causes of illness, and for the funding of public education (Blumberg, 1988). The policy issue or question relative to definitions of health/illness concerns priorities given to the use of resources and the types of programs provided for those in need of psychiatric/psychological/social help. When resources are limited, will services be provided to people with less severe emotional problems of living as well as those who suffer from severe and persistent mental illness? This policy decision depends in part on how mental illness and mental health are defined. When causation of mental illness is considered, an important policy question relates to the choices in the allocation of resources—that is, to programs that focus on changing the social environment and/or on changing the individual.

Case Study: Sheila Allen

Troubles for Sheila Allen, a 20-year-old airline flight attendant, began in March of 1978 when her legs gave out while she was dancing. In the next several months her legs continued to hurt, followed by pain and weakness in her arms and a general tired feeling. Visits to doctors, including a family doctor, an orthopedic specialist, a chiropractor, a psychologist, and a psychiatrist, revealed no physical basis for her health problems. Various medicines were prescribed, but none seemed to improve her condition. She continued to obtain medical care from an internist, a neurologist, and several psychiatrists, all of whom agreed that her problem was psychosomatic.

Finally, in October of 1978, Sheila decided that "the best way I could get hospitalized was to talk depression and suicide." A friend took her to a community hospital where she "asked to be admitted for psychiatric help." Her name, she said, was Sheila Allen, her age was 24, and her complaint (as later interpreted and standardized and noted on her chart) was bizarre behavior, with looseness of thought associations and severe depression associated with suicidal thoughts. She was admitted to the psychiatric wing of the hospital and was tested, observed, and examined for the next few days. The physician examining her noted: "She was sitting on the edge of the bed... with a beautiful figure, a beautiful face, and beautiful, wide-apart eyes. She was also pathetic. She didn't seem to have any strength at all. She couldn't walk. She could hardly sit up. She could hardly lift her arms." When the physician indicated that he wanted her to be examined by a neurologist, she said, "I don't want to see a neurologist. I've seen a dozen neurologists. I'm a kook. I'm in the kook hospital. I want you to fix up my kookiness." The neurologist examined Sheila and determined that she had myasthenia gravis, a serious muscle disease. Some five years after this examination, with appropriate medication and a thymus operation, Sheila was back at work as a flight attendant, noting that "The only trouble I have now is trying to hold myself back. I don't want to walk…I want to run. I'm so full of strength and energy."

Exercise

Read "The Hoofbeats of a Zebra" (Roueche, 1984). Look for illustrations of the interdependence of the several dimensions of health, including physical health, mental health, social functioning, role functioning, and general well-being. Identify how numerous doctors searched for an explanation for Allen's condition and prescribed a variety of medical and psychological treatments. Using Chapter 2 as a frame of reference, consider the complications of distinguishing between mental illness and physical illness, and the implications of diagnosis and treatment for this patient's well-being.

Reference:

Roueche, Berton. "The Hoofbeats of a Zebra," *The New Yorker,* June 4, 1984.

Case Study: Sylvia Frumkin

"The Journey of Sylvia Frumkin" is a study "about a young New York woman battling schizophrenia, the most severe…and, in her case, nearly untreatable…mental illness" (Sheehan, 1995). Sylvia Frumkin (a pseudonym) began her journey as an adolescent, evaluated by a psychiatric social worker after "she told her parents that she was afraid of having a nervous breakdown and asked if she might seek psychiatric help. Her parents told her she was being silly, that 'no daughter of ours needs psychiatric help'" (Moran, Freedman, & Sharfstein, 1984). However, after Sylvia made a suicidal gesture, her parents sent her to a social worker for evaluation. The social worker told Sylvia's parents that she needed professional help from a child psychiatrist. After a brief period of therapy, Sylvia, at age 16, entered a private psychiatric hospital when "her behavior became extrmely bizarre and inappropriate, indicating the emergence of an acute psychosis requiring immediate hospitalization" (Moran et al., 1994).

From the time of Sylvia's first hospitalization in 1963 to 1980, she "experienced 45 changes in treatment settings over a period of 18 years, bouncing back and forth between her family home, various hospital settings, and community residential settings" (Moran et al., 1994). This pattern continued beyond 1980 until her death in 1994 at the age of

46. Sylvia died at the Rockland Psychiatric Center, where she had been a patient for two years.

Sylvia's real name was Maxine Mason (Sheehan, 1995). She lived with her family, including father, mother, and sister, at various times during her career as a mental patient. Her treatment included a diverse group of therapies, psychological and medical, with the primary treatment being medications. "About one-quarter to one-third of the moves Miss Frumkin made from one institution to another were for economic rather than clinical reasons" (Moran et al., 1984).

From time to time Sylvia was able to work, but her illness and disability prevented any long-term employment. Family support appeared to be the single most important factor in Sylvia's ability to cope with her illness and life in the community. At the same time, her journey "illustrates the enormous emotional and financial impact caring for a chronically mentally ill relative has on a family" (Moran et al., 1984).

Exercise
Read "The Journey of Sylvia Frumkin" (Moran et al., 1984) and "The Last Days of Sylvia Frumkin" (Sheehan, 1995). In their analysis of Sylvia's journey as represented in Sheehan's book, *Is There No Place on Earth for Me?*, Moran et al. (1984) provide insights into the "key problems of providing and financing care in the community for the catastrophically mentally ill," noting that the case "offers valuable information to clinicians and policymakers." Draw upon Chapter 1 to identify the mental health policies and services that affected the care of Sylvia over most of her lifetime. Review the section on severe mental illness in Chapter 2 and examine the special demands Sylvia's care placed on the mental health system, the community, and the family. Keep this study in mind as you consider issues related to mental health programs and services discussed in Chapter 5 and issues on financing presented in Chapter 6. Return to this case study as you read the final chapter of the book, and identify the features of a future mental health system that would respond more effectively to the mental health needs of people like Sylvia.

References:

Moran, A. E., Freedman, R. I., and Sharfstein, S. S. "The Journey of Sylvia Frumkin: A Case Study for Policymakers," (1984) *Hospital and Community Psychiatry*, 35(9).

Sheehan, Susan. *Is There No Place on Earth for Me?* New York: Vintage, 1982.

Sheehan, Susan. "The Last Days of Sylvia Frumkin," *The New Yorker*, February 20–27, 1995.

3.
Epidemiology of Mental Disorders

An essential step in policy making and program development is needs assessment, a process by which information is gathered for the development of service programs and the allocation of resources. Needs assessment for mental health purposes depends heavily upon concepts of mental health and mental illness discussed in Chapter 2. These concepts guide epidemiological studies that focus on the distribution and determinants of mental disorders and of mental health service utilization (Rosenfield, 1989). In particular, epidemiologists seek to measure rates related to disease/health, such as incidence (new cases in a specific period of time) and prevalence (all cases over a period of time, both new and preexisting). Of special interest is the study of factors that may predispose individuals or groups to certain illnesses, such as age, gender, ethnic group status, social class, occupation, and marital status. This identification of risk factors provides direction for service delivery, especially in regard to the allocation of resources to various levels of prevention.

Epidemiological studies must be closely linked to conceptualizations and measurements of mental health and mental illness in order to contribute to mental health policy making and service delivery (Rosenfield, 1989). The measurement of mental illness in epidemiological research has been enhanced through the development of the *Diagnostic and Statistical Manual* by the American Psychiatric Association (APA,

1994). For example, DSM-III was used as the foundation for Epidemiologic Catchment Area studies sponsored by the National Institute of Mental Health (Regier et al., 1984). The DSM classification system was particularly appropriate for these studies because it included criteria for discrete mental disorders, in contrast to more general definitions based on a continuum of health to illness.

Historically, two major types of epidemiological research have been used to determine the nature and extent of mental illness in American communities: treatment rate studies and community surveys. Treatment rate research focuses on patients with mental disorders who are receiving or have received services in such locations as hospitals, outpatient clinics, or the private offices of mental health practitioners. In contrast, community survey studies usually include treated persons with mental disorders as well as untreated populations with and without illness.

Psychiatric epidemiology as a mode of scientific research gained momentum following World War II. Since that time, epidemiological studies have contributed to policy making by providing insights into the causes of mental illness, the risk of becoming mentally ill, environmental factors related to prevention and intervention, relationships between physical and mental disorders, and the course of psychiatric disorders (Regier et al., 1984; Klerman, 1986). Of special note are the NIMH ECA studies and the National Comorbidity Survey (Kessler et al., 1994; Regier et al., 1993; Robins & Regier, 1991). Selected findings from these studies are included in this chapter to provide the reader with a picture of the extent and nature of mental illness and the utilization of mental health services in the United States. We also consider the impact of ethnicity on utilization of services and issues related to the epidemiology of mental illness and homeless people.

EPIDEMIOLOGIC CATCHMENT AREA PROGRAM

The National Institute of Mental Health sponsored the single most significant set of epidemiological studies on mental illness through its Epidemiologic Catchment Area program. A major purpose of the program was to provide scientific data to guide public policy in the mental health field. Reviews of psychiatric epidemiological surveys conducted since World War II provide a historical context in relation to the development of the ECA program in 1977–1978 (Regier et al., 1984; Klerman, 1986). The President's Commission on Mental Health (1978) identified major epidemiologic and services research gaps in the field of mental health and illness, supporting the ECA program as a response to these concerns. The program incorporated "improvements in mental disorder diagnostic criteria, standardized diagnostic interviews, survey research design, and computerized data processing" (Regier et al., 1984, p. 934). The objectives of the ECA program were to obtain prevalence rates of specific mental disorders, to collect data on the correlates of disorders in terms of population groups at risk, and to link prevalence data to the study of health services use. Some of the principal features of the ECA program included the following:

- collection of data from a sample of approximately 20,000 people living in five sites (New Haven, Baltimore, Saint Louis, Los Angeles, and Durham);
- use of the DSM-III classification of mental disorders;
- collection of demographic information thought to be correlated with specific disorders;
- inclusion of treated and untreated individuals in institutions and in the community;
- sample size sufficient to make generalizations about prevalence rates;
- a longitudinal design that included interviews one year apart;
- use of an interview instrument, the Diagnostic Interview Schedule, based on DSM-III criteria for mental disorders (APA, 1987; Eaton et al., 1984; Regier et al., 1984; Robins & Regier, 1991).

Collection of data for the ECA studies was carried out by trained lay people through interviews with respondents 18 years of age and older. A Diagnostic Interview Schedule was designed to "elicit the elements of a diagnosis, including symptoms, their severity, frequency, distribution over time, and whether or not they are explainable by physical illness, use of drugs or alcohol, or the presence of another psychiatric disorder" (Myers et al., 1984, p. 960). Data collected through structured interviews were analyzed through a computer program in order to generate diagnoses for 30 separate disorders at various time periods, such as the previous six months, last year, and lifetime.

The first reports from the ECA program include a description of the program (Regier et al., 1984), the design of the ECA surveys (Eaton et al., 1984), lifetime prevalence of specific psychiatric disorders in three sites (Robins et al., 1984), six-month prevalence of psychiatric disorders in three communities (Myers et al., 1984), and utilization of health and mental health services in three communities (Shapiro, Skinner, & Kessler, 1984). In an introductory editorial to these ECA reports, Freedman (1984) suggested that "Policy makers can now, with some confidence, know where to focus attention. The data bank of the ECA can indeed be appropriately helpful in considerations of health ser-vice needs, health finances, or in public health or professional educa-tional or manpower needs" (p. 933). Additional reports based on ECA data have focused on special topics, such as psychiatric diagnoses of medical service users (Kessler et al., 1987), service contacts with health professionals (Leaf et al., 1985), comparisions of utilization of mental health services of Mexican-Americans and non-Hispanic whites (Hough et al., 1987), and the relationship between psychiatric disorders and violence (Swanson et al., 1990).

More recently, the major findings of the initial ECA studies have been reported in *Psychiatric Disorders in America* (Robins & Regier, 1991). This book includes a chapter on the procedures used in the ECA studies, an overview of disorders based on data from five sites, as well as chapters using data about specific disorders, such as schizophrenic disorders, affective disorders, alcohol abuse and dependence, syn-dromes of drug abuse and dependence, panic and phobia, generalized anxiety disorder, obsessive-compulsive disorder, somatization disorder, antisocial personality, and cognitive impairment.

Data used for the studies cited above were obtained in the first wave of interviews with adults in the five study sites during the peri-od from 1980 to 1985. Data were also collected in a second wave of in-terviews one year after the initial interviews. We draw upon both sets of studies—those using wave 1 data and those using wave 1 and wave 2 data—in presenting a picture of the prevalence of mental disorders in the United States. Our consideration of prevalence of specific disor-ders is based on wave 1 data analyzed by Robins, Locke, and Regier (1991) in a chapter of *Psychiatric Disorders in America* (Robins & Regier, 1991), and wave 2 data from reports by Bourdon et al. (1994), Regier et al. (1993), and Narrow et al. (1993). Data presented in this chapter per-tain to adults. At present, there are no comparable data on the preva-lence of mental disorders in children and adolescents or on their use of mental health services. However, NIMH is currently funding a research study on mental disorders in children and adolescents that will inform the development of mental health policy for this population (Bourdon et al., 1994).

OVERALL PREVALENCE OF DISORDERS

ECA wave 1 findings estimated that approximately 20% of the Amer-ican adult population had an active mental disorder within one year of the time of interview, and approximately 32% had a mental disorder within their lifetime (Robins et al., 1991). ECA wave 2 findings, collected one year after wave 1 interviews, indicated rates of active mental and addictive disorders to be 28.1% (Regier et al., 1993; Bourdon et al., 1994). Based on 1990 census data, this estimate constitutes approximately 51.3 million adults, with 40.4 million of this group affected by a nonaddictive mental disorder (Bourdon et al., 1994). Wave 2 data generated the finding that new and recurrent cases constitute a one-year incidence rate of 12.3%. Other selected results included the following:

- one-third of those with an addictive disorder also suffered from a comorbid mental disorder in the same year;
- addictive conditions appear to be episodic as indicated by the onset of more new cases during the year than were diagnosed at wave 1;
- schizophrenia shows a more chronic course…more than twice as many had the disorder at wave 1 as suffered a new or recurrent onset of the disorder;
- unipolar affective disorder appears to be the most episodic of the affective disorders;
- the phobic disorders, which had the highest prevalence rate of any specific diagnosis, show a chronicity level somewhere in between that of the addictive disorders and schizophrenia;
- antisocial personality shows a relatively high one-year incidence rate of one percent and an annual prevalence rate of 1.5 percent;
- cognitive impairment status improved over the year for nearly half (0.8) percent of the 1.7 percent with cognitive dysfunction at wave 1, while 0.9 percent continued with the same level of cognitive function (Bourdon et al., 1994, p. 24).

Of special interest to mental health policy makers and program planners are findings on the association between group membership and psychiatric disorder. While the ECA findings do not establish causal relationships, they display some interesting associations between disorders and demographic and social factors. In gender comparisons, wave 1 data show that men are more likely than women to have had a lifetime disorder (36% compared to 30%). However, there were no gender differences in reports of disorders during the past year (20% for both groups). The data on age groups present a surprising finding that younger persons had somewhat higher rates of mental disorder than older persons, both in terms of lifetime rates and active case rates. Various possible explanations for this finding have been examined, such as older adults attributing symptoms of mental disorder to physical illness, or lack of recall of symptoms. However, none of these artifacts seemed to account for the general age findings (Robins et al., 1991). When ethnic groups were compared, African-Americans had higher active and lifetime rates than non-Hispanic whites or Hispanics, with Hispanics second highest, although not significantly different from either African-Americans or other whites.

ECA wave 1 data were collected on the respondent's own current educational level, income, and occupation. Relationships of these factors to the presence of mental disorders are difficult to establish, since they may be risk factors (causes) or consequences of mental disorder. ECA data show that education is related to mental disorder in that individuals not completing high school had higher active rates (23%, as compared to 18%) and higher lifetime rates (36%, as compared to 30%). When indicators of poverty are used, individuals on welfare or receiving disability payments from Social Security were more likely than other persons to have a mental disorder. High rates of disorder were also found among men who had a history of unemployment. Marital status was found to be related to both lifetime and active disorders, with higher rates among individuals who were separated or divorced, or had cohabited without marriage.

PREVALENCE OF SPECIFIC DISORDERS

ECA wave 1 data provide a picture of the prevalence of specific mental disorders. Disorders with lifetime rates higher than 10% and active rates higher than 5% are phobias (14.3% lifetime, 8.8% active) and alcohol abuse/dependence (13.8%, 6.3%). These disorders were the most common of active disorders in wave 2, with a rate of 10.9% for phobias and 7.4% for alcohol abuse/dependence (Regier et al., 1993). Other wave 1 and wave 2 common disorders were generalized anxiety, major depressive episode, and drug abuse/dependence (Robins et al., 1991; Regier et al., 1993).

ECA wave 1 data show that the rates of specific mental disorders differ in terms of gender, age, education, ethnic group membership, job status, and marital status (Robins et al., 1991). Men's lifetime rates are higher than women's for alcohol abuse and antisocial personality; lower than women's for somatization disorder, obsessive-compulsive disorder, and major depressive episode. For active disorder rates, men were higher than women for antisocial personality, drug abuse/dependence, and alcohol abuse/dependence, while women were higher for somatization, depressive episode, generalized anxiety, and panic/phobia. Findings on age groups show that the younger (lower half) cohort had higher lifetime rates than the older cohort, especially for disorders of antisocial personality, drug disorders, and manic episodes. No differences in age cohorts were found in five disorders: somatization, generalized anxiety, phobia, panic, and cognitive impairment.

With regard to education, high rates for individuals who did not complete high school were due largely to the disorders of somatization, antisocial personality, and cognitive impairment. Ethnic group differences are viewed as closely associated with educational levels, so that the overall differences may be more related to educational level than ethnicity. However, the major differences between African-Americans and others appear to come mainly from higher rates of cognitive impairment. The relationship between job status and active mental disorder was examined only for men aged 30 to 64, with the finding that the unemployed had twice the rate of disorder compared to the employed for all disorders except drug abuse. There are few clear patterns of relationship between marital status and disorder for the specific disorders, except that single people are much more likely than others to have the disorder of drug abuse.

Indicators of socioeconomic status (SES) are used to examine specific disorders. In three instances, a scale (education, earnings, occupational status) developed by Nam and Powers (1965) was used to analyze data on the specific disorders of schizophrenia, panic and phobia, and generalized anxiety. In the case of schizophrenia, the lifetime prevalence of this disorder in the lowest socioeconomic class was almost five times higher than in the highest class (2.5% and 0.5%, respectively). The difference between highest and lowest socioeconomic groups held for all time intervals. When data on panic and phobic disorders were analyzed in terms of the Nam and Powers (1965) index of occupational status, there was little difference in the rates of phobic or panic disorders among economic groups. Using financial dependence as a measure of SES, individuals with high dependence were most likely to have panic or phobic disorders. Using the Nam and Powers (1965) index with the data on generalized anxiety, one-year prevalence decreases as occupational status increases.

COMORBIDITY

Rates of comorbidity reflect the co-occurrence of mental disorders. ECA wave 1 studies produced data on comorbidity rates showing that 60% of individuals who had at least one lifetime disorder had at least one more disorder (Robins et al., 1991). Similar findings were obtained in the National Comorbidity Survey (Kessler et al., 1994), with 56% of the respondents with at least one lifetime disorder also having one or more additional disorders. In the ECA studies, people with some specific disorders, such as somatization, antisocial personality, panic, and schizophrenia, had rates of comorbidity of over 90%. Of special interest are the findings with regard to the co-occurrence of alcohol abuse/dependence and/or other drug abuse/dependence with another mental disorder. ECA data show that 52% of individuals with a lifetime disorder of alcohol abuse/dependence, and 75% with drug abuse/dependence, had at least one other mental disorder (Robins et al., 1991).

NATIONAL COMORBIDITY SURVEY

In addition to the ECA program, a major study sponsored by NIMH on the prevalence of mental disorders in the United States was conducted at the University of Michigan. From 1990 to 1992, Kessler and his colleagues interviewed a probability sample of 8,098 respondents from 48, coterminous states (Kessler et al., 1994). Respondents were from a noninstitutionalized population, with an age range from 15 to 54. Psychiatric diagnoses were based on DSM III-R, with trained lay interviewers using a modified version of the Composite International Diagnostic Interview. This study found that 29.5% of the respondents reported having had a mental disorder within the past year, with 48% reporting at least one disorder at some point in their lives. These rates are considerably higher than the ECA wave 1 estimates of 20% (one year) and 32% (lifetime) rates, but similar to wave 2 reports of 28.1% for active disorders. A rather dramatic finding of the National Comorbidity Survey was the fact that about 14% of the population have three or more lifetime disorders. The researchers described this group as having a pileup of problems and most likely to be low-income, low-educated, city-dwelling white women in their 20s and 30s (Kessler et al., 1994). Most people with severe mental disorders were in this pileup group.

National Comorbidity Survey findings on specific disorders show major depression and alcohol dependence to be the most common lifetime disorders. When disorders are grouped, highest lifetime rates of disorder are found for substance abuse/dependence (26.6%), followed by any anxiety disorder (24.9%), and any affective disorder (19.3%). Annual rates show highest rates for any anxiety disorder (17.2%), with similar rates for any affective disorder (11.3%) and any substance abuse/dependence disorder (11.3%). Major depression (10.3%) and simple phobia (8.8%) are the most common active disorders (Kessler et al., 1994).

Demographic correlates of disorder were examined in the National Comorbidity Survey, with some findings consistent and others inconsistent with the ECA studies. For example, men (48.7%) were slightly more likely than women (48%) to have any lifetime disorder (consistent with ECA data), with women (31.2%) more likely than men (27.7%) to have active disorders (inconsistent with ECA data). With regard to age, findings were similar to those of the ECA studies, with higher rates among younger groups. The findings on race were somewhat inconsistent with the ECA studies, as rates for African-Americans were not significantly higher than those of whites, and Hispanics had higher rates than non-Hispanic whites. As with the ECA study findings, National Comorbidity Survey findings showed a decline in disorders as education and income increased (Kessler et al., 1994).

UTILIZATION OF MENTAL HEALTH SERVICES

Data about utilization of mental health services provide an important source of information for policy making and planning for mental health services. Treatment rate studies have informed mental health professionals and policy makers about the use of services by individuals who have been diagnosed with mental or emotional problems. However, these studies are limited to individuals who seek help and receive services. Community surveys, on the other hand, are able to provide information about both users and non-users of services.

Examples of the use of community surveys to study service utilization in mental health are the ECA Program and the National Comorbidity Survey. These studies provide estimates of one-year service use rates of the four service sectors of the mental health delivery system: speciality mental health, general medical, human service professionals, and voluntary support network. ECA wave 2 data on service utilization are presented in several forms, such as the proportion of the total population using the services of the four sectors; the proportion of persons using services in relation to those who report disorders; service use in relation to specific disorders; and the inpatient service use in various facilities.

From the first perspective, 14.7% of the population used one or more service sectors during the past year. Recognizing some overlap between outpatient sector use, 5.9% of the adult population used the speciality mental health sector, 6.4% the general medical sector, 3% the human services sector, and 4.1% the voluntary support network. The 14.7% consists of 8.1% with a defined illness receiving services and 6.6% with no defined illness receiving services. The 8.1% with defined illness receiving services represents less than one-third of the 28.1% reporting an active mental disorder (Bourdon et al., 1994; Regier et al., 1993).

Of the group who had at least one active disorder, the speciality mental health sector was used by 40%, the general medical sector by 43%, the human services sector by 20%, and the voluntary support network by 28%. Seventeen percent of those seeking service went to more than one sector. A third perspective involves the distribution of outpatient treatment services by specific disorders. The highest service use was by persons with somatization disorder (69.7%), followed by schizophrenia (64.3%), affective disorders (45.7%), anxiety disorders (32.7%), antisocial personality (31.1%), and severe cognitive impairment (17%). Thirty-seven percent of individuals with comorbidity of a mental disorder with an active alcohol or other drug disorder received some kind of treatment. About 21% of this group were helped in the speciality mental and addictive disorders sector, 16% in general medical sector, 8% from other human service professionals, and 11% from voluntary support networks (Regier et al., 1993).

Finally, the ECA data provide a picture of utilization of inpatient treatment over a one-year period by an estimated 1.6 million adults. These individuals were served in various types of facilities, including general hospital psychiatric units (43.3%), state and county mental hospitals (35.2%), county mental health centers (4.2%), Veterans Administration hospital psychiatric units (7.1%), alcohol/drug treatment centers (7.2%), and nursing homes (3.3%) (Bourdon et al., 1994; Regier et al., 1993).

Findings from the National Comorbidity Survey indicated that about 40% of individuals with lifetime disorders got help for their illness, leaving a large proportion of ill persons untreated. Also, less than one-half of the individuals with three or more lifetime disorders received help from the mental health speciality service system. For individuals with active disorders in the past year, this study found approximately 20% received care. Based on these findings on utilization, Kessler et al. (1994) establish the "importance of more outreach and more research on barriers to professional help-seeking," especially in regard to persons with comorbid disorders (p. 8).

ECA and National Comorbidity Survey findings that a large proportion of individuals with disorders do not receive any kind of service raise policy questions in relation to who should be served, given limited financial resources. For example, individuals with the most severe illnesses might be targeted for the most service. Individuals with less severe illness might be covered only partially by insurance or entitlement, with high co-pay requirements. There is also evidence of low reliance on self-help groups, and high reliance on family members for care, highlighting the potential for self-help care for reducing the burdens now placed on families.

ETHNICITY AND UTILIZATION OF SERVICES

Due to the sizable population of Hispanics in the Los Angeles area, ECA survey data from this location were used to examine the health service utilization patterns of Mexican-Americans (Hough et al., 1987). Prior research suggested that this ethnic group underutilized mental health services in comparison to the general population. Hough et al. (1987) analyzed data on service experiences over a six-month period of time, focusing on the relationship of utilization to mental disorder, ethnicity, and geographic location. These authors found that "Mexican-Americans with a recently diagnosed mental disorder were only half as likely as non-Hispanic whites (11% vs. 22%) to have made a mental health visit" (p. 702). In addition, the number of visits by Mexican-Americans was about one-half (11.1% vs. 21.7%) that of non-Hispanics.

Another way of stating this underutilization is that of the Mexican-American population in Los Angeles with a recent mental disorder, about 44% are untreated, 45% are treated in the general medical sector, and 11% are treated in the mental health speciality sector. A number of possible barriers to utilization were suggested for future analysis, including "lack of easily accessible services or information about where to find them, financial constraints, lack of culturally appropriate services, or reluctance to use services as a consequence of felt stigma or other mental health care related attitudes and beliefs for that population" (Hough et al., 1987, p. 708).

ECA study reports on utilization of mental health services provide a first step toward understanding help-seeking patterns of the population in general, as well as those of specific ethnic minority groups. Other national studies, such as a study of adult African-Americans (Neighbors, 1985), also provide information on help-seeking patterns for people with mental health problems. For example, Neighbors (1985) found that when African-Americans have mental problems, such as "nervous breakdowns" or emotional problems, only a very small proportion seek out professional help, with 83% seeking help from individuals within an informal social network. In Neighbors's study, only 9% of individuals with mental health problems contacted a community mental health center, psychiatrist, or psychologist.

In a study of use of outpatient mental health services in the private sector, Padgett et al. (1994) analyzed data on non-Hispanic whites,

Hispanics, and African-Americans who were federal employees insured by Blue Cross/Blue Shield. These investigators employed the Andersen and Newman (1973) model of predisposing, enabling, and need factors in relation to service use. They found highest use by non-Hispanic whites, followed by Hispanics, with blacks displaying the lowest level of utilization. This same pattern obtained for women in the study (Padgett et al., 1994a).

A major question left unanswered by epidemiological studies is why individuals use or do not use mental health services. Neighbors (1985) has suggested that the stigma attached to being a "case" in a mental health agency, or the perception that help available will be ineffective, are possible reasons African-Americans do not use these services. Padgett et al. (1994, 1994a) found that sociodemographic factors, such as age, geographic region, plan option, and education did not explain the lower use of services by African-Americans and Hispanics. These authors suggest that cultural and attitudinal factors and characteristics of the service delivery system, e.g., lack of ethnic mental health personnel, constitute barriers to utilization.

Several reasons for lack of use of services among the general population have been identified by Mechanic (1989). These factors need to be taken into account when considering service utilization by members of ethnic minority groups. Mechanic listed the following reasons:

- unwillingness of many patients to define themselves as having a mental or emotional disorder, or to seek care for such a problem from a mental health professional;
- perceived stigma associated with mental health services and the lack of support from significant others in using such services;
- barriers to access to appropriate care including the lack of a regular source of medical care, inadequate insurance coverage for mental health services, and high levels of co-payment in using such services;
- lack of knowledge or sophistication among physicians in recognizing mental health problems and making appropriate referrals, or attitudes among physicians that inhibit appropriate care and referral (1989, p. 55).

Another approach to the question of the relationship of mental health services policy to service use comes from health services research. Regier (1986) notes, "Determination of who receives health services and the quantity and quality of those services depends on diagnosis as well as other variables, such as nondiagnostic patient characteristics, treatment effectiveness characteristics, health service provider characteristics, health facility characteristics, and the organization and financing of care" (p. 327). For example, some individuals have more social supports than others, a factor that may influence their use of mental health services. Another factor involves beliefs of primary care physicians and patients about the effectiveness of treatment. In relation to health facility characteristics, some communities provide more and better services than others.

HOMELESS MENTALLY ILL PERSONS

The emergence of homelessness as a public health problem is in large part due to the health and mental health problems of this population. As policy makers and service providers have struggled with questions of how to meet the needs of the homeless, special attention has been given to the generation of epidemiological data on homeless mentally ill persons. While researchers have provided useful data on the number of homeless mentally ill people and their characteristics and needs, there also has been a recognition of the special methodological problems related to the study of this population.

While there is an absence of any national surveys on the homeless and the homeless mentally ill, the review of a large number of studies on regional, state, and community levels indicates that a significant proportion, but definitely not a majority, of homeless adults suffer from mental disorders. The most commonly stated estimate of serious mental illness among the homeless is one third, with a substantial proportion (20%–45%) having alcohol-related problems (Dennis et al., 1991). It is recognized that the basis for prevalence figures involves various definitions of mental illness and of homelessness. Studies about mental illness among homeless persons conclude that these individuals are socially heterogeneous, have multiple needs, are likely to have had contact with the police, to have few family members or other social supports, to encounter extensive barriers to employment, to have problems involving alcohol or other drugs, to have needs in addition to mental health care, to have low service utilization, and to need special treatment and service interventions (Dennis et al., 1991; Morrissey & Levine, 1987; Piliavin et al., 1994).

Evaluations of the studies that have produced these findings have identified some basic research problems pertaining to the definition and measurement of homelessness and of mental illness (Dennis, 1987; Susser et al., 1989). Definitions of homelessness are based on criteria ranging from rather narrow to broad and inclusive factors. For example, many studies define the homeless as anyone who sleeps in a shelter or public place, sometimes labeled the literal homeless (Rossi, 1989; Susser, Conover, & Struening, 1989). More inclusive definitions include people in marginal living arrangments, such as doubling up with friends or relatives, or living in skid row flophouses. Given a definition of homelessness, the researcher is confronted with an even more problematic factor—the development of sampling procedures and the selection of a sample of homeless people that will permit generalizations. Because of the wide range of living sites and the geographic movement of the homeless population, it is difficult to specify a sampling frame for social surveys and to locate a sample population.

These research problems are magnified with regard to studying the mentally ill homeless. In this instance, there must be a definition of mental disorder and ways of measuring whether or not a homeless person is mentally ill. In some studies the clinician, in a hospital, shelter, or on the streets, interviews the homeless person and makes a clinical diagnosis. In other cases, a lay interviewer may use a Diagnostic Interview Schedule (in total, or modified) or scales used to ascertain disorders, such as the Center for Epidemiological Studies Depression Scale, the General Health Questionnaire, and the Psychiatric Epidemiology Research Interview (PERI) scale (Susser et al., 1989). Another method of ascertaining mental disorder is to rely on the homeless person's self-report of illness and/or hospitalization. Each of these approaches involves problems of validity and reliability of measurement.

A strong argument has been made that information from ethnographic research is likely to be more useful than survey data in understanding homelessness. Various studies of mentally ill homeless people have used ethnographic methods such as participant observation in order to ascertain "the meanings which behavior and social life have for the people under study" (Koegel, 1987, p. 8). Such studies include research on homeless mentally ill in the skid row of Los Angeles (Farr, Koegel, & Burnham, 1986), on homeless adults in the streets of New York City (Baxter & Hopper, 1981), and various studies of homeless mentally ill women (Koegel, 1987).

Despite the methodological problems in the conduct of research on homeless mentally ill people, the findings from such studies have produced profiles of heterogeneous groups, with varying degrees of mental illness, and with a documentation of a range of needs (Dennis et al., 1991). These studies have led to special efforts on the part of service providers to develop innovative practice approaches to treatment of mentally ill homeless persons.

REVIEW

Epidemiological findings about mental disorders have significant implications for policy making and development of mental health services. To illustrate this fact, selected findings from the Epidemiologic Catchment Area Program of NIMH and the National Comorbidity Survey are presented in terms of the prevalence of mental disorders, social and demographic correlates of disorders, and the utilization of mental health services. The designers of the ECA studies had high hopes that the findings would bring about more informed development and allocation of services aimed at both treatment and prevention. Knowledge is now available about the frequency of specific mental disorders in the general population and about groups that are underserved. While the ECA findings have highlighted the unmet needs of people with psychiatric disorders, Pardes (1986) indicates that "We will need to look carefully at how to use it (ECA) to influence the development of our services systems as such"—that is, for prevention and intervention programs (p. 340). An example of the influence of these data on educational programs is the DART (Depression Awareness, Recognition, Treatment) program of the National Institute of Mental Health (Regier et al., 1988). Finally, research on homeless mentally ill persons has been introduced as an example of the use of epidemiological methods to provide knowledge for policy making and service delivery. The special methodological problems of research with this population have been cited, along with the recognition that a decade of research provides a knowledge base for the delivery of services to mentally ill persons among the homeless population.

4.
History of Mental Health Policies and Services

Historical perspectives on the development of mental health policies and care in the United States provide a context for understanding current mental health issues. These perspectives are usually organized around one or more themes, such as cycles of reform, political climates, treatment modalities and technology, or the locus of care. Such themes are found in numerous accounts of the history of U.S. mental health policy and care (Bell, 1989; Bloom, 1984; Cameron, 1989; Dorwart & Epstein, 1993; Grob, 1987, 1991, 1992, 1994; Rochefort, 1993; Rothman, 1971, 1980; Thompson, 1994). Drawing from the historical literature, in this chapter we explore the development of mental health policy and services in the United States. This presentation is organized in terms of a "cycles of reform" theme, following Rochefort's (1993) observation that "Both its widespread adoption and its intrinsic appeal as a coherent intellectual framework make the cyclical concept an important model for students of the mental health policy process" (p. 99).

As you read about policies and services associated with the various historical cycles, keep in mind the questions posed in the policy framework of Gilbert and Specht (1986): (1) What benefits are offered? (2) To whom are they offered? (3) How are benefits delivered? (4) How are they financed? When appropriate, these questions should be answered in terms of the various policy and program alternatives, the social values of the policy makers, and the assumptions or theories related to the alternatives (Gilbert & Specht, 1986).

Another useful framework for analyzing public mental health policies in terms of cyclical changes is provided by Rochefort (1993). Rochefort suggests four key descriptive themes for examining historical cycles: (1) periodic rediscovery of mental illness and the mentally ill as a problem on the national political agenda; (2) peak/trough levels of policy and program activity, with peaks such as the mental health center movement and troughs such as the incompleteness of deinstitutionalization; (3) recurrence of past concepts and themes, such as the debate concerning biological vs. social and environmental causes of mental disorders; and (4) recurrence of bygone policy and program approaches, e.g., ways of organizing and delivering mental health services. These themes are apparent in laws enacted by Congress in the various historical periods. Selected laws are cited in this chapter to illustrate the development of mental health policy at the federal level. These laws also demonstrate the intergovernmental relations and division of responsibility between federal, state, and local community governments in the provision of mental health care (Grob, 1994a; Rochefort, 1993).

The cycles of reform discussed in this chapter include (1) the asylum/mental hospital/moral treatment period, from the 1770s to around 1900; (2) the mental hygiene movement/psychopathic hospital period, from about 1900 to about 1945; (3) deinstitutionalization and the community mental health movement, from the early 1950s to the present; (4) the Nixon/Ford/Carter presidential period, from 1969 to 1980; (5) the Reagan/Bush presidential period, from 1981 to 1992; (6) the Clinton presidential period, from 1993 to the present. For the reader interested in placing this examination of mental health policies into a broader context of American social welfare policies, Jansson's (1993) *The Reluctant Welfare State* serves as an excellent reference.

THE ASYLUM/MENTAL HOSPITAL/MORAL TREATMENT PERIOD

In Colonial America most persons with mental disorders were cared for in their own homes by family members or in households subsidized by the local government (Dembling, 1995). Later, mentally ill persons were included in almshouses or poorhouses with indigent people as wards of the community. Thus, almshouses came to include a mix of indigent people, physically and/or mentally ill, mentally retarded, and the aged. It was an accepted principle that the responsibility for care of mentally ill persons should be lodged with the family or the local community. For the most part, the "insane" or "lunatics" were viewed as constituting a social and economic problem, not a medical problem (Grob, 1994). By the early 1770s, some general hospitals began to admit mentally ill people, however, and a public mental hospital was established in Williamsburg, Virginia, in 1773.

The usual treatment of the mentally ill in almshouses and hospitals was inhumane (Bell, 1989). However, some changes in care came from the idea that persons with psychiatric illness could benefit from humane care in institutional settings. A "moral treatment" approach to care of the mentally ill originated in 1793 with the work of a French physician, Philippe Pinel, in a Paris hospital for the "insane." Pinel believed that patients should be treated with humane, sympathetic, and personal care in a hospital or asylum setting. The name given to this approach to treatment of mentally ill persons came from the French term, *traitement moral*, which did not mean "moralistic content," but "psychologically oriented therapy." "The hospital, retreat, asylum—whatever its designation—which focused on the insane alone was at the heart of his [Pinel's] therapeutic system" (Grob, 1994, p. 27). This movement in the United States did, however, have a moralistic flavor related to the idea that bad habits lead to tendencies toward mental disorders (Rochefort, 1993).

Another major influence on care of mentally ill persons during this period came from England, where William Tuke established the York Retreat in 1792. Based on religious principles, the treatment approach of the Retreat "was to assist patients in developing internal means of self-restraint and self-control" (Grob, 1994, p. 28). In the United States, private asylums that used moral treatment as a mode of institutional care usually excluded the poor. However, by the 1830s and 1840s superintendents of state institutions began using a moral treatment approach with a focus on medical treatment.

In response to a perceived need for hospital care for indigent mentally ill persons, Dorothea Dix led a movement in the 1840s supporting the development of a state mental hospital in Massachusetts (Bloom, 1984; Grob, 1994). Dix based her advocacy efforts on the belief that "the state had a moral, humanitarian, medical, and legal obligation toward the mentally ill to provide the benefits of asylum care" (Grob, 1994, p. 47). As a result of the efforts of Dix and her followers, more than 30 state hospitals were established during the 1840s, mainly to serve poor people who were mentally ill and could benefit from "asylum"—that is, separation from home or local community. The hospital environment was considered to offer better care than local community almshouses or jails. As these hospitals were established, the fiscal responsibility for institutional care was assumed jointly by each respective state and its local communities. Gradually, care for seriously mentally ill persons moved from the local community to state institutional facilities, with more than 300 state mental hospitals established between about 1845 and 1945 (Bloom, 1984). This development came in response to the fact that appropriate community alternatives for the care of the mentally ill were not available, and it was fostered by the assumption that hospitals could provide humane care and treatment.

During the period up to about 1890, most patients entering state hospitals were "acute cases," hospitalized for less than one year. Most mentally ill people remained in their local communities or in municipal almshouses (Grob, 1992). After 1890, however, states began assuming more fiscal responsibility for care and treatment of the mentally ill. States hoped to improve the quality of care through centralization of responsibility. In practice, however, many patients remained in these hospitals for long periods of time and the focus of the hospital became custodial rather than treatment oriented. As state hospitals became overcrowded and lacked adequate staff, these conditions "contributed to the creation of a depressing internal institutional environment that appeared to have few redeeming qualities" (Grob, 1987, p. 412). As Bloom (1984) observes, "By the late 19th century, state mental hospitals had grown in size and number, but the quality of the treatment had so deteriorated that they were hardly better than the community programs they had been built to replace" (p. 9). The patient population increasingly became composed of long-term, aged, and chronically ill persons. Overcrowding was due in large part to the lack of adequate state funding and the reluctance of professionals to work in these institutions. The dependence on state hospitals for mental health care represented public mental health policy until after the end of World War II in 1945.

THE MENTAL HYGIENE MOVEMENT

Around 1900 it had become clear to many professionals in psychiatry and psychology that persons with mental disorders were not being treated effectively in state hospitals. At the same time, there emerged a belief in the treatability of mental illness, particularly through psychotherapy (Tessler & Goldman, 1982). This treatment approach developed into what has been called "dynamic psychiatry" and the "mental hygiene" movement (Grob, 1994). Although hospital care was not replaced, the new movement gained acceptance through its emphasis on psychology and psychodynamic psychiatry. A major impetus came through the efforts of Clifford Beers (1908), who described his experiences as a patient in a mental hospital in a book entitled, *A Mind That Found Itself*. Beers emphasized the need for citizens, as well as professionals, to become involved in promoting changes in psychiatric care. Beers gained the support of leaders in the field of psychiatry, especially Adolf Meyer and William James, in establishing a National Committee for Mental Hygiene in 1909, an organization which provided leadership for the mental hygiene movement and later became the Mental Health Association.

Supporters of the mental hygiene movement advocated that care be provided in the local community, in psychopathic hospitals devoted to treatment of acute cases, and in community clinics, especially child guidance clinics. Some of these hospitals and clinics had university research and training interests, such as the Psychopathic Hospital at the University of Michigan, the Boston Psychopathic Hospital, and the Phipps Psychiatric Clinic of Johns Hopkins University. The treatment approaches of these organizations included psychodynamic and psychoanalytic psychiatry, with a focus on early treatment in the community to avoid hospitalization (Grob, 1987, 1994). As increased attention was given to the relationship between personality development and the individual's place in the social environment, social workers became involved in the treatment of the mentally ill as well as in preventive work with families and schools.

As a sign of the mental hygiene movement, "mental illness" gained currency as a replacement for the term "insanity" (Bell, 1989). With the expansion of the mental hygiene movement in the 1920s and 1930s, the provision of mental health services was expanded from the seriously ill in hospitals to individuals living in the community with a broad range of disorders and emotional problems. Still, state hospitals continued to be the major institutions for care of the seriously mentally ill until after World War II (Rothman, 1971, 1980; Grob, 1992).

DEINSTITUTIONALIZATION AND THE
COMMUNITY MENTAL HEALTH MOVEMENT

Beginning in the late 1940s, deinstitutionalization evolved over time as a policy that strongly favored the provision of care and treatment in the community. As Rochefort (1993) has observed, deinstitutionalization represented "a major innovation in both the philosophy and the practice of mental health services delivery," offering "a compelling case study of the complexities of modern social policy making" (p. 214).

The impetus for this policy is attributed to several sources, including the experiences of mental health professionals in working with war draftees and military personnel during World War II. These experiences generated the belief that brief treatment interventions and psychosocial treatment techniques could be successful (Tessler & Goldman, 1982; Grob, 1994). Another powerful force promoting deinstitutionalization was changes in state hospitals, especially the introduction of new medications that permitted discharge of patients to the community (Rochefort, 1993).

During the period after World War II, the federal government became a major force in the development of mental health policies and the funding of mental health programs, especially through the leadership of Robert H. Felix in the National Institute of Mental Health. These policies and programs had a significant influence on the deinstitutionalization movement (Grob, 1994; Rochefort, 1993). In its emergence as mental health policy, deinstitutionalization came to be defined as "the process of (1) preventing both unnecessary admission to and retention in institutions; (2) finding and developing appropriate alternatives in the community for housing, treatment, training, education, and rehabilitation of the mentally disabled who do not need to be in institutions; and (3) improving conditions, care and treatment for those who need institutional care" (U.S. G.A.O., 1977, p. 1).

While deinstitutionalization has received mixed support from mental health professionals, the movement gained impetus from those who "became convinced that hospitalizing patients who were undergoing an acute episode of mental illness often did more harm than good," leading to an increase in outpatient care and brief hospital stays for those admitted (Jencks, 1994, p. 25). Mental health professionals of this persuasion participated in the closing of many state psychiatric hospitals, setting off a dramatic decline in the number of patients remaining in these hospitals.

The federal role in mental health policy making became firmly established with the passage of two major Acts of Congress. In July 1946, the National Mental Health Act (Public Law 79-487) created the National Institute of Mental Health, with the purpose of promoting research on etiology, prevention, and treatment of mental illness; training of mental health personnel; and improving state and local mental health services through a grant-in-aid program (Bell, 1989; Rochefort, 1993). NIMH generated support for the Mental Health Study Act of 1955 (P.L. 84-182), which "called for a truly comprehensive review of the mental health system in the United States" (Rochefort, 1993, p. 54). The Act established a Joint Commission on Mental Illness and Health, which produced a report in 1961, *Action for Mental Health*. This report provided a foundation for further deinstitutionalization through the development of community mental health care. The report recommended the following:

- immediate and intensive care for acutely disturbed mental patients in outpatient community mental health clinics…, inpatient psychiatric units located in every general hospital with 100 or more beds,… intensive psychiatric treatment centers…;
- improved care of chronic mental patients in other converted state mental hospitals…;
- improved and expanded aftercare, partial hospitalization…and rehabilitation services;
- expanded mental health education (Bloom, 1984, pp. 19, 20).

COMMUNITY MENTAL HEALTH CENTERS

President John F. Kennedy used the report, *Action for Mental Health*, as a basis for a 1963 message to Congress in which he noted that "mental illness and mental retardation are among our most critical health problems. They occur more frequently, affect more people, require more prolonged treatment, cause more suffering by the families of the afflicted, waste more of our human resources, and constitute more financial drain upon both the Public Treasury and the personal finances of the individual families than any other single condition" (U.S. House of Representatives, 1963). The program proposed by President Kennedy became law as the Mental Retardation Facilities and Community Mental Health Centers Construction Act of 1963 (P.L. 88-164), usually referred to as the Community Mental Health Centers Act. The Act focused on comprehensive community care, construction of comprehensive community mental health centers, initial staffing costs of such centers, and facilitation of community plans for these services.

The mental health program enacted under President Kennedy emphasized community care over institutional care. It provided for Centers that would include five essential services: inpatient care, outpatient care, emergency services, partial hospitalization, and consultation and education. The concept of "continuity of care" was to be ensured by requirements "that a person eligible for treatment in one element of a community mental health center be eligible in all elements;… that patients be readily transferable from one element to another;… that clinical information about patients be shared by all elements of the mental health center; … that staff members be able to move among treatment elements in order to follow their patients; and that no minimum period of residence in the catchment area be imposed as a requirement for treatment" (Bloom, 1984, p. 25).

The community mental health movement as social policy has been highly criticized as an ideology not grounded in scientific findings (Bloom, 1984; Cameron, 1989). As an ideology, the movement represented a set of beliefs that the etiology of mental illness is directly related to the social environment. This conception led to efforts on the part of professionals to change the environment and to take social action to eliminate some of the barriers to good health, especially for ethnic minorities and the poor (Grob, 1992). Supporters of community mental health care also argued that community care would save taxpayers money, a goal seldom achieved.

MEDICARE/MEDICAID HEALTH PROGRAMS

In addition to enactment of the Community Mental Health Centers Act in 1963, the federal government supported deinstitutionalization through the establishment in 1966 of Medicare and Medicaid health care programs for poor and disabled people (Rochefort, 1993). These programs allowed for the transfer of large numbers of elderly and poor people into nursing homes. In 1972, the federal government's program of Supplemental Security Income provided payments for the aged, blind, and disabled who were not covered by the Social Security Program. Income from this program facilitated the movement of many state hospital patients from state hospitals to the community. In some instances this process became one of trans-institutionalization, rather than deinstitutionalization. The deinstitutionalization movement was also influenced by changes in laws and practices concerning involuntary hospitalization. These changes at the state governmental level established new requirements for civil commitment, such as danger presented to self or others, resulting in fewer involuntary admissions to state hospitals.

THE NIXON/FORD/CARTER PRESIDENTIAL PERIOD:
1969–1980

The community mental health movement continued to have the support of Congress during the period from 1963 to 1980, despite a lack of support from the administrations of Presidents Nixon and Ford (1969–1976). As Rochefort (1993) has observed, "Along with several other components of the legacy of the New Frontier and Great Society, the community mental health program came under Republican siege during the mid-1970s" (p. 61). Despite this opposition and a veto by President Ford, Congress expanded the role of Community Mental Health Centers through 1975 legislation that specified several additional services for mental health centers: specialized services for children and the elderly; screening services to promote alternatives to hospitalization; follow-up services for patients discharged from inpatient status; and programs for the prevention and treatment of alcohol and drug abuse (Cameron, 1989).

Renewed support for the community mental health movement came with the election of President Carter in 1976. Carter established the President's Commission on Mental Health "to review national needs and to make necessary recommendations," with his wife Rosalynn taking an active role as honorary chairperson of the Commission (Grob, 1994, p. 284). The work of the Commission established a foundation for the passage of the Mental Health Systems Act of 1980 (P.L. 96-398). This Act was designed to support the ongoing activities of community mental health centers and to recognize the needs of special groups such as chronically mentally ill persons, severely disturbed children and adolescents, and other underserved populations. The Mental Health Systems Act of 1980 also directed the National Institute of Mental Health to

(1) design national goals and establish national priorities for (a) the prevention of mental illness, and (b) the promotion of mental health; (2) encourage and assist local entities and state agencies to achieve the goals and priorities described in paragraph 1; (3) develop and coordinate Federal prevention policies and programs and to assure increased focus on the prevention of mental illness and the promotion of mental health (U.S. Congress P.L. 96-398).

Shortly after the election of President Reagan, this Act was rescinded, and the federal role in regard to mental health policy and funding was transferred back to the states with the passage of the Omnibus Reconciliation Act of 1981 (P.L. 97-35) (Grob, 1994).

PSYCHOSOCIAL REHABILITATION/COMMUNITY SUPPORT SYSTEMS

In response to strong criticisms of policies of deinstitutionalization, the National Institute of Mental Health began to give increased attention to the needs of a special group of persons perceived to be chronically mentally ill. It was recognized that "The new community mental health policy often overlooked the need for supportive services to ensure that severely mentally ill persons would have access to housing, food, social networks, and recreation; it also created a bifurcated system with weak or nonexistent linkages between centers and mental hospitals" (Grob, 1994, p. 278). A small number of programs in local communities had already responded to some of the needs of severely mentally ill persons through the development of innovative psychosocial rehabilitation programs. Two of these programs established models of care that are currently duplicated throughout the United States. The first was Fountain House in New York City, a "clubhouse" model of rehabilitation of ex–mental patients started by J. H. Beard in 1947. The second was a model of community care developed in the early 1970s by Stein and Test (1975) and their colleagues in Madison, Wisconsin. This program, Assertive Community Treatment (ACT), included a strong emphasis on psychosocial rehabilitation and continues to be replicated in various forms throughout the United States (Thompson, Griffith, & Leaf, 1990).

At the federal level, in 1974 a group of individuals in the Division of Mental Health Service Programs at NIMH began developing the idea of serving chronically mentally ill persons through Community Support Programs. The purpose of these programs was to "provide a network of caring for the chronically mentally ill living in community settings, based upon a diversity of health, mental health, rehabilitation, and social welfare services" (Tessler & Goldman, 1982, p. xii). The Community Support Program became a prime example of a federal mental health policy for a specific group of mentally ill persons: those with severe illness. The Program called for federal funds to be granted to state mental health agencies, which would in turn work with local communities to assure that services were delivered to this population. The Community Support Program was incorporated into the Mental Health Services Act of 1980, and even though the Act was rescinded in 1981, this program model continues to be advocated by NIMH.

THE REAGAN/BUSH PRESIDENTIAL PERIOD: 1981–1992

Mental health policies at the federal level during the Reagan and Bush administrations appear to be a "cycle of reform," although a general term for this period is lacking. The major policy shift was in the pattern of funding of mental health services. As a part of the Omnibus Budget Reconciliation Act of 1981 (OBRA) (P.L. 97-35), the pattern of direct funding of community projects or state formula-based programs (categorical grants) changed to a model of block grants to the states. Thus, the direct line of categorical funding from the federal government to community mental health centers was eliminated, and the responsibility for allocation of federal funds for mental health services was placed with the states (Rochefort & Logan, 1989; Rochefort, 1993). The federal government still retained jurisdiction over decisions about who would be eligible for services and the purpose of the services, but it was left to the states and local communities to decide what programs would best serve these purposes (Rochefort & Logan, 1989). Thus, the states were required to allocate a certain portion of funds for some specific client groups and purposes, such as prevention and early treatment of alcohol and drug abuse, alcohol and drug abuse services for women, and new services for underserved areas or populations (e.g., severely disturbed children and adolescents) (Rochefort & Logan, 1989). In addition to the change in the pattern of funding of mental health programs, the Reagan administration reduced the allocations of specific funds for substance abuse and mental health services.

The OBRA legislation on mental health policy and services raises several issues regarding the mental health system. First, when states make the decision on priorities for funding, this leaves open the possibility of some states minimizing services for mental health and for some client groups within the service population. Second, an emphasis on services to chronically mentally ill persons may have the effect of moving the community mental health centers into serving a very narrowly defined clientele, thereby undermining the broad goals of the community mental health movement (Rochefort & Logan, 1989). Third, changes in the federal funding for services under Medicaid, Medicare, and Supplemental Security Income programs affect where services are provided by curtailing community-based services to mentally ill persons. These programs, as well as private insurance plans, have favored hospitalization over community care (Kiesler, 1992).

A second example of a federal mental health policy established during this period is the State Comprehensive Mental Health Services Plan Act of 1986 (P.L. 99-660). This Act required the states to develop, establish, and implement state comprehensive mental health plans that focus on an organized community-based system of care for chronically mentally ill individuals. This Act illustrates the various components of policy making identified in Chapter 1, that is, who gets what services and how they delivered and financed. Thus, the Act requires needs assessment: "The State plan shall contain quantitative targets to be achieved in the implementation of such system, including numbers of chronically mentally ill individuals residing in the areas to be served under such system." The development of program activities is illustrated in the Act: "The State plan shall describe services to be provided to chronically mentally ill individuals to enable such individuals to gain access to mental health services, including access to treatment, prevention, and rehabilitation services. The State shall provide for activities to reduce the rate of hospitalization of chronically mentally ill individuals."

The State Plan Act specifically identified a special group of chronically mentally ill persons to receive services—that is, the homeless: "The State plan shall provide for the establishment and implementation of a program of outreach to, and services for, chronically mentally ill individuals who are homeless." For this special population, the Act created demonstration grants for services provided to homeless chronically mentally ill individuals. Federal mental health policy in relation to the homeless is found not only in the State Comprehensive Mental Health Services Plan Act of 1986, but in other legislation as well. For example, the National Affordable Housing Act of 1990 (P.L. 101-625) provided for funding of housing and services programs directed toward homeless mentally ill people and/or substance abusers. Under this Act, funding for special programs for the mentally ill homeless is provided by two federal agencies, Housing and Urban Development and Health and Human Services. Thus, HUD sponsors programs such as Shelter Plus, "designed to provide housing and supportive services on a long-term basis for homeless persons with disabilities, primarily those with serious mental illness, chronic problems with alcohol and/or drugs, and AIDS and related diseases" (HUD, 1992).

Another example of a mental health policy directed toward the homeless mentally ill is the Stewart B. McKinney Homeless Assistance Act of 1987 (P.L. 100-77). This Act has funded a number of demonstration projects designed to provide this population with mental health and related services, including outreach services in nontraditional settings, intensive, long-term case management, mental health treatment, staffing and operation of supportive living programs, and management/administrative activities related to a comprehensive system of care. In addition, the Act provided block grant program funds to states for five services: outreach, case management, mental health treatment, support and supervisory services in housing for homeless mentally ill persons, and training for service providers (Levine & Rog, 1990). The Center for Mental Health Services within the Substance Abuse and Mental Health Services Administration coordinates programs funded by the McKinney Act, such as Projects for Assistance in Transition from Homelessness (PATH). The Center collaborates with HUD and other federal agencies through Access to Community Care and Effective Services and Support (ACCESS).

Federal legislation in 1987 and 1990 has created new policies with regard to mentally ill residents of nursing homes. This legislation sought to establish goals of mental health care for nursing home residents, so that these individuals' mental health service needs would not be neglected by reason of residency in homes without treatment programs. The Nursing Home Reform Amendments in the 1987 Omnibus Budget Reconciliation Act (P.L. 100-203) established requirements for screening of individuals before entering nursing homes. The screening was to determine if the person seeking entry into a nursing home was mentally ill or retarded and needed specialized mental health treatment. The amendments called for the discharge from nursing homes of individuals who had resided at the nursing home less than 30 months, needed intensive mental health treatment, and could not receive this treatment within the nursing home. Penalties for noncompliance with the law included a cutoff of Medicare and Medicaid payments to the nursing home. This law represented a policy change with regard to the use of Medicare and Medicaid funds for the care of mentally ill and retarded individuals.

Considerable controversy resulted from the efforts of the Health Care Financing Administration to establish rules to implement the federal legislation regarding care in nursing homes. The major focus of the rules was on the review process, labeled Pre-Admission Screening and Annual Resident Review. Additional amendments with regard to nursing home care of mentally ill and retarded persons were enacted in 1990, particularly with regard to the rules for PASARR, the definition of mental illness, and the meaning of active treatment and specialized services.

A final example of a federal mental health policy enacted during the presidency of George Bush is the Americans with Disabilities Act of 1990 (P.L. 101–336). This Act recognizes the special needs of individuals with physical or mental disabilities. Discrimination against these individuals is defined as a "serious and pervasive social problem" (Sec. 2). The Act was created in response to the fact that "people with disabilities, as a group, occupy an inferior status in our society, and are severely disadvantaged socially, vocationally, economically, and educationally" (Sec. 2).

THE CLINTON PRESIDENTIAL PERIOD

The future of mental health policy at the federal level is uncertain. A new "cycle of reform" in mental health policy and services may be generated under health care reform proposals of the Clinton administration. Even if a new cycle does not begin during this presidential period, these proposals for health care reform provide a useful study of potential changes in the mental health system.

One of President Clinton's major campaign promises was to reform the U.S. health care system. Shortly after inauguration, the president established a Task Force on National Health Care Reform, chaired by Hillary Rodham Clinton. The report of this task force led to the proposal to Congress in November 1993 of an American Health Security Act. One of the working groups of the task force, led by Tipper Gore, focused on mental health and substance abuse policies and services. This work group made recommendations on mental health benefits to be included in the plan. The group dealt with issues of universal coverage, insurance reform, regional alliances with managed competition, and accountable health plans by health care organizations (Plaut & Arons, 1994).

The Clinton health reform discussions recognized a number of problems in the mental health system: lack of insurance coverage for a large number of Americans; an emphasis on costly inpatient care; lack of parity of mental health services with general health services; differences in quality of care between the private and public sectors; and lack of coordination of care for children and adolescents (Arons & Buck, 1994). In response to these problems, the mental health and substance abuse work group proposed new goals for the mental health system:

- They would ensure that persons with MH/SA (mental health/substance abuse) disorders, and their families, had access to specialized services.
- They would guarantee that health plans had the flexibility to provide the appropriate types, mix, and level of services for each individual consumer.
- They would encourage the development and use of alternatives to hospitalization, in the least restrictive environment appropriate to the needs of the individual.
- They would reduce the shifting of costs and responsibilities to the public sector and encourage the integration of the public and private delivery systems (Arons & Buck, 1994, p. 3).

In addition to the Clinton plan, a number of other health reform proposals have been developed under the sponsorship of members of Congress. They vary in relation to employer mandate, single-payer national health insurance, tax credits and deductions, and managed competition. Rochefort (1993) has suggested that health care reform proposals be analyzed in terms of these dimensions, as well as four basic criteria: universal insurance coverage, comprehensiveness of benefits, cost control, and organization of services. As Arons and Buck (1994) have noted, the debate over mental health services in health care reform is over cost estimates of benefits, the possible effects on the access and quality of care for the seriously mentally ill, and the effectiveness of treatment for persons with mental health/substance abuse problems.

It is evident from examining various health care reform proposals that there is a continuing dependence of mental health services on federal health policy. Kiesler (1992) takes the position that this dependence has been detrimental to mental health care, and without some independence from health care policy, mental health policy is doomed to failure. Thus far, health care policy has influenced mental health services through shifts in inpatient care from state and county mental hospitals to general hospitals, care in private psychiatric hospitals, and care in residential treatment centers for children. Hospital care has overtaken the idea of general health care both for health and mental health patients. This *de facto* policy has been supported by fiscal plans of Medicaid, Medicare, and commercial insurance companies. In turn, community-based treatment and support services, which are less expensive and often more effective, remain inadequately supported and financed.

An important issue related to the influence of health care policy on mental health services concerns the possible effects of health care reform on the role of state mental health agencies. If health care reform reinforces the trend toward privatization and insurance coverage for hospital care, the question arises as to the future functions of state departments of mental health. The dramatic decrease from 1950 to 1990 in beds (from more than 500,000 to less than 100,000) and reduction from 1950 to 1993 in state-operated mental hospitals (from 322 to 256) suggest that state mental health agencies may not be needed (Glover & Petrila, 1994; Lutterman, 1994). On the other hand, a number of activities remain that may best be carried out at the state level. These include the provision of forensic services, services for seriously mentally ill persons, development of "computer-based technologies for evaluating issues of access, appropriateness of services, consumer satisfaction, and outcome in systems of care," and support for nontraditional services such as self-help groups and psychosocial programs (Glover & Petrila, 1994, p. 912). Finally, state mental health agencies are likely to continue to function as a conduit of federal monies into local community programs.

ASSESSMENT OF DEINSTITUTIONALIZATION

The deinstitutionalization movement has continued as public mental health policy throughout the Reagan/Bush presidential years and into the Clinton administration. There is considerable disagreement concerning the extent to which the policy of deinstitutionalization has achieved its goals and objectives (Belcher & Bentley, 1994; Johnson, 1994; Mechanic & Rochefort, 1990; Surles, 1994). It is clear that the census of state hospitals has declined in favor of community residential care and treatment (Rochefort, 1993). Inpatient stays in state hospitals have changed from long-term care to treatment for brief periods of time.

With deinstitutionalization, state and county mental hospitals are no longer the central facilities of state and county mental health systems. Most inpatient care for mental disorders has changed to care in the private sector by general hospitals. One of the major reasons for the decline in hospital populations was the provision of entitlements under Medicare and Medicaid, allowing hospitals to discharge older adult patients to nursing homes. In addition, many severely mentally ill persons returned to the community into "board and care homes, halfway houses, supervised apartments, and other residential facilities" (Rochefort, 1993, p. 224). These nontraditional community care settings were thought to provide less restrictive settings for patients discharged from hospitals.

Numerous critics of deinstitutionalization have identified some major problems leading to an assessment of this movement as "one of the era's most stunning public policy failures" (Mechanic & Rochefort, 1990, p. 302). These problems include the lack of adequate funding for mental health and supportive services in the community, poor quality of service, lack of service delivery coordination, and lack of attention to the severely mentally ill. Some of these limitations of the movement are associated with care in state mental hospitals. For example, in the early period of deinstitutionalization, patients were moved into the community by "opening the back doors," and in a later period, this phase continued, as well as a new phase of "closing of the front doors" of state hospitals (Mechanic & Rochefort, 1990, p. 309; Morrissey, 1989).

Current critics of deinstitutionalization, such as Lamb (1992a), have proposed a moratorium on this movement, due to a continued lack of community resources, especially for persons with severe mental illness. Some mental health advocates support reinstitutionalization of patients who cannot function in the community, such as homeless mentally ill persons. In their assessment of deinstitutional-ization, Mechanic and Rochefort (1990) argue that it is difficult to im-prove the public mental health system and to overcome the problems of deinstitutionalization, as a result of "the low standing of mental health issues on the national social agenda" (p. 323). They assert that for a deinstitutionalized system to work, health and welfare entitle-ments must be assured. A safety net must be established to assure protection and support for mentally ill individuals in the communi-ty. Of special concern is the emergence of a group of severely men-tally ill young adults who remain in the community but are resistant to treatment, often have a dual diagnosis of mental illness and substance abuse, and usually need substantial social supports (Rochefort, 1993). Some of these individuals are a part of the diverse homeless mentally ill population not served well by the process of deinstitutionalization.

Assessments of the success of deinstitutionalization range from very negative to modified positive. In declaring that deinstitutional-ization has failed, Johnson (1994) observes that "In the end, deinstitu-tionalization was a slogan masquerading as a reform, the status quo disguised as change, a goal without a program" (p. 218). On a more positive note, Gerhart (1990) has observed that "important goals of the deinstitutionalization movement have indeed been realized," as evi-denced by reports of ex-patients residing in the community, by im-provements in inpatient care, and by innovations in community-based care services (p. 13).

REVIEW

The development of mental health policies is viewed from the per-spective of "cycles of reform." This approach to understanding the his-torical dimensions of mental health policy makes use of time periods and themes of policy changes, such as the asylum/mental hospi-tal/moral treatment period (1770s to 1900), mental hygiene movement (1900 to 1945), deinstitutionalization and community mental health movement (1950s to the present), the Nixon/Ford/Carter presidential period (1969 to 1980), the Reagan/Bush presidential period (1981 to 1992), and the Clinton presidential period (1993 to the present). The principal policy features and examples of major federal mental health legislation for each of these periods are identified. As Grob (1994) has suggested, cyclical reforms of mental health policies and services have usually involved "unrealistic expectations and rhetorical claims" that are unfulfilled (p. 310). Although there has been some success in each of the reform periods, the search continues for policies and programs that will prevent, treat, and cure mental disorders. In Rochefort's (1993) terms, "providing decent care and treatment to all who are within this population is a public policy challenge still unmet" (p. xiv).

5.
Mental Health Programs, Services, and Service Delivery

Public mental health policies are implemented through mental health programs and their related services. These programs are designed to improve the quality of life for all citizens, ranging from members of the general population to persons with severe mental illness. Difficulties in defining, classifying, and measuring mental health services have been identified by George (1989). For example, it is unclear whether the term *mental health services* refers solely to treatment of mental illness or whether it includes other social or human services, such as supportive services involving housing, financial assistance, and job skill training. George (1989) differentiates between social and mental health services by defining the latter as having a purpose of identification, diagnosis, and treatment of mental health problems. Other authors, however, include both psychiatric treatment and social supports when defining mental health services (Morrissey, 1989). Such a broad definition of services is especially appropriate in relation to the mental health needs of persons with persistent and severe disorders.

Our discussion in this book recognizes that mental health programs (treatment and services) are delivered by several professional and nonprofessional groups. The four core mental health disciplines are psychiatry, psychology, social work, and psychiatric nursing (Dial et al., 1990). In addition, public services are provided by staff with various levels of education and training, such as paraprofessional mental health workers, hospital aides, community workers, and residential care managers. Considering the public services of professionals, the smallest group of providers is medical personnel, including general physicians and psychiatrists, who are often employed full- or part-time in hospitals and community mental health centers. Psychologists also constitute a small group of professional mental health providers, again most often on a full- or part-time basis in hospitals and community centers. The largest numbers of professionals serving mental health clients in the public sector are social workers in hospitals and community mental health centers and nurses in hospitals (Reamer, 1989; Cameron, 1989; Redlick et al., 1994).

Our focus in this chapter is on programs developed for persons who have mental disorders or who are at risk for developing these problems. In discussing mental health programs, we look at a number of dimensions, such as characteristics of the illness of the client/patient, the nature of the services and who provides them, the location or setting of the services, and how service delivery is organized. Policy implementation is understood through examination of these features of mental health programs—that is, who gets what kind of service and how the service is delivered within a mental health system.

Mental health programs, which are configurations of interventions and activities directed toward mental health policy goals and objectives, are often described in terms of program setting, such as institutional vs. community-based services, inpatient or outpatient services, or hospitalization vs. non-hospitalization. In the past, the major location for public institutional care has been the state mental hospital, with the patient usually separated from his or her local community. However, deinstitutionalization and privatization have left the state mental hospital providing care for a minority of hospitalized patients. In the last decade there has been a dramatic increase in the use of psychiatric units of local community general hospitals and private psychiatric hospitals through purchase of service contracts or health insurance plans. Other types of institutional care for mentally ill persons include partial hospitalization, residential treatment centers, nursing homes, and residential group homes. While these settings may be classified as non-institutional, community-based programs, they often resemble institutional care. Outpatient services under public auspices are provided mostly through hospitals and community mental health centers.

This chapter includes a description of the major organizational units in mental health service delivery systems. The community support program is examined as a systems approach to the organization and delivery of mental health services. This discussion is followed by a consideration of some of the innovative community-based programs developed for persons with severe, chronic mental illness. Finally, we identify several alternative mental health programs, such as self-help, coordinating mechanisms, and advocacy groups. As Brown (1985) has indicated, "In the last two decades we have witnessed dramatic changes in the mental health system: the decline of the traditional state hospital, the birth of the community mental health center, the expansion of psychiatric services in general hospitals, the creation of huge nursing home populations of chronically mentally ill persons, and the production of a corps of urban bag people" (p. 1).

EMERGENCY SERVICES

Emergency services are established to respond to psychiatric crises (Gerhart, 1990; Hillard, 1994). These services are usually provided through hospital emergency rooms and community mental health centers. The provision of these services is likely to be centralized in one or more local community sites, depending on the size of the community and the organizational structure of the local community mental health system. Services include diagnosis, referral, and both outpatient and inpatient treatment. The providers of these services serve as gatekeepers for entry into a state hospital, community psychiatric hospitals, or local community general hospital psychiatric units.

The current trend is for community mental health centers to assume major responsibility for crisis intervention with persons in the community who seek public psychiatric services. Centers may serve as the entry point for hospitalization, or they may have arrangements with local community hospitals for emergency patient assessment and care. Community mental health centers respond to the ongoing emergency needs of severely mentally ill persons residing in the community, including individuals living with families, in private dwellings, in apartments, and in residential care homes. Crisis intervention, including psychiatric treatment and social services, is extended to this population through mental health center programs and/or contracted service/treatment organizations.

HOSPITALIZATION

Mental hospitalization may be defined as the inpatient treatment in a hospital of a person with a diagnosed mental disorder (Kiesler & Sibulkin, 1987). Public mental hospitals are operated by a state, county, or federal agency. A number of problems are associated with these institutions, including issues such as involuntary commitment to them, quality of care, and whether or not comparable care can be provided on an outpatient basis.

Persons entering state hospitals are usually admitted on an involuntary basis under state civil commitment procedures. Such patients are diagnosed as mentally ill and meet commitment criteria pertaining to dangerousness to self and/or others and to disability. The care provided in state hospitals includes medical treatments, such as psychotropic medications, and psychological treatments, such as social learning and skills training and various forms of therapy, counseling, and discharge planning (Gerhart, 1990). The state hospital provides short-term treatment for most inpatients, but for a limited number of people, it may serve as a long-term custodial care facility.

Why hospitalize patients with mental illness? Kiesler and Sibulkin (1987) have identified a number of reasons. First, it is easier for the mental health professional to make an assessment and provide treatment in a hospital. The patient is available for a psychiatric examination, medical tests, medications, and other therapy. Patient compliance with treatment plans is more likely to occur in a hospital than in the community. Second, insurance coverage usually favors inpatient care, especially when care is funded by Medicaid and Medicare. Third, the professional in charge, usually a psychiatrist, has more control over the patient and over staff within the hospital than in outside treatment environments. Fourth, hospitalization usually makes life easier for the patient's family.

Goals regarding hospital care have been a prominent part of the policy of deinstitutionalization. These goals are concerned with reducing admissions into the public hospital, improving quality of care and decreasing lengths of hospital stays, and re-integrating current patients into the community. Such goals have emerged from concerns about care in state mental hospitals, as highlighted in *Action for Mental Health*, a 1961 report of the Joint Commission on Mental Illness and Health. This report emphasized the adverse effects of treating large numbers of patients in a single location, and the need in state hospitals for treatment goals as well as custodial care. Criticisms of state hospitals include Goffman's (1961) now-classic view that "the effects of mental hospitalization can be negative and anti-therapeutic" (p. 142).

Talbott (1978) has summarized the principal problems of state hospitals in the past as follows: the physical plants were generally poorly designed and poorly kept; the patients were mostly severely mentally ill persons, often readmissions; the staff often were not well qualified; treatment programs were limited, and mainly relied on medications; the hospital was not part of a broader community service system, nor were its programs linked very well to other agencies, state departments of mental health, state government, or to consumers. These state hospitals were generally underfunded and often not fully accredited.

In recent years, major improvements have occurred in many state mental hospitals, with some professionals urging the continuation of such hospitals on a small scale. For example, Gralnick (1985) has promoted the idea that the state hospital system can be revitalized: "The state hospital system, despite having been maligned and nearly destroyed, has great therapeutic potential. It could provide extended care to acutely ill patients before they become chronically ill; restore the capability to pinpoint responsibility for patient care, which has been lost under community care; and provide a stimulating academic environment conducive to research into treatment of the mentally ill" (p. 738).

The Future of State Mental Hospitals

Four major options continue to be available for state mental hospitals: closure, maintenance of the status quo, radical reform, or alterations in function (Talbott, 1980). These options are not mutually exclusive, as many states have closed some hospitals and altered the functions of others. Over the past two decades, the most dramatic change has been a reduction in the number of state hospital beds—from 361,765 in 1972 to 93,647 in 1990, amounting to a decrease of 73% (Lutterman, 1994; Witkin et al., 1990; Rosenstein, Milazzo-Sayre, & Manderscheid, 1990). During the same period, the number of state hospitals declined from 321 to 267. As of 1993, states operated 256 state hospitals, with 42 states planning to downsize their state hospital systems. Twelve states were in the process of closing one or more hospitals (Lutterman, 1994). In some communities, state hospitals appear to remain open due to "policy gridlock," which results from political and administrative barriers to closure (Becker, 1993). Becker (1993) refers to this process as "the politics of closing state mental hospitals," demonstrating that a number of actors may resist closure, such as legislators, hospital employees, mental health officials, consumer advocacy groups, and local community residents (p. 103).

A policy environment framework is useful for examining the future role of the state hospital (Talbott, 1978). Bachrach (1986) uses this framework to demonstrate that the state hospital is not an independent organization but is part of a service delivery system. Consequently, the hospital is subject to the influence of and the changes in four policy environments: core level, specific, supportive, and general environments. The core level environment concerns the internal operations of the hospital, its personnel, and values and norms. The specific environment includes the various agencies and organizations that have exchange relationships with the hospital. The supportive environment consists of organizations that exert some control over the operations of the hospital, such as funding, accreditation, and staffing. Finally, the general environment involves a broad range of social, economic, political, and professional influences that affect the hospital (Bachrach, 1986).

These policy environments do not have equal influence on the role of the state hospital. For example, the availability of appropriate community-based services and the service delivery patterns and resources of local community mental health centers determine to some extent the role of the state hospital. Certainly, state political policy makers have a major influence on the place of the hospital within the total mental health care system funded by the state. A central issue is the extent to which the state hospital is a vital part of a state and community mental health system. Thus, the hospital may be regarded as a last resort for the chronically mentally ill, or as a treatment center that has strong connections with community-based programs. In this regard, Waslow (1993) has argued that hospital care needs to be available for those who need it, at the times they need it, with asylum provided through "humane, unlocked hospitals that provide shelter, food, and compassionate care and treatment" (p. 208).

COMMUNITY MENTAL HEALTH CENTERS

The Mental Retardation Facilities and Community Mental Health Centers Construction Act of 1963 (P.L. 84-164) established community mental health centers as the primary locus of community care for mentally ill people. The centers were seen as fulfilling the following roles:

- replacing institutional care with community care;
- providing service to the entire community, especially through prevention (expressed in terms of comprehensiveness of services, education, and consultation);
- planning for services for the mental health of the entire community, and changing the community's environment;
- providing continuity of care, directed toward least restrictive settings for care.

Community Mental Health Center (CMHC) programs were designed to serve citizens in catchment/service areas (geographic areas with defined boundaries). Catchment areas were identified in local communities in each of the states, and the mental health needs of the populations within these areas were identified (Bloom, 1984; Hasen-feld, 1986). Funding was provided to establish a community mental health center in each of the catchment areas, some 1,500 in all. Funds were allocated differentially to the states, depending on their needs. The total construction cost was not borne entirely by the federal government, as state and/or local money was required as well. Federal funding for staffing costs began at 75% and decreased in succeeding years. As already noted, centers were expected to provide five essential services: inpatient care, outpatient care, emergency services, partial hospitalization, and community services of consultation and education. Additional services were added through amendments passed in 1975 (P.L. 94-63), including "specialized services for children and the elderly, screening services in order to promote alternatives to hospitalization, follow-up services for patients discharged from inpatient status, and programs for the prevention and treatment of alcohol and drug abuse" (Cameron, 1989, p. 134).

The 1975 amendments expanded the range of persons and illnesses to be served by the community mental health centers. However, adequate funding for these services was not forthcoming, leading to strong criticism of the community-based services system for its failure to provide aftercare services meeting the needs of chronically mentally ill persons. On the positive side, 763 community mental health centers had been established by 1980, and the claim was made that these centers put "clinical care, preventive services, and social services within reach of over 110 million people, or 50% of the population" (Bloom, 1984, p. 31). Within this spirit, the Mental Health Systems Act of 1980 (P.L. 96-398) included provisions for strengthening community mental health centers and adding new services. After the election of President Reagan, the budget for the Mental Health Systems Act was repealed, however, so these provisions were not supported with funds. Current levels of services were maintained as federal funds incorporated into block grants allowed states to continue to receive funds for mental health centers.

CMHCs Under a State System

The structure of service delivery of mental health centers in Michigan illustrates how community mental health centers may operate. In Michigan, the Department of Mental Health oversees the delivery of public mental health services. Policies governing the goals and operations of the State Department and County Mental Health Boards are established in the Mental Health Code (State of Michigan, 1990a). Michigan has 83 counties, and because of the small population of some of the counties, groups of two to three counties in the low-population areas form a single Community Mental Health Board. This has resulted in the establishment of 54 Community Mental Health Boards throughout the state.

In Michigan, mental health boards oversee the allocation of funds and the determination of mental health policies and programs within federal, state, and county mandates. The purpose of mental health boards is to provide "a range of mental health services for persons who are located within that county" (State of Michigan, 1990a, Sec. 330.1206). A service is defined as any of the following: prevention, consultation, collaboration, educational, or informational service; diagnostic service; emergency service; inpatient service; outpatient service; partial hospitalization service; residential, sheltered, or protective care service; habilitation or rehabilitation service; any other service approved by the department (Sec. 330.1208). These mental health services may be provided through community mental health centers or through public or private agencies funded by a Board through purchase of service contracts.

An example of the operations of a community mental health center is provided with reference to a center serving the southwest part of the city of Detroit, Michigan. Southwest Detroit Community Mental Health Services Inc. operates a number of service programs, including services for children, adults, and families; services for continuing care; and a day program for psychosocial rehabilitation.

The major program services include diagnostic services, clinical services, psychosocial rehabilitation and prevention, and consultation and education. Some of the programs for children, adults, and families include parenting programs, teen support, weight loss programs, Department of Social Services consultation, stress management training, housing programs (e.g., residential training center, Fairweather Lodges), and a Hispanic outreach project. The continuing care program includes special services such as court screening, hospital liaison/case management, psychosocial assessments at intake, nursing services, transition to independence services, adult foster care home program, family education, services to substance abuse clients, an Assertive Community Treatment program, AIDS education, and self-help consumer groups. The effectiveness of these service programs depends in large part on the levels of federal, state, and local funding.

Residential Care Programs

The context for a significant proportion of the mental health services of a community mental health center is the residential care system, the major alternative to hospitalization (Segal & Kotler, 1989). This system involves family care, family foster care, board and care, residential care, nursing homes, group care homes, single-room-occupancy hotels, and homeless shelters. An important part of the mental health service provider's responsibility is to assure that the living circumstances are appropriate and are in the least restrictive setting possible. Mental health center personnel are in constant contact with mental health consumers and care providers in community residential care settings. Providing services to these residents also requires interchanges with other human service organizations, such as the Department of Social Services and Public Health Department.

Evaluation of CMHC Programs

Dowell and Ciarlo (1989) provide a perceptive evaluation of the goals of the CMHC program in the United States "as the centerpiece of federal mental health policy for most of two decades" (p. 196). These authors review data on community mental health centers in terms of the major goals of the community mental health movement:

1. Increase the range and quantity of public mental health services;
2. Make services equally available and accessible to all;
3. Provide services in relation to existing local needs;
4. Decrease state hospital admissions and residents;
5. Maximize citizen participation in community programs;
6. Prevent development of mental disorders;
7. Coordinate mental health–related services in the catchment area;
8. Provide services as efficiently as possible;
9. Provide services which reduce suffering and increase personal functioning (p. 196).

The Dowell and Ciarlo (1989) review confirms the fact that community mental health centers have increased services to catchment-area residents and that the range of services has become more specialized and comprehensive. However, with federal funding cutbacks, the centers have become less comprehensive and less community-oriented in their provision of services. In some communities, state and local funding has not been generated to replace federal funds, leading to considerable instability in the organizations. There is some evidence that mental health services have become more accessible to people in poverty and ethnic minorities as a result of the establishment of community mental health centers. At the same time, these groups remain underserved, as do the elderly, children, severely disabled clients, dually diagnosed persons, and rural clients.

PREVENTION SERVICES AND RESEARCH

The major objectives of the community mental health movement have been the prevention of mental illness and the promotion of mental health (Lorion & Allen, 1989). The President's Commission on Mental Health (1978) recommended that preventive interventions be supported, and preventive research centers have been developed under the National Institute of Mental Health. Under the sponsorship of the Department of Health and Human Services, the Institute of Medicine created a Committee on Prevention of Mental Disorders to study the status of mental health prevention and prevention research. This committee reported its findings and recommendations in a 1994 publication entitled *Reducing Risks for Mental Disorders* (Mrazek & Haggerty, 1994). In this report, the committee "recommends that an enhanced research agenda to prevent mental disorders be initiated and suported across all relevant federal agencies...as well as state governments, universities, and private foundations" (p. xii). Areas to be developed through a prevention research agenda include the following:

- Building the infrastructure to coordinate research and service programs and to train and support new investigators.
- Expanding the knowledge base for preventive interventions.
- Conducting well-evaluated preventive interventions (p. xii).

The inclusion of prevention as a service strategy supported by federal mental health policies is consistent with the public health view that disease and illness can be controlled through prevention. However, there are controversies over the definition of health and illness and their causes, suggesting that some mental disorders may not be controllable through prevention, due to lack of known etiology.

An important issue in regard to preventive mental health services concerns ways in which prevention is defined. The Committee on Prevention of Mental Disorders has promoted the view that the concept of prevention should be defined narrowly, that is, as "those interventions that occur before the initial onset of a disorder" (Mrazek & Haggerty, 1994, p. xii). However, the Committee recognized that the concept of prevention is often extended to include intervention at three levels: primary, secondary, and tertiary. These three levels are differentiated as follows: "Primary prevention seeks to decrease the number of new cases of a disorder or illness (incidence). Secondary prevention seeks to lower the rate of established cases of the disorder or illness in the population (prevalence). Tertiary prevention seeks to decrease the amount of disability associated with an existing disorder or illness" (Mrazek & Haggerty, 1994, p. 20).

This "three levels" classification approach to prevention can be applied to some of the activities of community mental health centers. Centers often develop programs of education and consultation in order to carry out primary prevention, especially with regard to children and adolescents in schools and other community programs. Secondary prevention usually involves early case finding, through such activities as crisis intervention. The targeted population for such services includes individuals who are in the early stages of illness and who can be expected to benefit from early treatment. An example of tertiary prevention is the treatment of severely and persistently mentally ill persons in psychosocial rehabilitation programs.

While these definitions have some utility for clinical and community practice, the Committee on Prevention of Mental Disorders (Mrazek & Haggerty, 1994) determined that prevention research should be focused on "interventions that occur before the initial onset of a disorder" (p. 23). This focus includes incorporation of aspects of Gordon's (1983) classification system: universal, selective, and indicated prevention. Under this system,

- Universal preventive interventions are targeted to the general public or a whole population group that has not been identified on the basis of individual risk.
- Selective preventive interventions for mental disorders are targeted to individuals or a subgroup of the population whose risk of developing mental disorders is significantly higher than average.
- Indicated preventive interventions for mental disorders are targeted to high-risk individuals who are identified as having minimal but detectable signs or symptoms foreshadowing mental disorder (pp. 25, 26).

In adopting this intervention spectrum and recognizing possible overlaps of the parts, the Committee on the Prevention of Mental Disorders recommended that this scheme be applied to "all research and service related to interventions for mental disorders" (p. 27).

Interest in prevention services has been stimulated by renewed activities in prevention research (Steinberg & Silverman, 1987; Mrazek &

Haggerty, 1994). Researchers have investigated the identification of at-risk populations; standards for measuring outcomes of prevention programs; the types of people and disorders that may benefit from prevention services; the impact of culture, ethnicity, and race on interventions; and the potential negative implications of prevention programs (Albee & Ryan-Finn, 1994; Wiggins, 1994; Mrazek & Haggerty, 1994). Topics such as these have been included in the prevention research agenda recommended to the federal government by the Committee on Prevention of Mental Disorders. The Committee has recommended that the federal government initiate prevention programs in areas where knowledge about mental disorders is sufficient to merit prevention interventions. The focus of research on such interventions is to be placed on "potentially modifiable biological and psychosocial risk and protective factors for the onset of mental disorders" (Mrazek & Haggerty, 1994, p. xiv).

The concepts of risk factors and protective factors have guided the development by Coie et al. (1993) of a conceptual framework for a national research program on prevention. Risk factors include "variables associated with a high probability of onset, greater severity, and longer duration of major mental health problems" (p. 1013). Protective factors "refer to conditions that improve people's resistance to risk factors and disorder" (p. 1013). An important feature of this framework is the recognition in etiological models of "complex interactions among genetic, biomedical, and psychosocial risk and protective factors" (p. 1013). Equally important is the idea that prevention research involves an interplay between science and practice, so that new knowledge must be "translated into practical applications that will 'sell' in schools, hospitals, playgrounds, homes, clinics, industries, and community agencies nationwide" (p. 1020).

INNOVATIVE COMMUNITY-BASED PROGRAMS

Community treatment involves programs that are directed toward individuals who have never been hospitalized as well as toward those who enter hospitals and return to the community. A major issue concerns whether or not an individual can obtain adequate and effective care in the community. Does community treatment for patients discharged from a hospital help prevent rehospitalization, does it result in fewer days in a hospital after readmission, or does it have other positive effects on the individual? There are a number of types of community care now developed for individuals in relation to these goals. Some of these innovative programs operate out of community mental health centers or state hospital systems, while others are conducted by private agencies under public funding. To illustrate such programs, we will describe some that have been evaluated through research studies. These programs include community support systems, rehabilitation services, and assertive community treatment programs.

Community Support Programs

The Community Support Program of the National Institute of Mental Health is a model of service provision that emphasizes the coordination of services for chronically mentally ill persons (NIMH, 1982; Rochefort, 1993). The program was developed with the idea that social support networks are lacking for many mentally ill persons in their communities. The goal of the Community Support Program is to "provide a network of caring for the chronically mentally ill living in community settings, based upon a diversity of health, mental health, rehabilitation, and social welfare services" (Tessler & Goldman, 1982, p. xii). The need for a coordinated approach to serving this population was recognized by a work group at NIMH who found that:

- the needs of people with chronic mental illness extended well beyond the boundaries of the mental health system;
- even within the mental health system, it was necessary to promote the development of local agencies willing and able to make long-term commitments to chronic patients who needed some services not easily reimbursable by third-party insurers;
- there was a pervasive need to better clarify lines of responsibility for the chronic patients at all levels of government (Tessler & Goldman, 1982, pp. 12–13).

In the implementation of the Community Support Program, NIMH gave funds to state mental health agencies, who in turn were expected to work with local communities in their development of community support systems. Contracts were given to 19 states to carry out the intent of the NIMH. In order to have a community support system, Community Support Program guidelines called for staff and resources to implement the following ten functions:

1. Identification of the target population, whether in hospitals or in the community, and outreach to offer appropriate services to those willing to participate;
2. Assistance in applying for entitlements;

3. Crisis stabilization services in the least restrictive setting possible, with hospitalization available when other options are insufficient;
4. Psychosocial rehabilitation services, including but not limited to: goal-oriented rehabilitation evaluation; training in community living skills, in the natural setting wherever possible; opportunities to improve employability; appropriate living arrangements in an atmosphere that encourages improvements in functioning; opportunities to develop social skills, interests, and leisure-time activities to provide a sense of participation and worth;
5. Supportive services of indefinite duration, including supportive living and working arrangements, and other such services for as long as they are needed;
6. Medical and mental health care;
7. Backup support to families, friends, and community members;
8. Involvement of concerned community members in planning and offering housing or working opportunities;
9. Protection of client rights, both in hospitals and in the community;
10. Case management, to ensure continuous availability of appropriate forms of assistance (Tessler & Goldman, 1982, p. 16).

The NIMH request for proposals listed four prerequisites for constituting a community support system:

- The comprehensive needs of the population at risk must be assessed;
- There must be legislative, administrative, and financial arrangements to guarantee that appropriate forms of assistance are available to meet these needs;
- There must be a core services agency within the community that is committed to helping severely mentally disabled people improve their lives;
- There must be an individual person (or team) at the client level responsible for remaining in touch with the client on a continuing basis, regardless of how many agencies get involved (Tessler & Goldman, 1982, p. 17).

The activities related to a community support system occur at the federal, state, and local levels. The federal government is the contractor and provides monitoring, technical assistance, advocacy, and interagency collaboration. States provide coordination and system-building activities, such as the design and implementation of community support strategies. At the local level, the ten components of the Community Support Program identified above must be included in a community system. The outcome of these activities is expected to be improvement of the quality of life for the chronically mentally ill (Tessler & Goldman, 1982).

The Community Support Program demonstrates a federal initiative directed toward dealing with some of the problems brought on by deinstitutionalization of severely mentally ill persons. In an evaluation sponsored by the federal government, community support systems in local communities were found to have achieved a number of program goals (Tessler & Goldman, 1982). The Community Support Program was implemented to some extent by pilot programs in several states prior to the passage of the Mental Health Systems Act of 1980. Its development has been limited since the beginning of the Reagan administration, but it continues as a major framework for service at the local community level.

REHABILITATION SERVICES

Psychiatric rehabilitation, also referred to as psychosocial rehabilitation, has become an effective method of service delivery with the severely mentally ill (Bachrach, 1992; Lamb, 1994; Peterson, Patrick, & Rissmeyer, 1990; Sartorius, 1992). In a review of studies of psychiatric rehabilitation, Wallace (1993) found considerable evidence of program effectiveness—"severely mentally ill individuals learn skills, use them in their own environments, and may receive other clinically meaningful benefits" (p. 537). The goals of psychiatric rehabilitation are based on a philosophy and technology that "focus on treating the consequences of the mental illness rather than just the illness per se" (Anthony, 1992, p. 165). A useful approach to rehabilitation has been developed from a model of illness generated by the World Health Organization. WHO's model focuses on the illness (impairment) and the consequences of the illness (disability and handicap). This focus has been translated into a rehabilitation model guided by the concepts of impairment, disability, and disadvantage. These concepts are illustrated in Exhibit 1 (Anthony, Cohen, & Farkas, 1990).

In keeping with this model, many psychiatric rehabilitation programs follow two strategies: "development of clients' skills and development of clients' supports," with the assumption "that if people's skill levels and/or the supports in their immediate environments are changed, those with psychiatric disabilities will be able to perform the

Exhibit 1   The Rehabilitation Model for Severe Mental Illness

	Stages		
	Impairment	Disability	Disadvantage
Definitions	Any loss or abnormality of psychological, physiological, or anatomical structure or function	Any restriction or lack of ability to perform an activity and/or role in the manner or within the range considered normal for a human being (resulting from an impairment)	A lack of opportunity for a given individual that limits or prevents the fulfillment of a role that is normal (depending on age, sex, social, or cultural factors) for that individual (resulting from an impairment and/or a disability)
Examples	Hallucinations, delusions, depression	Lack of work adjustment skills, social skills, or ADL skills, which restricts one's residential educational, vocational, and social roles*	Discrimination and poverty, which contribute to unemployment and homelessness

*ADL is activities of daily living.

Source: W.A. Anthony, M.D. Cohen, & M.D. Farkas, *Psychiatric Rehabilitation* (Boston: Boston University, Center for Psychiatric Rehabilitation, 1990).

activities necessary to function in specific roles of their choice" (Anthony, 1992, p. 166). These strategies must confront a number of restrictions to a person's well-being, including "discrimination, lack of economic resources, disincentives, and lack of reasonable accommodations," and must recognize "that the restricted range of opportunity experienced by many mentally ill persons contributes to the person's rehabilitation outcome" (p. 166).

Programs of psychosocial rehabilitation include day hospitals, day treatment, partial hospitalization, psychosocial rehabilitation centers, self-help programs, and assertive treatment programs (Anthony, 1992). The reader interested in psychiatric rehabilitation will find articles in the *Psychosocial Rehabilitation Journal* of special relevance, as well as educational materials developed at the Center for Psychiatric Rehabilitation of Boston University.

As we have already noted, one of the ten principal functions to be performed in a community support system is the provision of "such psychosocial rehabilitation services as goal-direction, rehabilitation, evaluation, transitional living arrangements, socialization, and vocational rehabilitation" (NIMH, 1982, p. 1). The purpose of providing psychosocial services is to "improve or maintain clients' abilities to function in normal social roles" (p. 210). These services include, but are not limited to, the following:

- Help clients evaluate their strengths and weaknesses and participate in setting their own goals and planning for appropriate services.
- Train clients in daily and community living skills such as medication use, diet, exercise, personal hygiene, shopping, cooking, budgeting, housekeeping, use of transportation, and other community resources.
- Help clients develop social skills, interests and leisure time activities, including opportunities for age-appropriate, culturally appropriate daytime and evening activities.
- Help clients find and make use of appropriate employment opportunities, vocational rehabilitation services, or other supported or sheltered work environments. Provision must also be made for people who may not be able to use these opportunities and services, but who need a chance to be useful and a meaningful way to structure their time (p. 210).

These services are framed within a philosophy of treatment that focuses on the client's learning of community living skills in a service setting located in the community. A number of types of psychosocial rehabilitation programs follow the goals and philosophy developed by the Community Support Program model and have demonstrated effectiveness (Lamb, 1994).

While these programs have gained in popularity among clients and their advocates, there are a number of policy considerations that affect program development. As Anthony (1992) has noted, "Effective integration of psychiatric rehabilitation into mental health systems depends on the skills, knowledge, and attitudes of the various personnel who interact with the client; the programs used by the personnel; and the service systems that support the people and programs" (p. 167). The issue with regard to personnel is the need for appropriate educational training for this type of mental health service. The programs themselves must be developed and administered in keeping with the principles of psychosocial rehabilitation, especially with an emphasis on the client's life in the community. Psychosocial rehabilitation cannot operate well without being supported with funding and integrated into a community mental health system. Thus, policy makers must assure such support and integration if rehabilitation programs are to be successful. These principles have been enunciated in the Community

Support Program model described earlier in this chapter. We now present descriptions of several examples of rehabilitation programs currently operating in a number of American communities.

The Fountain House Model

The Fountain House model emerged out of a voluntary organization established by a small group of patients at a state mental hospital and a small group of volunteers from the community. The group took on the name "We Are Not Alone," with the purpose of assisting mental patients in their planning for release from the hospital and for their adjustment in the community. Recognition is given to J. H. Beard for his leadership in developing the organization's rehabilitation programs. Around 1948 the "We Are Not Alone" group was able to purchase a building near Times Square in New York City to serve as a "clubhouse" for its members. Descriptions of the principles and services during the early development of this clubhouse model of rehabilitation are provided by Beard (1978). The focus of the program is on the transition of individuals from mental hospitals to the community. The locale for the service is the clubhouse, a building where the ex-patients come as members, where individuals participate in the day-to-day activities of the clubhouse, and from which members keep in touch with other members through home and hospital visits.

In the early 1950s, the National Council of Jewish Women became involved in efforts to provide services for the mentally ill discharged into the community. This organization helped establish the Fountain House model in Chicago, Cleveland, Pittsburgh, and Louisville. As Peterson et al. (1990) have noted, current versions of this model vary to some extent in their services and staffing, but they generally adhere to the basic principles of Fountain House. There is a review process provided by Fountain House in New York for organizations seeking to use this model. Within the clubhouse, staff and members work together in units related to vocational training, in activities related to upkeep, thrift shop, snack bar, clerical office, kitchen-dining room, and administration. An apartment program focuses on helping individuals locate appropriate living quarters. Special attention is given to work-related activities, such as a transitional employment program leading to independent work arrangements. Clubhouses also have social and recreational programs for members. Rehabilitation centers that employ the Fountain House model may be involved in additional activities, most notably outreach activities with natural support systems and with community agencies, and in social advocacy activities. A number of program evaluation studies have been completed in rehabilitation centers using the Fountain House model, demonstrating successful attainment of program objectives (Beard, 1982; Peterson et al., 1990; Rosenfield & Neese-Todd, 1993).

ACT Model of Community Care

Perhaps the best-known models of community-based care for severely mentally ill persons are those developed in Madison, Wisconsin, especially the Assertive Community Treatment Team program (ACT). As Test (1981) points out, these programs include a major focus on comprehensive psychosocial treatments. The principal actors in the development of the Madison models were Leonard Stein, Mary Ann Test, and their colleagues at the Mendota State Hospital and the Dane County Mental Health Center in Madison, Wisconsin (Stein et al., 1975). These models of care have undergone several phases of development since 1970. Programs are always based on the premise that for most people the community is a better place for treatment than a hospital. A historical review of the ongoing development of the Madison model is provided by Thompson et al. (1990). The first model, Total In-Community Treatment, focused on a target population of "difficult-to-discharge patients," by providing inpatient psychosocial activities designed to prepare patients to leave the hospital and return to the community. Follow-up community care was oriented toward maintaining the patient in the community and avoiding rehospitalization. In a second phase, a program entitled Training in Community Living was developed to reach "patients presenting for admission" and thereby prevent hospitalization (p. 628).

Using an experimental model of treatment and evaluation, Stein and Test compared patients treated in the Mendota Mental Health Institute (a hospital setting) to patients in a community-based treatment program. The results of these studies demonstrated that the Training in Community Living program was "effective as an alternative to hospitalization for a large majority of patients presenting to a public facility for admission" (Thompson et al., 1990, p. 628). Out of this program emerged two other versions of the model, an Assertive Community Treatment Team approach and a Mobile Community Treatment model. These last two models have been replicated throughout the United States, and the special role of the assertive community worker has been described in the professional literature by Witheridge (1989). Research by Stein and Test and their colleagues, as well as evaluations of other applications of the Assertive Community Treatment Team model (Olfson, 1990), have "demonstrated that they are highly effective in reducing the need for psychiatric hospitalization of chronic mentally ill patients" (Taube et al., 1990, p. 642).

Community Residential Care Programs: Fairweather Lodge

Residential care is one of the major program components of Community Mental Health Centers. Residential care placement often follows one of three models: "residential care as a part of the treatment continuum; residential care as a residual system of custody; residential care as a developmental context for the mentally ill" (Segal & Kotler, 1989, p. 238). Care is usually provided in one of four types of facilities: family care, board and care homes, halfway houses, and satellite house programs. The principles of psychosocial rehabilitation are sometimes employed in these facilities, especially in halfway houses and satellite house programs.

An example of an innovative residential care program which involves psychosocial rehabilitation and serves as an alternative to hospitalization is the Fairweather Lodge program. As conceived by George Fairweather, mentally ill patients are trained on small group wards for discharge into the community into a Lodge, a residential care home with 6 to 15 patients (Fairweather, 1964; Segal & Kotler, 1989). The Lodge home provides for a supportive living situation and for employment opportunities. The hospital training program emphasizes self-management, problem-solving skills, mutual responsibility in decision making, and self-support abilities through a peer reference group. While the training is going on, hospital staff locate a residence for the group. There is also a development of employment opportunities for the Lodge members, usually through a small business venture such as a custodial service, lawn service, mailing service, car wash, or landscaping business. Whenever possible, a Lodge group owns and operates a small business. A home coordinator is available to the Lodge members as a program coordinator, but does not reside with the members. Lodge members control the activities of the house but may call upon the coordinator for technical advice.

As an alternative to hospitalization and to other types of community care, Lodge programs have been found to be effective in preventing rehospitalization and providing employment for members, and to be less expensive than hospitalization (Fairweather, 1980). The creation of Lodge programs often involves State Departments of Mental Health, State Psychiatric Hospitals, and Community Mental Health Centers. The Lodge residences provide an opportunity for consumer-directed mental health services in the community.

Community Mental Health Care: Nursing Homes

For some years, nursing homes have been "the largest single set-ting for the care of the mentally ill" (Linn & Stein, 1989, p. 267). This circumstance was the result of deinstitutionalization, the financial benefits of older adults covered under the Medicaid program, and other federal and state laws. A number of other forces made the trans-fer of older adults from state and county mental hospitals to nursing homes a frequent occurrence, such as the use of psychotropic med-ications, the discharge practices of state hospitals, and the aftercare programs of community mental health centers. Unfortunately, mental health services have not been provided to a large proportion of nurs-ing home residents with mental disorders, including both older and younger adults. Recognizing this problem, Congress enacted the Nursing Home Reform Act of 1987 (P.L. 100-203). This act required screening for mental disorders of individuals seeking admission to, or residing in, a Medicare or Medicaid certified facility (Gottlieb, 1992). The Act also required that mental health treatment and services be provided for mentally ill persons residing in nursing homes.

SELF-HELP AND MENTAL HEALTH SERVICE

Self-help groups are an important part of the mental health ser-vice system. The Surgeon General's Workshop on Self-Help and Pub-lic Health (U.S. DHHS, 1987) noted that "The essence of these groups is that their members help each other cope with or overcome a health or other problem that they all share, with mutual aid and emotional support as a central purpose" (p. 1). In the mental health area, Rootes and Aanes (1992) have defined self-help groups in terms of the fol-lowing criteria:

- A self-help group is supportive and educational.
- Its leadership comes from within the group.
- The group addresses a single major life-disrupting event.
- Group members participate voluntarily.
- The group has no monetary interests or profit obligation.
- Membership is anonymous and confidential (p. 379).

Under this formulation, "the focus of self-help groups is personal growth, which is accomplished primarily through education and sup-port" (p. 381).

Some individuals with mental health problems participate in self-help groups, at times in place of professional help, and at other times in conjunction with professional services. The self-help system is one of three major helping systems available to people with mental health problems (Powell, 1987). The first is the professional mental health system, including hospital and other institutional care, community mental health programs, and psychosocial rehabilitation programs. The second is the community caregiving system, including informal care through family and social networks. The third is the self-help system. Two central questions arise with regard to these three helping systems. First, how are they similar and how are they different from each other? (Powell, 1987). Second, what kinds of interrelationships, competing or complementary, occur between these systems? (Hasenfeld & Gidron, 1993; Powell, 1987).

Powell (1987) has responded to the first question by noting four major ways in which the three major helping systems differ: in regard to the role of the provider, basis of power, specificity of function, and role of the participant. Provider roles of the professional are sanctioned by educational training, and these providers are paid to perform specific tasks based on professional credentials. In contrast, the nonprofessional informal helper is not paid and does not carry out professional tasks. Self-help group members rely on their personal experiences rather than "expertise" to help each other. Professionals have technical expertise as their basis of power, self-help groups have experientially based expertise, and community caregivers have social expertise. The functions of the three helping systems appear to differ in that community caregivers usually have nonspecific functions, while professional and self-help groups usually have specialized purposes. Finally, the role of the participant differs in the various helping systems. In self-help, the participant's role is mutual, self-directed; in professional helping, the participant's role is nonmutual, other-directed; in informal community care, the participant's role varies with regard to mutuality and direction.

A major problem within the mental health system is the relationship of the various helping systems to each other. In particular, there is a tension between mental health organizations and self-help groups (Powell, 1994). Yet, as Hasenfeld and Gidron (1993) suggest, "there is a growing recognition of the benefit of linking the services each provides" (p. 218). Hasenfeld and Gidron (1993) use an organizational perspective to examine two patterns of interaction between self-help groups and human service organizations: competition and conflict vs. cooperation. These patterns are said to depend on the nature of the self-help group and the human service organizations, that is, their domain and mission, dependence on external resources, service technology, and internal structure. In the mental health field in particular there continue to be efforts to reduce the tensions between service agencies and self-help groups and to promote positive interrelationships.

According to the ECA studies, the participation of individuals with mental health problems in self-help is low. These studies show life-time participation rates of 3.6% for men and 2.2% for women. The life-time rate for non-Hispanic whites respondents was 3.6%, compared to 3.2% for Latinos and 1.1% for African-Americans (Lieberman & Snowden, 1993). Epidemiological study findings on self-help groups are very limited, and given the vast diversity in types of groups, there is a need for more extensive research in this area (Powell, 1993; Snow-den & Lieberman, 1994).

Self-Help Agencies

Client/consumer-run self-help agencies represent a somewhat dif-ferent form of self-help. As of 1993, a total of 38 state mental health agencies sponsored consumer-run agencies. The 261 agencies funded under state mental health systems varied considerably in regard to their purposes, including peer/mutual support, client-staffed busi-nesses, technical assistance, policy development, case advocacy, crisis intervention, vocational rehabilitation, case management, social ser-vices, transitional housing, and residential crisis facilities (Lutterman, 1994).

The distinguishing characteristics of consumer-run, self-help agen-cies are examined by Segal, Silverman, and Temkin (1993). These agen-cies have an overriding goal of empowerment of consumers "within the organization through exercising control over their collective expe-riences" (p. 710). In these agencies empowerment at individual, organ-izational, and societal levels is a major objective of clients. As Segal et al. (1993) note, clients help each other obtain resources, develop coping skills, enhance members' self-concepts and reduce stigma, give mem-bers control in the agencies' governance, administration and service delivery, and foster members' involvement in social policy making. These features of the self-help agency are similar to independent living programs and different from traditional psychiatric rehabilitation pro-grams. These latter programs usually are unable to empower clients, as they rely primarily on the professionals to define client problems and direct the resolution of them.

Segal and his colleagues (1995) provide an interesting picture of the members of four self-help agencies in the San Francisco Bay Area. These researchers studied the consumers of services in drop-in centers that provided "mutual support groups, drop-in space, resources for survival in the community, and direct services" (p. 270). Eighty-seven percent of the respondents had confirmed mental disorders, and 50% had a dual diagnosis of mental disorder and substance abuse. The principal function of the self-help agency was to provide material resources, such as food, clothing, telephones, and help in finding shelter. A principal conclusion of the study was "that self-help agencies, in combination with community mental health agencies, can serve a poor, primarily African-American and often homeless population. . . subgroups that are traditionally less well served by the mental health system" (p. 274). Of special note was the fact that the self-help agencies were able to reach mental health consumers who otherwise might not have used services, and that the agencies were able to connect them with mental health agencies for medical and psychotherapeutic care.

Consumer-run agencies are also illustrated in the work of Mowbray et al. (1988). Such agency programs include a project employing four advocates to assist patients in their transition to the community; a program in which volunteers help clients practice social skills and engage in normal social activities; a program directed toward helping clients with skills to remain independent in the community; and a drop-in center for social activities and mutual support. Evaluation of these programs led to the conclusion that they were successful, "indicating the productivity and diversity of services possible from consumer groups" (p. 155).

COORDINATION OF MENTAL HEALTH CARE

In our description of various parts of the mental health system, it is apparent that mental health services are often "fragmented, incomplete, and often inefficient" and there is a "need for improved coordination of services" (Rochefort, 1993, p. 133). A number of policy initiatives have been made to improve coordination of services. For example, coordination of services has been a major goal of community mental health centers. This emphasis on coordination has appeared in numerous reports and legislative acts, such as the President's Commission on Mental Health (1978), the Mental Health Systems Act of 1980, the State Comprehensive Mental Health Services Plan of 1986, and the Steward B. McKinney Homeless Assistance Act of 1987.

A number of mechanisms developed to achieve coordination of mental health services have been identified by Rochefort (1993). These include strategies at the client, organization, and systems levels of service. The most common strategy has been some form of case management, which "assigns responsibility for the multiple services needs of clients to an individual or team" (p. 136). This approach to service is only one part of a broader plan for coordination inherent in community support systems, which seek to coordinate various programs at the local community level. In some communities, coordination is achieved through the incorporation of public mental health agencies into an "integrated services" model, whereby a number of public services are organized under one umbrella, such as public health, social services, vocational rehabilitation services, employment training, and substance abuse programs. In regard to coordination of funding for mental health services, one model has involved the creation of mental health authorities (Goldman, Morrissey, & Ridgely, 1990). Each of these strategies for coordination has its own set of limitations and obstacles, due in part to the nature of mental illness, the bureaucratic features of service organizations, and the power and control problems inherent in interorganizational relationships (Rochefort, 1993).

Dorwart and Epstein (1993) have examined mental health systems in an effort to explain why they "are so often perceived to fail, to be inadequate in meeting the needs of patients, or worse, to be inhumane and harmful" (p. 148). These authors conclude that a major factor limiting success for mental health systems is their relationship to other more dominant systems, including medical, long-term care, social service, and justice. The mental health system often becomes a residual system, taking on functions related to other systems without primary responsibility or adequate funding to carry out its mission. This circumstance leads to a need for integration, that is, "organizing the organizations" to achieve coordination of "public-private, federal-state, institution-community dimensions of a mental health system" (p. 153).

RURAL MENTAL HEALTH

ECA studies have shown that rural rates of disorder are similar to those in urban areas. There are some differences in specific disorders, with rates of alcohol abuse/dependence and cognitive deficit higher in rural areas (Wagenfeld et al., 1993). Yet, mental health services for rural populations are much more limited than those for residents of urban areas (Human & Wasem, 1991; Wagenfeld, 1981). Most of the programs and service delivery patterns described in this chapter are urban models and have not been available and/or appropriate in a rural context. For example, rural areas usually lack hospital psychiatric emergency services and adequate services for children, adolescents, and other special populations. The special needs and service delivery problems for rural populations have been recognized by the Office of Rural Health Policy in the U.S. Department of Health and Human Services. The need for increased access to mental health services has been identified as the major problem for residents of rural areas, especially since "groups at greater risk for mental disorder...the elderly, the chronically ill, the poor, and the dependent...are disproportionately represented in rural areas" (Human & Wasem, 1991, p. 233).

The United States government's Office of Rural Health Policy has a major responsibility at the federal level to help resolve rural mental health issues, such as access to services and coordination between physical and mental health systems. At the same time, other federal agencies are involved in supporting health services for rural populations, such as the Health Resources and Services Administration; Health Care Financing Administration; Alcohol, Drug Abuse, and Mental Health Administration; U.S. Department of Agriculture; and U.S. Department of Education (Human & Wasem, 1991). Of special note is the significant relationship between health care, including mental health care, and the economic conditions of rural America. Service needs and service delivery problems are often associated with poor economic conditions in rural areas. As a consequence, there is a call for a comprehensive policy of rural resource development in order to prevent mental health problems as well as to meet mental health needs (Pulver, 1988). Other recommendations for the development of rural health care policies include attention to critical elements that affect policy making. These include data and research on rural mental health needs; the need for mental health professionals; financial access to health care; dissemination of information about innovative service programs; community and health professional involvement and cooperation; and the need for outreach, coordination, and case management (Human & Wasem, 1991).

ADVOCACY FOR SERVICES: THE NATIONAL ALLIANCE FOR THE MENTALLY ILL

The National Alliance for the Mentally Ill is the major national voluntary organization that advocates for services for mentally ill persons. This organization, with its membership of parents, relatives, and others associated with mentally ill persons, has characteristics of a mutual support group and a social movement (Hatfield, 1991). The organization and movement emerged in 1979 from parents' "dissatisfaction about (1) lack of services for their mentally ill relatives, (2) stigma that devastated both patients and parents, and (3) inability of professionals to serve this population in a caring way" (Hatfield, 1991, p. 96).

The national organization of NAMI is made up of local and state chapters throughout the United States. Some of its advocacy activities include public education, including anti-stigma campaigns, and support of public mental health services. A special interest of the organization has been to advocate for research on mental illness, particularly through support for the National Alliance for Research on Schizophrenia and Affective Disorders (Johnson, 1989). NAMI's organizational ideology is based on the following beliefs (Hatfield, 1991, p. 98):

- Mental illness is not a mental health problem; it is a biological illness.
- Mental illness is a no-fault disease.
- The family is important in support and treatment.
- Society has an obligation to provide treatment and care.

These beliefs provide a foundation for members to support each other in local chapter groups, not unlike other self-help groups, and at the same time to advocate, along with mental health professionals, for people with mental illness.

The role of NAMI in the mental health field has been the subject of controversy, as noted in the following question, "Does NAMI represent the needs of all families with psychiatric patients?" (Johnson, 1994; Unzicker, 1994). In a discussion of this issue, Johnson (1994) has argued that NAMI represents families as well as mentally ill persons, specifically people with persistent and serious illnesses. While these two groups, families and recovering patients, may have somewhat different needs, NAMI claims that it is organized to advocate for the interests of both. Unzicker (1994) holds the opposite view—that NAMI does not, and cannot, represent mentally ill people, because this role can only be appropriately carried out by those who are ill. Unzicker argues that NAMI is only interested in supporting a small segment of people with mental disorders, those with specific, severe, diagnoses, and that the family members represent an elite part of the society, leaving many ethnic and social class groups unrepresented.

REVIEW

The major programs and services provided by the mental health system are identified in terms of institutional care, community-based services, prevention services, and innovative programs. Efforts to evaluate these various programs are highlighted. The federal government's Community Support Program is discussed in terms of its focus on serving seriously mentally ill people through the coordination of the federal, state, and local governmental entities. Specific community-based programs that have as a major goal the social rehabilitation of individuals in the community, such as residential and clubhouse programs, are given special attention. The mental health service needs of people in rural areas are identified. Finally, self-help groups and advocacy groups are examined in regard to their relationships to mental health service programs.

6.
Financing of Mental Health Services

The financing of mental health programs and services is an inherent and crucial consideration in policy making. Policy issues about who gets what mental health services and how they are delivered are closely related to funding patterns. Cycles of reform in mental health care are often associated with changes in funding, especially when federal and state governments seek to expand or curtail expenditures for health and social service programs.

Experts involved in developing mental health policies for the Clinton administration's health care reform proposal recognized that "Over time, the delivery and financing of mental health and substance abuse care have evolved into a complex patchwork of services" (Arons et al., 1994, p. 192). Health care reform proposals in the 1990s have responded to these problems with a major focus on new funding arrangements for mental health care. For example, the Clinton health care reform proposal includes a goal of providing "basic coverage for mental health/substance abuse care for all Americans," as well as the goal "to fully integrate mental health/substance abuse services into the mainstream of health care" (Arons et al., 1994, p. 193). These goals of coverage and integration represent two of the most significant demands for change in the financing of mental health care.

PUBLIC/PRIVATE FINANCING

A significant feature of mental health care financing is the blurred line between public and private funding in relation to the provision of services. This blurring is found in the trend toward privatization, which refers to "both the growing number of private nonprofit and for-profit facilities carrying out mental health care and the increasing purchase by public authorities of services from private agencies" (Dorwart & Epstein, 1993, p. 59). Despite the increased use of public funds for the purchase of services from the private sector, public funding and private insurance plans for mental health care represent a continuation of a "two-class" system of public- and private-sector care. This leaves people with severe illness and lack of private insurance dependent on a "complex, uncoordinated mix of federal, state, local, and private funds to purchase services" (Arons et al., 1994, p. 194).

Traditionally, federal, state, and local community governments have assumed responsibility for mentally ill persons who were unable to finance their own care through "out-of-pocket" funds or through private insurance. The public sector finances care for the uninsured, as well as for people with entitlements under Medicare and Medicaid. The policy question concerns how much responsibility the various levels of government are willing to assume for mental health care financing.

As our review of the development of mental health policy in the United States indicates, the major responsibility for funding of mental health care has moved from the private sector (family), to the local community, to the states, to the federal government, and back to the states and local community. Currently, mental health care continues to be funded by several sources, generally divided into the private sector (e.g., Blue Cross/Blue Shield, commercial insurers, self-insured, and self-pay) and the public sector (e.g., state/county programs, Medicaid/Medicare, Supplemental Security Income). Service providers such as hospitals, community mental health centers, and professionals in private practice often receive payment through both private and public sectors.

A substantial number of Americans, estimated in 1990 to be about 36 million people, have no insurance coverage for mental health services (Arons & Buck, 1994). Private-sector insurance plans usually lead to higher quantity and quality of services compared to those provided by the public sector. This conclusion comes from comparisons of state mental hospital care vs. private mental hospital and general hospital care, and comparisons of public community mental health services vs. private-sector services in the community (Dorwart & Schlesinger,

1988). However, benefits are usually restricted under private insurance coverage, leading at times to shifts in costs to the public sector, especially for rehabilitative and extended care services (Arons & Buck, 1994).

There is some consensus among mental health consumers and professionals that funding levels for the public mental health system are inadequate, both in relation to institutional care and community-based care, especially for the severely mentally ill, the elderly, and the homeless. There is disagreement concerning which levels of government should finance public mental health care for these individuals. Public funding varies widely, as federal funding is distributed differentially to the states, and different funding patterns are found among the states and local governments. As a consequence, it is difficult to make generalizations about public- and private-sector funding of mental health services at any given point in time. Nevertheless, we will identify some of the major funding patterns for mental health care and examine policy issues related to the goal of providing mental health care for all Americans.

EXPENDITURES FOR MENTAL ILLNESS

The costs of mental illness can be expressed in general terms, such as economic burdens on individuals, families, and society, as well as in specific dollar terms. Estimates of dollar figures are based on complex methods for calculating costs (Rice, Kelman, & Miller, 1992; Taube, 1990). The work of Rice and her colleagues (1992) provides a foundation for such estimates. Their cost figures include core costs directly connected to illness and related costs involving direct treatment and support, lost productivity, and caregiver services. Based on this framework, estimated costs to society for mental and substance abuse range from 273 billion dollars in 1990 to 370 billion dollars in 1992 (Arons & Buck, 1994; SAMHSA, 1994c).

FEDERAL/STATE MENTAL HEALTH POLICY
AND FUNDING

Public funding patterns are derived from both *de jure* and *de facto* mental health policies. As Kiesler and Sibulkin (1987) have noted, the *de jure* mental health policy of the United States can be characterized as one of deinstitutionalization, including a shift of services from state hospital care to community-based outpatient care. These authors argue, however, that federal insurance coverage has supported a *de facto* mental health policy of institutional care. The funding arrangements of the federally funded programs of Medicare and Medicaid support this argument, as they foster inpatient care and include financial disincentives for outpatient and community care.

Both the Medicare and the Medicaid programs were created by amendments to the Social Security Act in 1965. (Medicare was established for aged [65 and over] and disabled individuals who contributed to the Social Security system. These persons became eligible for mental health services financed through Medicare.) A majority of the Medicare funds used for mental health care are applied to inpatient care in hospitals or nursing homes. Medicaid is a Supplemental Security Insurance program through which the federal government shares with the states the funding of health care for individuals not eligible for Medicare. Medicaid covers some mental health services for the "poor," that is, the aged, blind, disabled, and Aid to Families with Dependent Children (AFCD) families, while excluding intact families, the working poor, single people, and childless couples (Kiesler & Sibulkin, 1987). Medicaid is an important source for mental health funding because it is linked to the Supplemental Security Income program. A large number of Supplementary Security Income recipients have a need for both acute and continuing mental health care (Frank & McGuire, 1994). Under Medicaid, some health services are mandated under amendments to the Social Security Act, while others are optional to the states. The states may limit the extent of coverage for all services, with variation between the states in optional and mandatory services. Coverage applying to mental health care includes physician services, outpatient hospital services, clinic services, and all of the institutional services (Kiesler & Sibulkin, 1987).

In addition to federal funds for mental health services through the Medicare and Medicaid programs, funding is administered through the states under the block grant format of The Omnibus Budget Reconciliation Act of 1981 (P.L. 97-35). Most states have allocated a higher proportion of their mental health dollars (both federal funds and state funds) to institutional care than to community-based care programs (Rochefort & Logan, 1989; Frank & McGuire, 1994). Federal and state programs not only provide for mental health services but also pay for a range of health and social welfare benefits to mentally ill persons (Cain, 1993). These benefits include Social Security income and entitlements for retired persons, blind persons, disabled persons, and certain family members of individuals covered by Social Security. Individuals in these groups who are not covered by Social Security benefits may be eligible for Supplemental Security Income through a financial means test. Income for disabled persons is provided through the Social Security Disability Insurance program. In many states, public welfare departments provide emergency relief based on financial means tests—income that is considered essential for the physical and mental health of mentally ill persons (Cain, 1993). The federal, state, and local funding of social welfare benefits is the major policy force that allows mentally ill persons to reside in their local communities.

PRIVATIZATION

As the history of state mental hospitals in the United States attests, the responsibility for inpatient care of the seriously mentally ill in public hospitals has been assumed by the states for more than 200 years. Recently, however, privatization arrangements have made it possible for state funds to be used to cover the cost of some inpatient care in private-sector hospitals. Over the past two decades, a number of factors have encouraged a move to privatization of mental health services, such as more liberal insurance coverage, Medicare and Medicaid programs, community mental health center development, briefer hospital stays, and the reduced role of the federal government with regard to the states' programs (Dorwart & Schlesinger, 1988). Privatization is apparent in the growth of the private psychiatric hospital sector. For example, from 1970 to 1987, the number of inpatient beds in private facilities increased from 7% to 35%, while the number of general hospital inpatient beds increased from 4% to 20%, with multi-hospital corporations operating more than 7% of private psychiatric hospitals (Dorwart & Schlesinger, 1988).

There are several reasons for this change in the organization and sponsorship of mental health services through the growth of the private sector (Dorwart & Schlesinger, 1988). First, there has been an increasing demand for mental health services. This is attributed to several factors: insurance coverage for psychiatric hospital care has expanded; the public appears to be more willing to use mental health services; employers are more willing to provide coverage for mental health services, especially through their employee assistance plans; and the media supports the treatment of mental disorders and of drug and alcohol abuse. While the general health care system has had problems in terms of profitability, the mental health care sector offers opportunities for growth and profit, especially for system-affiliated hospitals. State-level mental health administrators have encouraged the use of local community private mental health services through the purchase of service contracts. Thus, as Dorwart and Schlesinger (1988) conclude, "the privatization of mental health care involves the growth of both for-profit inpatient care, primarily in system-affiliated psychiatric specialty hospitals, and private nonprofit treatment, primarily in psychiatric units of community general hospitals" (p. 547).

Some issues related to the privatization of mental health services, as noted by Dorwart and Schlesinger (1988), include the following possibilities: services may be inaccessible to individuals who cannot pay for them; a higher quality of care may be available in private facilities than in public facilities; and private systems may be less responsive to community needs and may limit investment in teaching and research. These possible effects of privatization on mental health care delivery have generated the following policy issues:

- A three-tiered structure has emerged: public, private nonprofit, and private for-profit providers of mental health services. Issues regarding this structure involve the accessibility, quality, and cost of care in each of these sectors.
- With the expansion of inpatient services in the private sector, there may be problems with coordination/fragmentation of services, aftercare, and monitoring of quality of care.
- If and when expansion of mental health services slows, profits may decline, and new alternatives for payment may be necessary.
- In order to consider policy alternatives, research on the relationship of ownership arrangements to aspects of care is needed, especially with regard to the place of inpatient and community programs within the mental health care system.

These policy issues demonstrate that privatization has made an already complex system of mental health service financing even more complex. The prior dichotomy between private and public sectors and the dominance of the public sector has changed as a result of new policies and practices in the mental health field and the general health care field.

MANAGED CARE AND PAYMENT PLANS

The interdependence of health care financing policies and delivery of mental health services is apparent in discussions of managed care and various types of reimbursement plans (Dorwart & Epstein, 1993; Hoge et al., 1994; Mechanic, Schlesinger, & McAlpine, 1995). The growth of managed-care health systems is attributed to the policy initiatives of the federal government, especially the passage of the Health Maintenance Organization Act of 1973 (P.L. 93-222) and subsequent amendments. This Act provided financial subsidies for the development of new HMOs meeting federal qualifications. For example, these HMOs were required to offer a number of basic services, such as outpatient mental health care, crisis intervention services, and treatment of alcoholics and drug abusers. The Congress has continued to support the expansion of managed care through legislation that provided for administrative flexibility and for increased use of HMOs by Medicare and Medicaid recipients (DeLeon, VandenBos, & Bulatao, 1991).

From a managed-care perspective, mechanisms must be developed to contain costs of care and to prevent overuse of services. Managed care consists of these mechanisms, that is, "organizational arrangements that alter treatment decisions that would otherwise have been made by individual patients or providers" (Mechanic et al., 1995, p. 20). Mechanisms for meeting the policy goal of reducing utilization include "(a) pretreatment authorization, (b) concurrent utilization review, (c) benefit plans designed to provide financial incentives or constraints to receive care from efficient providers, and (d) increasing requirements for greater employee-user cost sharing" (Broskowski, 1991, p. 8). Mechanisms for controlling the cost of care include "(a) capitated payments for a defined group of beneficiaries, (b) negotiated fee-for-service payments to preferred providers selected for quality and efficiency, (c) prospective fixed payments for DRGs, (d) claims review, and (e) insurance coverage extended to cover less expensive but equally effective treatment alternatives" (Broskowski, 1991, p. 8).

The most prominent managed-care systems are HMOs, preferred provider organizations, and review/utilization management mechanisms. These approaches to care management all have implications for the delivery of mental health services, because they affect the organizational setting (e.g., inpatient or outpatient care) and the financial arrangements for payment of services. Managed care occurs in organizations that influence patient care "through case-by-case assessments of the appropriateness of care prior to its provision" (Dorwart, 1990, p. 1088). HMOs establish service arrangements with providers and set up procedures to control members' access to health care. PPOs "generally consist of groups of independent providers who have agreed to provide health care at a reduced rate by contract with a given payer such as a major employer or insurance carrier" (Ridgely & Goldman, 1989, p. 357). Both HMOs and PPOs have some type of utilization review, a strategy that may have negative effects on patient care and may result in rationing of psychiatric care. Managed-care systems are sometimes criticized for not meeting the mental health needs of individuals, particularly since they often provide minimal levels of service and use "a physician gatekeeper who is typically untrained in the mental health area" (DeLeon et al., 1991, p. 22).

The major models of reimbursement are based on a prepayment or prospective payment arrangement. Most employ a third-party payment plan, with the parties involved being the patient, the payer, and the provider of services. Under such a model, the patient does not pay the provider directly, but the provider receives reimbursement from a payer, such as an HMO or Blue Cross/Blue Shield. Usually payment comes after the service has been provided, and the payment may be limited due to co-payment provisions or other restrictions in the patient's coverage.

A number of variations of prospective or prepayment reimbursement plans have been developed for reimbursing health care. Two major variations are diagonosis-related group (DRG) arrangements and capitation payment.

These forms of reimbursement usually have been applied to general health care. There has been a concern that they may not be applicable to mental health care. Thus, psychiatric programs have been exempt from the prospective payment system developed for Medicare services. This has led to consideration of the goals of these cost-containment prepayment plans and the extent to which it would be appropriate to apply them to psychiatric services. Under a DRG plan, a hospital is paid a fixed amount of money for each hospital stay, based on the patient's location in a DRG created on the basis of diagnosis and selected other factors. Payment is based on the average cost of service to people in a particular group, not on the cost for an individual patient. The provider, such as a hospital, computes the average amount of time allotted to each illness or hospital stay.

Mental health professionals involved in the financing of mental health care have identified some of the problems of a DRG system in relation to psychiatric care, such as variations in length of stay for psychiatric patients (Jencks, Goldman, & McGuire, 1985). These variations come from the diagnostic system of psychiatry, the lack of standardized treatment for many mental disorders, and problems in relation to chronic disorders for which outside resources are necessary for care, such as family and support groups. In addition, there is considerable variation in the types of settings in which psychiatric services are delivered, such as psychiatric hospitals and general hospitals, as well as in staff providing the services. In this regard, Goldman et al. (1984) have posed several policy questions relative to prospective payment plans for services in psychiatric hospitals and psychiatric units of general hospitals:

- Are DRGs an appropriate system for classifying mental disorders? Can they be modified to better predict resource utilization?
- Are the alternatives such as negotiated contracts for per diem rates, capitation financing, or the retention of cost reimbursement better than prospective payment?
- Should psychiatric units in general hospitals continue to be exempted along with psychiatric hospitals?
- Is exclusion from prospective payment a benefit in the short run? (p. 463).

These questions must be considered in relation to the goals of a prepayment plan: efficiency, cost containment, quality of care, and assignment of resources in keeping with need (equity).

CAPITATION PLANS

Capitation plans involve payment of a fixed dollar amount for services delivered to an individual during a specified period of time, such as a period of one year (Lehman, 1987). Capitation is the mechanism used in HMO and individual practice association plans. Services under capitation plans are usually "bundled," that is, grouped by individual procedure, episode of illness, and coverage period (Lehman, 1987, p. 31). Lehman (1987) summarizes some of the pros and cons of capitation plans in relation to mental health care. Under such plans, the patient is thought to be more likely to seek care early and to take advantage of preventive services. The provider is guaranteed income and can coordinate services for an individual or group of individuals.

Arguments against capitation include the fact that the consumer may not have sound knowledge about alternatives and may have a limited choice of services. Providers may fear that the demand for services will exceed the amount for which the payment has covered. High-risk groups may be excluded from services by organizations under capitation plans. Lehman (1987) notes that the empirical literature on these issues "is both extensive and inconclusive" (p. 32).

An example of a capitation plan is provided in a study of mental health services in Philadelphia. The Philadelphia plan involved a restructuring of the mental health system within the community by focusing on Medicaid recipients (Schinnar & Rothbard, 1989). This capitation plan consolidated funding sources, introduced changes in the management of services, and targeted special groups for services. The Philadelphia plan was expected to have an impact on providers because of the financial incentives and management of services by a central funding authority. This is illustrated by the staffing possibilities, such as increased use of psychiatrists for high users, increased mix of professionals in relation to the case management model, and a mix of treatments. It is uncertain how the plan affects client care and outcome, especially for high users, the chronically mentally ill, the young, and the elderly. Some evaluation questions posed in regard to the Philadelphia plan include the following:

- Will targeting special programs to high users change their service utilization patterns and improve their mental health status?
- Can outpatient care be effectively substituted for inpatient care, and will the result be less costly services?
- Will targeting services to high users have a negative impact on the care of moderate users, and what unintended system changes does such targeting produce? (Schinnar & Rothbard, 1989, p. 683).

FUNDING FOR SPECIAL GROUPS: SEVERE MENTAL ILLNESS

There is an unusual degree of consensus among mental health professionals about care for people with severe and persistent mental illness: that "there is no system of treatment and care for the chronic mentally ill, and no simple method for funding services" (Talbott & Sharfstein, 1986, p. 1126). Talbott and Sharfstein (1986) identify a number of goals for a funding system that would meet the needs of severely mentally ill persons:

- comprehensive services, including treatment, shelter, support;
- fixed fiscal, administrative responsibility for this population;
- maintenance of adequate funding;
- coverage of all chronic mentally ill persons;
- integration of funding for treatment, shelter, support;
- provision of incentives for systems changes in institutional and community settings, in keeping with cost-effective and quality care;
- provision of some choice on the part of patients in types of care.

Maintaining that these goals cannot be reached under prevailing mental health funding arrangements, Talbott and Sharfstein (1986) have proposed a new funding system: "The program would take all existing funds regardless of the source or the service provided... medical, psychiatric, social, vocational, or other support service...and pool them into a single Social Security title for the chronic mentally ill" (p. 1129). Under such a plan, funds from the federal government would be granted to the states under a capitation plan. The state would then fund local community agencies for providing services to the chronic mentally ill, including hospital, day hospital, and support of families in home care. A principal feature of this proposal is the involvement of the federal and state governments in a capitation method of financing, with responsibility for services placed on the local community agencies.

ETHICS AND FINANCING OF MENTAL HEALTH SERVICES

There are a number of ethical dilemmas within the public mental health system related to funding of services. The following questions illustrate these dilemmas:

- Who gets treatment? Elpers (1986) notes that "the question arises of whether available resources should be devoted to treating patients who are chronically and severely ill or to treating those who are less ill and therefore can be expected to stay in or return to the mainstream" (p. 671).
- What amount of resources should be devoted to the mentally ill (rehabilitation), in contrast to prevention and research?
- What amount of resources should be devoted to special groups, such as the elderly, young adults, the homeless, or severely mentally ill persons?
- What amount of resources should be devoted to patients with needs for "expensive" treatment, leaving less resources for other patients? (Eth, 1990).
- How does a funding mechanism such as DRGs affect the service provided to patients?
- Given the movement for rights of individuals to remain in the community and the limits to involuntary commitment, how can the state protect individuals and citizens from harm?
- To what extent are prepayment plans justified if they result in undertreatment, even if they are more efficient? (Goldman & Sharfstein, 1987).
- In what ways does the DSM system influence the occurrence of misdiagnosis in practice?

To illustrate ways in which these questions might be examined, we explore the ethical issue regarding misdiagnosis. Kirk and Kutchins (1988) have noted the possible relationships between the DSM classification system and financial reimbursement for mental health services. These authors suggest that there may be times when classification and diagnosis of mental disorders is deliberately inaccurate, violating legal and ethical standards of behavior. In a study of clinical social workers, Kirk and Kutchins found frequent occurrence of deliberate misdiagnosis. Clinicians often rationalized giving an over- or under-diagnosis by seeing it "as either harmless or in the client's best interest: the client is helped to avoid a stigmatizing label or to obtain needed services" (p. 231). A very high proportion (80%) of the respondents indicated that their diagnoses were influenced by the reimbursement system. Kirk and Kutchins suggest that there are serious ethical implications related to these findings, both in regard to the individual clinician's practice, as well as to mental health policy making and service planning based on inaccurate data about client problems and service delivery. If, in fact, there is widespread misuse of DSM by social workers or other mental health professionals, then Kutchins and Kirk (1987) argue that "social workers need a new system for assessing clients for reimbursement as well as for case planning" (p. 209). In the use of DSM, these authors suggest procedures to help "maintain a practice that is ethically and legally sound:

- All diagnoses should be made with scrupulous regard for correct procedures.
- Careful attention should be paid to organic conditions.
- A physician should be routinely consulted about the medical aspects of a diagnosis.
- Every diagnosis should be accurately reported to the client and to the insurer.
- Clients should be advised, preferably in writing, that no diagnosis is meant to indicate a definitive judgment about any physical condition.
- Clients should be referred to physicians for the evaluation of any medical condition (p. 209).

HEALTH CARE REFORM AND MENTAL HEALTH

In the past decade there have been a number of health care reform proposals developed at the federal government level. Major features of these plans include variations in employer mandates for coverage, single-payer vs. multiple-payer arrangements, tax credits and deductions, and managed competition (Rochefort, 1993). A health care reform proposal of the Clinton administration, the American Health Security Act of 1993, included attention to the financing and delivery of mental health and substance abuse services. The proposed Act stated that "Mental health and substance abuse services form an integral component of a national system of health care" (American Health Security Act of 1993, Sec. 27). The Act also called for a comprehensive array of services and required states to develop a plan by the year 2001 to "move from the traditional two-tier structure for separate public and private mental health and substance abuse services" to an "integrated, comprehensive managed system of care" (Sec. 27). Research and demonstration projects were proposed to support "the development of improved outreach stategies for AIDS and HIV-infected drug abusers, the homeless, individuals involved in the criminal justice system, and populations with co-morbidity" (Sec. 186). The Act also includes funds to support "development of systems that link substance abuse and mental health treatment with primary care, target rural and remote areas and culturally distinct populations and facilitate the transfer of knowledge" (Sec. 186).

The proposal included a number of restrictions in mental health coverage that are not applied to the care of physical disorders (SAMHSA, 1993d). Differences in coverage for these two types of illness constitutes a major policy issue in regard to funding for mental health services. In this debate over parity between psychiatric disorders and physical illnesses, the American Psychiatric Association called for "non-discriminatory coverage of all medical disorders including mental illness (which includes substance abuse) for any medically necessary treatment...and (insurance benefits that) should be equal to other medical illnesses with respect to dollar limits (annual and lifetime), deductibles, coinsurance, and stop-loss provisions" (Savitz, Grace, & Brown, 1993, p. 7).

The Clinton plan did not propose equity, but contended that such coverage must be phased in due to the high costs of mental health services. Thus, the plan proposed hospital treatment with (a) a 60-day maximum a year; (b) a 30-day maximum for each visit, unless the patient poses a threat to his/her own life or someone else's life; (c) an end to these day limits in 2001; (d) no fee for patients in HMO-style plans, with patients in higher-cost plans paying 20% of fees. For psychotherapy, there would be (a) a 30-day maximum; (b) a fee of $25 per visit for patients in HMO-style plans, with patients in higher-cost plans paying 50% of fees; (c) an end to the day limit in 2001, as well as a drop in fees to $10 or 20% of fees (Miller, 1993; SAMHSA, 1993d).

The overall long-term goal of the Act was to achieve by the year 2001 "a comprehensive, integrated system of care with improved benefits" (American Health Security Act of 1993, Sec. 27).

As the Clinton Health Care Reform proposal suggests, there are a number of issues pertaining to mental health care (Plaut & Arons, 1994; Arons & Buck, 1994; Frank & McGuire, 1994). Some issues are related to the "complexity of relations between acute and long-term care, between medical and social services, and between services provided by physicians and those offered by other health care professionals" (Mechanic, 1993, p. 349). The question of who should receive what services is controversial, especially since "the population of users of mental health services is heterogeneous, varying by disorder, degrees of discomfort, disability, and voluntary participation" (p. 351). It appears that individuals with severe, persistent illness are most disadvantaged by the proposed insurance plans, especially since these individuals require long-term care that includes both medical and social services, and the costs for their care are often unpredictable. Other issues involve questions of how to provide services in underserved areas (rural, inner-city); how to improve access to services; how to integrate public and private systems of care; how to integrate medical and psychiatric services; and how the roles of federal, state, and local governments are defined (Plaut & Arons, 1994).

One of the most perplexing problems related to mental health care in the Clinton plan is how the Medicaid program would operate (Buck & Koyanagi, 1994). The current financial arrangements for Medicaid are complicated by the fact that the various states have different eligibility requirements, financial formulas, and benefits. Under the Clinton proposal, "The most fundamental change in the Medicaid program would be that beneficiaries would receive services through the same health plans as other Americans. As proposed, these services would include acute mental health treatment in inpatient, residential, intensive nonresidential, and outpatient settings" (Buck & Koyanagi, 1994, p. 884). States would still be required to ensure provision of some acute and long-term services, and they would be permitted to offer optional benefits and to impose some cost-sharing for premiums and services. The Clinton proposal would affect financing of mental health services by states in regard to levels of payment and care in mental hospitals, allowing payments for inpatient care but reducing federal support for such care. Finally, the proposal would expand Medicaid services to children and adolescents in low-income households (Stroul et al., 1994).

The policy debates over inclusion of mental health services in health care reform also focus on preventive mental health services. Advocates of prevention, such as the member organizations of the

National Mental Health Association, have recommended the inclusion of preventive mental health services in health care reform (NMHA, 1993). Proposed preventive mental health interventions include the following services:

- screening for developmental delays and mental health problems for children and adolescents, and for mental health problems in adults;
- counseling for individuals and families at high risk of developing mental or emotional disorders;
- intensive interventions for high-risk individuals, especially pregnant women, parents, and infants;
- support of self-help groups for people with mental health problems or life situations of stress or change (NMHA, 1993).

REVIEW

Mental health care financing policies have a major impact on the delivery of mental health services. The positive effects of these policies are apparent to the extent that large numbers of Americans benefit from psychiatric care from hospitalization and from community-based care. The negative effects of current mental health policies come from the fact that a two-class system prevails, wherein the quality of care provided by the public sector is considerably inferior to services provided in the private sector. In some instances, the care of individuals who rely on public funding is improved by the privatization of services covered by the public sector.

The high costs of mental health care, both in the public sector and the private sector, have had negative effects on the level of services available to all Americans. Various mechanisms have been introduced to contain the costs of care, such as forms of managed care, funding arrangements such as DRGs and capitation, and methods of monitoring services and costs through utilization reviews. Individuals covered by insurance in the private sector have their care rationed by these mechanisms. For individuals receiving care through the public sector, the major obstacle to services is inadequate public funding from governmental units at the federal, state, and local community levels. The inadequacy of funding is most pronounced in state hospitals that lack accreditation, have insufficient staff, and have poor physical facilities. It is most visible in communities where community-based mental health care is not available or accessible, as evidenced by the number of severely mentally ill and homeless mentally ill people who do not receive mental health care or social services. Public financing of mental health care is determined through the political process. We have identified the principal features of a health care reform plan by the Clinton administration as they pertain to mental health. At present, it is unclear how the states and the federal government will resolve the complex issues of health care reform and how such reforms will affect mental health services.

7.
Individual Rights and the Mental Health System

$\mathbf{T}$he purpose of mental health policies is to protect the rights of people who receive mental health services. Policies regarding patient/client rights are found in "a broad range of statutes (i.e., legislation), case law (i.e., decisions and opinions of courts), and administrative regulations, rules, orders, and decisions (i.e., the actions of administrative agencies) pertaining to mental health research and practice" (Shah & Sales, 1991, p. 1). Mental health policies include various laws pertaining to civil process, criminal process, juvenile and family law process, and administrative law process (Shah & Sales, 1991; Weiner & Wettstein, 1993). Thus, mental health law involves the rights of patients, the obligations and responsibilities of the state in operating a public mental health system, and the ethics and responsibilities of mental health professionals (Sales & Shuman, 1994). As Brooks (1988) has observed, "During the past twenty-five years, the role of law in the mental health system has expanded to where it now influences every aspect of care and treatment, both in the hospital and in the community" (p. 62).

The voluminous literature on the rights of mental health clients displays considerable disagreement and tension between the legal and mental health professions. Excellent discussions of policy issues surrounding patient/client rights can be found in the works of Brooks (1979, 1988), Keilitz (1989), Lamb and Mills (1986), Mechanic (1989),

Nurcombe and Partlett (1994), Reamer (1994), Reisner and Slobogin (1990), Simon (1992), Smith and Meyer (1987), and Weiner and Wettstein (1993). This literature forms a basis for examining the following policy areas:

1. Civil commitment/involuntary hospitalization;
2. Voluntary hospitalization;
3. Commitment and due process;
4. Right to treatment;
5. Right to treatment in the community;
6. Right to refuse treatment;
7. Involuntary outpatient civil commitment;
8. Rights of clients in the community;
9. Mental health and the criminal justice system;
10. Professional roles: duty to warn; confidentiality;
11. Legal rights of children;
12. Advocacy laws.

This discussion of the rights of mental health patients cites state laws, state court decisions, federal court decisions, and constitutional laws that pertain to the treatment of mentally ill persons. There are policy differences in the mental health statutes of the various states, in state court judicial rulings, and in administrative regulations and practices of state departments of mental health (Weiner & Wettstein, 1993). These patterns have emerged over the past three decades as the legal profession and advocate groups have influenced the mental health system through litigation for patient rights (Weiner & Wettstein, 1993; Sales & Shuman, 1994). An especially salient example of mental health policy formulated through the courts is found in litigation related to mentally ill people who are homeless. Stoner (1995) discusses court decisions involving homeless people, including those who are mentally ill, in areas such as mental health services, the right to shelter and emergency assistance, income maintenance, child welfare, evictions, voting rights, education, begging, loitering and sleeping in public, and arrests.

CIVIL COMMITMENT/INVOLUNTARY HOSPITALIZATION

Civil commitment may be defined as "the process of involuntarily hospitalizing mentally ill people who are thought to be dangerous" (Smith & Meyer, 1987, p. 611). All states provide for civil commitment of mentally ill persons, a process governed by state statutes, state mental health codes, and federal constitutional law. Until the early 1970s, the principal standard for civil commitment to a mental institution was the fact that the person was declared to be mentally ill. However, this standard is no longer sufficient for civil commitment, as reforms in mental health law have generated new processes and additional criteria.

Until new criteria of dangerousness and disability were established for civil commitment, the states generally followed the mental health profession's position that some mentally ill persons need to be confined to an institution for their own good—that is, for their own protection and for treatment (Brooks, 1988; LaFond, 1994). Under this philosophy, various states exercised their power of *parens patriae* and police power in hospitalizing mentally ill persons. The power of *parens patriae* is "the state's sovereign power of guardianship over persons of disability" (Brooks, 1979, p. 16). The state's police power permits it to confine a person in order to protect the citizens of the state, if the person is perceived as dangerous. As demonstrated in the history of use of state powers to hospitalize mentally ill persons, dramatic changes from the philosophy of *parens patriae* to police power (involving a criterion of dangerousness) have come about through mental health law. This is apparent in changes in the statutes of the various states, as well as through decisions of the courts.

No longer do most states intervene to care for the mentally ill unless other conditions, such as dangerousness and/or disability, are present (Smith & Meyer, 1987). Still, as Brooks (1979) notes, "The U.S. Supreme Court has never actually required dangerousness for purposes of involuntary commitment as a matter of constitutional law. On the contrary, the Court has implied that involuntary commitments for the purpose of care and treatment are constitutionally acceptable where appropriate care and treatment are actually provided" (p. 18). Current policies on civil commitment do not have the support of mental health professionals who give priority to the treatment needs of individuals over the patient's "liberty interests." The question that remains controversial in both mental health and legal circles is whether it should be easier to commit people involuntarily to treatment (Schwartz & Sibert, 1994; Mosher, 1994).

Civil libertarians usually support statutes and court rulings that emphasize liberty and the individual's right to remain in the community, regardless of the nature of his or her illness (Weiner & Wettstein, 1993). In response to these concerns, legal reforms have provided procedural protections against misuse of civil commitment. While the Supreme Court has not determined the exact conditions under which a person may be involuntarily confined to a hospital, it has acted on civil commitment in indirect ways. One such court decision is found in *O'Connor v. Donaldson* (422 U.S. 563, 1975). Donaldson had been a patient in a state hospital in Florida from 1957 to 1972. He refused medication and electroshock treatments, receiving no other treatment during his hospital stay. The Supreme Court took the position that a state "cannot constitutionally confine, without *more*, a nondangerous individual who is capable of surviving safely in freedom by himself or with the help of willing and responsible family members or friends" (*O'Connor v. Donaldson*, 1975).

The Mental Health Code of the State of Michigan provides an example of a state policy regarding civil commitment. The Code defines mental illness as "a substantial disorder of thought or mood which significantly impairs judgment, behavior, capacity to recognize reality, or ability to cope with the ordinary demands of life" (State of Michigan, 1990a, p. 30). For civil commitment purposes, the Code defines a "person requiring treatment" as any of the following:

> (a) A person who is mentally ill, and who as a result of that mental illness can reasonably be expected within the near future to intentionally or unintentionally seriously physically injure himself or another person, and who has engaged in an act or acts or made significant threats that are substantially supportive of the expectation.
>
> (b) A person who is mentally ill, and who as a result of that mental illness is unable to attend to those of his basic physical needs such as food, clothing, or shelter that must be attended to in order for him to avoid serious harm in the near future, and who has demonstrated that inability by failing to attend to those basic physical needs.
>
> (c) A person who is mentally ill, whose judgment is so impaired that he is unable to understand his need for treatment and whose continued behavior as the result of this mental illness can reasonably be expected, on the basis of competent medical opinion, to result in significant physical harm to himself or others (p. 30).

Most state commitment laws include three criteria of dangerousness (Segal et al., 1988). These criteria—danger to self, danger to others, and grave disability—were established first in California through the Lanterman-Petris-Short Act in 1969 (Cal. Welf. & Inst. Code). In this Act, grave disability is a form of dangerousness, defined as a "condition in which a person, as a result of a mental disorder, is unable to provide for his basic personal needs for food, clothing, or shelter" (Cal. Welf. & Inst. Code, 5008h). The inclusion of dangerousness as a standard for civil commitment was supported in 1972 by a federal district court in Wisconsin in *Lessard v. Schmidt* (349 F. Supp. 1078, 1972) wherein the court found the Wisconsin civil commitment statute unconstitutional "insofar as it permits commitment without proof…that the patient is both mentally ill and dangerous" (Reisner & Slobogin, 1990, p. 600). Initially, the concept of dangerousness was defined in terms of actual physical violence, but the meaning has been broadened considerably. The tendency has been to define danger "as a fairly serious, physical, imminent, threat to self or others" (Smith & Meyer, 1987, p. 593).

There has been ongoing debate concerning whether psychiatrists or other mental health professionals can predict dangerous behavior (Davis, 1991; Segal et al., 1988; Smith & Meyer, 1987; Brooks, 1988; Reisner & Slobogin, 1990). There is some limited evidence of the ability of mental health professionals to successfully predict dangerousness (McNiel & Binder, 1987; Rofman, Askinazi, & Fant, 1980; Segal et al., 1988). In a study of civil commitment, Segal and his colleagues (1988) were able to demonstrate that criteria of dangerousness can be reliably described in behavioral terms by clinicians in an emergency room. The development of instruments for this purpose has been helpful in establishing assessment standards in emergency psychiatric evaluations.

States have varying definitions of dangerousness. Some require that the danger be judged by recent acts or threats, while others require that the danger be imminent. In *Addington v. Texas* (441 U.S. 418, 1979), the Supreme Court ruled on the kind of evidence necessary to demonstrate dangerousness: "clear and convincing evidence, not merely by the usual civil law standard of a 'preponderance' of evidence, and not necessarily by evidence beyond a reasonable doubt, which is the standard used in criminal cases" (Brooks, 1988, p. 64).

Definitions of mental illness and dangerousness are normally provided in state statutes. Commitment procedures usually require that a psychiatrist or a psychologist determine whether the individual is mentally ill. Professionals do not always agree concerning whether an individual is mentally ill, dangerous, or disabled. The case of Joyce Brown, a homeless woman involuntarily committed to a hospital in New York City, illustrates difficulties that arise when professionals disagree concerning a diagnosis of mental illness (Cournos, 1989; Kaufman, 1988). New York City psychiatrists testified that Brown had "a serious mental illness which was demonstrated by her observed comportment on the street, including verbal aggressiveness, delusions, and an inability to take care of her own personal hygiene" (Rochefort, 1993, p. 155). Yet, according to the first judge in the case, American Civil

Liberties Union psychiatrists "offered nearly diametrically opposed guidance about Miss Brown's mental state" (Barbanel, 1987). They claimed that "Miss Brown did not have a serious mental illness, but was a 'professional street person' whose difficulties on the street were a natural consequence of being homeless" (Cournos, 1989, p. 737). While the judge ruled that "the city had failed to prove that the homeless woman was mentally ill or unable to care for herself," an Appellate Court upheld her involuntary hospitalization (Barbanel, 1987). She was subsequently released from the hospital when she refused medication (Cournos, 1989).

As illustrated in various court cases, civil commitment of mentally ill persons is a controversial issue (Smith & Meyer, 1987). And as noted in the case of Joyce Brown, professionals do not always agree on what constitutes mental illness as opposed to deviant behavior patterns. With regard to other criteria for commitment, there is considerable disagreement over the definition of dangerousness, so that in the Brown case, psychiatrists for the City of New York argued that she required hospitalization due to her illness and "by virtue of self-neglect, provocative behavior, and suicidal impulses" (Cournos, 1989, p. 737). While the New York State law "provided for involuntary commitment when a patient was in imminent danger of doing harm to self or others," the policy used by Mayor Koch to detain Joyce Brown defined dangerousness in terms of the "foreseeable" future, rather than imminent danger (Rochefort, 1993, p. 150).

VOLUNTARY HOSPITALIZATION

All states except Alabama permit a person to seek admission to a psychiatric hospital on a voluntary basis (Reisner & Slobogin, 1990). This is the customary form of admission with regard to entry into private psychiatric hospitals and psychiatric units of general hospitals. The procedures for voluntary admission to state mental hospitals are included in mental health codes, such as the Code of the State of Michigan, which reads: "When an individual asserted to be a person requiring treatment is deemed by a hospital to be suitable for informal or formal voluntary hospitalization, the hospital shall offer the individual the opportunity to request or make application for hospitalization as an informal or formal voluntary patient..." (State of Michigan, 1990a, p. 31). In Michigan, under informal admission to a hospital, the patient may terminate the hospital stay at any time. Under formal voluntary hospitalization, in order to leave the hospital the patient must indicate this intention and must be released within three days after the request is made.

The principal issue with regard to voluntary hospitalization is whether such an admission is really "voluntary" if pressures, such as the threat of formal proceedings, bring about entry into a hospital. A dramatic account of how a person may feel when relatives and friends seek to impose forced hospitalization is found in a personal story by Kate Millett, *The Loony Bin Trip* (1990). In this book, Millett describes her feelings when relatives, friends, and a doctor gathered at her apartment to make a "bust"—that is, to talk her into voluntarily entering a mental hospital (Millett, 1990; Schneider, 1990).

Voluntary commitment has a somewhat different meaning for children and adolescents than for adults (Nurcombe & Partlett, 1994). The rights of minors are generally superseded by the child-rearing rights of the parents, and the "Supreme Court has sanctioned the voluntary commitment by parents or guardians of minors, without the minor's consent" (p. 325). Yet, while parents are able to commit a child to a mental hospital, there are required review procedures to help protect against inappropriate hospitalization. These procedures usually involve a review by mental health professionals as "neutral factfinders" (Smith & Meyer, 1987; *Parham v. J.R.*, 442 U.S. 584, 1979).

COMMITMENT AND DUE PROCESS

Significant rights have been extended to mentally ill persons through changes in the procedures used in civil commitment. Until the 1970s, these proceedings were mainly informal and in the hands of mental health professionals, usually psychiatrists. Along with changes in the criteria for involuntary commitment, due process protections now help prevent inappropriate hospitalization. All states have formal policies for protection of patient/client rights in commitment procedures. However, state policies vary considerably in regard to procedures and implementation. Many of the rules and procedures for the handling of civil commitment to a mental hospital are derived from the due process and protection of liberty laws of the criminal system.

Some of the current and customary procedures of due process for the mentally ill include rights to a lawyer, to a hearing, to adequate notice, to a hearing with reasonable rules of evidence, to privilege against self-incrimination, and to trial by jury (Weiner & Wettstein, 1993). While the states may differ somewhat on these aspects of due process, all have somewhat similar legal procedures. State mental health codes include a specification of these procedures in relation to adults and children. States have different procedures for minors, which are often not as formal as those for adults (Nurcombe & Partlett, 1994; *Parham v. J.R.*, 442 U.S. 584, 1979; Brooks, 1979; Smith & Meyer, 1987).

Procedures for "emergency" detention of an individual in a hospital usually differ from those for non-emergency situations (Reisner & Slobogin, 1990; Smith & Meyer, 1987). They are usually less formal in process and have not been challenged to any great extent in the courts. Emergency detention may occur in a variety of ways: "by being apprehended by police; by being brought to a hospital by relatives or friends; by being converted from a voluntary patient to an involuntary patient when, after entering a mental health facility voluntarily, the person attempts to leave against the advice of the facility staff; or finally by being taken into custody as a result of a legal petition submitted to and validated by a court" (Reisner & Slobogin, 1990, pp. 698–699). Most states have limits on how long a person can be detained without a formal hearing, and after a formal hearing, how long a person can be hospitalized involuntarily without review.

Decisions about involuntary hospitalization are influenced by the expert witness of several people, such as psychiatrists, psychologists, and social workers. However, the final decision is made in the legal system by a court judge or appeals court decision. Some authors, such as Smith and Meyer (1987), suggest that "mental health professionals now effectively make most commitment decisions," because judges rely so heavily on their testimony (p. 604).

This circumstance leads to a debate over whether or not the process of commitment adequately protects the rights of individuals being hospitalized. A principal question in this debate has to do with whether mental health professionals should make, or strongly influence, commitment decisions, and if so, how well the legal rights of the patient are protected (Smith & Meyer, 1987).

THE RIGHT TO TREATMENT

Recognizing that some individuals will be confined to a mental hospital involuntarily through civil commitment procedures, the question is whether hospitalized patients have a right to treatment. In general, the courts have ruled that once patients have been hospitalized on an involuntary basis, they have a right to treatment. According to Brooks (1979), "The legal principle for the right to treatment is a simple one. If a patient is deprived of liberty in order that he be treated for his mental illness, he should, in fact, receive such treatment" (p. 28). Recognition is given to Dr. Morton Birnbaum for first developing the concept of the right to treatment in 1960 (Smith & Meyer, 1987). The nature of this right varies, depending on state statutes and on the jurisdiction covered in court decisions.

The basic federal court decision involving the right to treatment is found in *Wyatt v. Stickney* (325 F. Supp. 781, 1971). In this case it was determined that the Constitution "required the state to meet detailed minimum standards when treating involuntarily committed mentally ill patients" (Lamb & Mills, 1986, p. 477.) The *Wyatt v. Stickney* case involved a class action suit on behalf of patients in an Alabama hospital. "Generally, the Court found that defendants' treatment program was deficient in three fundamental areas. It failed to provide: (1) a humane psychological and physical environment, (2) qualified staff in numbers sufficient to administer adequate treatment, and (3) individualized treatment plans" (Reisner & Slobogin, 1990, p. 983). This suit was instigated by a group of employees who anticipated being laid off from the hospital. The suit highlighted the deplorable conditions of the hospital and brought about changes in the state mental health system. *Wyatt v. Stickney* changed the way in which the state hospital and the state mental health systems operated by increasing recognition of the rights of involuntarily hospitalized patients.

In considering what treatment means, most court decisions have emphasized the right to safety, comfort, and freedom from undue restraint, with some referring to limited mental health treatment or habilitation. Few legal decisions deal with the right to effective treatment (Smith & Meyer, 1987). Court decisions often do not relate directly to the question of the right to treatment of persons with mental illness, but the decisions have implications for such rights. For example, in the case of *Youngberg v. Romeo* (457 U.S. 307, 1982), the U.S. Supreme Court's rulings in relation to an institutionalized mentally retarded person determined the right to limited treatment or "habilitation" in relation to safety and freedom of the individual (Smith & Meyer, 1987). This case suggests that analogous rights would be granted to mentally ill persons. In the case of *O'Connor v. Donaldson* (422 U.S. 563, 1975), the U.S. Supreme Court did not decide on Donaldson's right to treatment, but rather indicated that he could not be confined merely on the determination that he was mentally ill. When the court found that Donaldson did not meet the civil commitment requirement of dangerousness, and was not receiving treatment, it was determined that he should be freed. As Smith and Meyer (1987) note, "The Supreme Court has not defined the specific nature of the right to safety, freedom from undue restraint, and limited treatment" (p. 641).

In addition to the right to humane care and treatment, hospitalized patients have a number of other rights that have been supported
by the courts, such as communication (mail, visitation, telephone), access to an attorney, presumption of competency, placement in the least
restrictive setting, periodic review, compensation for work, right to
manage funds, right to refuse to participate in research, right to personal possessions, religious freedom, and voting rights (Weiner &
Wettstein, 1993). An important element of treatment is the patient's informed consent to treatment (Reamer, 1994). Informed consent requires
that "prior to the acceptance of treatment, the patient must be apprised
of the diagnosis, the nature of the contemplated treatment, the risks
inherent in such treatment, his prognosis with and without treatment,
and any possible alternative approaches to alleviate the problem"
(Weiner & Wettstein, 1993, pp. 115, 116). Having received such information, the patient must "be legally competent and must give his consent voluntarily and knowingly" (p. 116).

RIGHT TO TREATMENT IN THE COMMUNITY

A central question of rights is whether a state, county, or local munic-
ipality must provide mental health treatment and services in the community, and if so, whether such treatment must be provided in the
"least restrictive" setting. The decision of *Goodwill v. Cuomo* (737 F. 2d
1239 2d Cir., 1984) suggests that there is no entitlement under the U.S.
Constitution for a community placement or a "least restrictive environment" (Reisner & Slobogin, 1990). This decision was based on
Youngberg v. Romeo (457 U.S. 307, 1982), which emphasized reliance on
a standard of professional judgment with regard to appropriate treatment. Currently, however, most states require that mental health professionals choose the least restrictive placement for care of people with
mental disorders (Perlin, 1994).

Issues over the concept of least restrictive care center around "the
clash between the legalistic goal of minimizing restrictions on liberty
and the clinical goal of determining the optimal treatment needs of
each severely mentally ill individual" (Munetz & Geller, 1993, p. 968).
The measurement of restrictiveness may be applied to the environment in which care is provided, or to dimensions of various treatment
alternatives of the individual. Such alternatives are required by most
state mental health laws (Munetz & Geller, 1993). With the passage of
the Americans with Disabilities Act of 1990, there is speculation that
there will be increased rights of the mentally disabled for treatment
and services in the community (Perlin, 1994).

RIGHT TO REFUSE TREATMENT

The legal profession and other advocates for the mentally ill have led the movement toward patients' rights in regard to mental health treatment, particularly the right to refuse treatments with known negative side effects (Bentley, 1993; Rosenson, 1993). As a result of past abuses within state hospitals in the administration of antipsychotic, psychotropic medications, electroconvulsive therapy, and psychosurgery, litigation against hospitals has argued for the patient's right to refuse treatment (Brooks, 1979; Cohen, 1988; Stone, 1981; Weiner & Wettstein, 1993). In the 1971 case of *Wyatt v. Stickney*, the court ruled "that confined mental patients had a right not to be subjected to treatment procedures such as lobotomy, electro-convulsive treatment, aversive reinforcement conditioning, or other unusual or hazardous treatment procedures without their express and informed consent after consultation with counsel or interested party of the patient's choice" (Brooks, 1979, p. 30).

In a 1978 New Jersey case, *Rennie v. Klein* (462 F. Supp. 1131), the judge ruled that "involuntarily hospitalized mental patients have a qualified constitutional right to refuse medication. The constitutional fulcrum is the evolving 'right of privacy,' which for all practical purposes insures the right of the individual to autonomy, a right to make significant decisions about intrusions on his or her mind and body" (Brooks, 1979, p. 32). Some qualifications to the right to refuse treatment are: "first, where there is a clear-cut emergency, limited to no more than seventy-two hours; second, where the patient is dangerous within the hospital setting; and third, where the patient needs care and has either no capacity or only a limited capacity to provide it for himself" (p. 33).

Many court decisions have recognized the patient's right to refuse treatment but have not established this as an absolute right. This is especially true of patients who have been judged incompetent. Thus, in the 1986 case of *Rivers v. Katz* (67 N.Y. 2d 485), a New York court "found a state constitutional right to refuse treatment which the state can invade only if the patient is dangerous or incompetent" (Smith & Meyer, 1987, p. 635). Three types of issues have been declared central to the question of right to refuse treatment:

1. What standards should be used for imposing treatment on an unwilling patient; that is, can treatment be imposed involuntarily except when the patient is incompetent or immediately physically dangerous to himself or others?
2. Who decides when involuntary treatment can be imposed? Should it be a judge? the treating physician? an independent mental health expert? a jury?

3. What procedure should be used to make this decision? Should it be a full evidentiary hearing with counsel and sworn testimony? Should it be an informal "hearing" at which the decision maker consults informally with the psychiatrist, reviews the "chart" and talks to the patient? (Smith & Meyer, 1987, p. 638).

In summary, some federal and state courts have ruled that patients have a right to refuse treatment under certain conditions, while other courts have ruled differently. The central issues are whether or not the patient is competent, and the circumstances under which forced treatment is permitted. At this time, for those who refuse treatment, there seems to be little research on the effects of this decision on the patient's health/illness (Kapp, 1994).

INVOLUNTARY OUTPATIENT CIVIL COMMITMENT

All states permit some form of involuntary outpatient civil commitment. In recent years a large number of states have either passed or modified statutes regarding involuntary outpatient commitment. Involuntary outpatient commitment "is the process whereby a commitment court, pursuant to a state's civil commitment laws, orders a person with mental illness to undergo community-based mental health care and related social services in lieu of compulsory institutionalization" (Keilitz, 1990, p. 368).

Three types of involuntary outpatient commitment have been identified: (1) trial or conditional release from institutional care; (2) outpatient commitment as the initial treatment in a least restrictive alternative; (3) preventive commitment (Stefan, 1987; McCafferty & Dooley, 1990; Wilk, 1988). Most states provide for one or both of the first two options, and few allow for preventive commitment. Under the first alternative, the physician makes the decision to release the patient from the hospital, usually to a community mental health center for continued treatment. The second option involves patients who are judged to meet inpatient commitment standards but are referred to the community instead of a hospital. An example of this type of commitment is found in the Mendota experiments using Assertive Community Treatment programs in contrast to hospitalization (Stein et al., 1975). The third type involves requiring treatment to prevent deterioration of an individual who does not meet the criteria for inpatient commitment.

There is an unusually high degree of variation in the states with regard to standards for outpatient commitment (McCafferty & Dooley, 1990). Most states take the position that some kind of outpatient civil commitment is appropriate when there is an indication that the patient's condition will deteriorate without treatment or that the person is unable or unwilling to obtain treatment voluntarily (Slobogin, 1994). However, many state statutes do not provide for due process protections for outpatient commitment or for protections against rehospitalization under conditions of noncompliance. Recognizing the need for clinicians to identify patients who might benefit from involuntary outpatient treatment, Geller (1990) has developed a set of guidelines for making the decision about appropriateness of such treatment. These guidelines focus on individuals who are severely ill, and "are based on patients' history, patients' capacity, and characteristics of the mental health system" (p. 751). The reader may wish to review these guidelines, especially in regard to the case illustrations provided in relation to each guideline.

It is noteworthy that some advocate groups, such as the Alliance for the Mentally Ill, have favored preventive commitment, as it appears to lessen the burden on family members and to help prevent hospitalization (Stefan, 1987). One of the arguments for outpatient commitment is that it leaves the patient with the liberties of the community, rather than the loss of freedoms inherent in institutional care. Generally speaking, however, ex-patients have not favored this type of commitment. Other advocate groups oppose outpatient commitment "on the grounds that it may extend intrusive social controls and expand the states' police powers in the absence of monitoring for possible abuses" (Swartz et al., 1995, p. 382).

Information obtained from a 1990–91 survey of states about outpatient commitment laws displays the variations among states in relation to a number of aspects of this type of commitment (Miller, 1992). Many states accept the principles of outpatient commitment, but states vary in relation to criteria and procedures. Survey findings from a study by Miller (1992) indicate that 35 states permitted initial commitment to outpatient treatment, 27 states used rehospitalization as the major means of dealing with noncompliance, and 27 states required judicial hearings before rehospitalization. Other research on outpatient commitment shows that such commitment "appears to provide limited but improved outcomes in rates of hospitalization and length of hospital stay" (Swartz et al., 1995, p. 381).

RIGHTS OF CLIENTS IN THE COMMUNITY

While the major emphasis on rights of mentally ill persons has been with regard to hospitalization, there is some recognition of the rights of individuals in community treatment programs. For example, on the state level, Michigan has established recipient rights for individuals receiving services in community mental health agencies (Raider, 1982). Specified rights are assured for clients in vendor agencies in which community mental health boards contract for services, in programs operated directly by community mental health boards, and in programs of the state's Office of Recipient Rights. Clients in community agencies that are funded by the mental health department must provide written statements of civil rights, treatment rights, and personal rights. Each agency and each community mental health board must have a rights adviser. The code assures individuals the right to treatment, and "is essentially a grievance system for clients" (p. 161). At the federal level, the enactment of the Americans with Disabilities Act of 1990 (P.L. 101-336) established rights for people with physical or mental disabilities. This Act is a "clear and comprehensive national mandate for the elimination of discrimination against individuals with disabilities" in the areas of employment, public services, public accommodations, and telecommunications (p. 2). A guide for professionals on the provisions and protections of this Act for individuals with mental disabilities has been published by the American Bar Association (Parry, 1994).

MENTAL HEALTH AND THE CRIMINAL JUSTICE SYSTEM

Mental health professionals, especially those involved in forensic psychiatry, are frequently involved with the legal system through their testimony in regard to competency, insanity, and guardianship (Quen, 1994). The concepts of mental illness, civil commitment, incompetence, and insanity are often confused with each other. Consequently, we will briefly discuss these terms and their interconnections, recognizing that a thorough understanding of these topics requires a more extensive and complex literature review.

Competency is a legal concept that refers to "someone's mental ability to make rational decisions" (Weiner & Wettstein, 1993, p. 273). Incompetency refers to the fact that "a court has determined that the person does not have the necessary mental or physical capacity to make decisions regarding his property and/or his person" (p. 273). While mental disorder may be an underlying reason for a person to be declared incompetent, "Few mentally ill persons have been declared legally incompetent; most mentally ill persons are capable, when their illness is under control, of making decisions related to their welfare" (p. 275). Mental health experts deal with this concept when called to testify with regard to several kinds of competency, such as a person's capacity to stand trial, to make a will, and to manage his or her own affairs (Smith & Meyer, 1987). While the mental health professional is likely to be involved in the determination of competency, "there is little consensus about the minimum standard of capacity which renders a person competent or incompetent in the eyes of the law" (p. 300).

In regard to criminal court cases, a person may be mentally ill and still be competent and able to stand trial. Persons are usually considered incompetent to stand trial if, at the time of the trial, they are "unable to understand the charges against them, adequately to participate in their own defense, or understand the legal process" (Smith & Meyer, 1987, p. 576). One of the most controversial aspects of this claim has to do with whether or not a defendant can refuse medication that would restore competency and hence the ability to stand trial. In contrast to the ability to stand trial, the term insanity may be used to refer to the mental state of the defendant at the time a crime was committed. Insanity may be a defense to the crime, asserting that the person did not know what he or she was doing at the time of the crime (Quen, 1994). As with competency tests, this area is complex and rests on the testimony of individuals within a court of law, and the decision is made by a judge or a jury.

As with other areas of mental health law, our focus is on the fact that the courts constitute an arena in which the rights of the mentally ill are defined. There are a number of mental health civil rights issues involved, all of which have to do with striking a balance between upholding the rights of the person and protecting the person from harm. Thus, a declaration of incompetence ends the person's "right to make decisions which may be harmful to him and establishes a guardian to protect his interests" (Smith & Meyer, 1987, p. 284). It also "provides protection of society," making known to the public "that this person no longer has the capacity to make decisions, and that his decisions will not be legally enforceable" (p. 285).

PROFESSIONAL ROLES: DUTY TO WARN

There is a legal responsibility of mental health professionals to warn and/or protect third parties from the violent actions of patients/clients (Simon, 1992; Weiner & Wettstein, 1993; Kopels & Kagle, 1993). A central foundation for this "duty to warn" and "duty to protect" is based on the *Tarasoff* case (*Tarasoff v. Regents of U. of Calif.*, 529 P. 2d 553, Calif. Sup. Ct. 1974; 1976). In this case, a University of California student told his psychologist that he intended to harm a fellow student, Ms. Tarasoff. Although the psychologist notified the police, he did not directly inform Tarasoff of danger, and she later was killed by the patient. The California Supreme Court ruled in favor of Tarasoff's family, who contended that the psychologist was negligent in failing to warn the victim.

Since the *Tarasoff* case, a number of courts and state legislatures have established that a "duty to exercise reasonable care to protect others arises when a psychotherapist determines, or should have determined, based on the standards of the profession, that a patient poses an imminent threat of serious harm to a third party" (Simon, 1992, pp. 125, 126). Simon (1992) calls this area of mental health law "one of the most controversial and vexing," as it is open to various interpretations (p. 126). Most statutes require that a potential victim be identified and warned and/or that the police be notified. The professional is expected to "assess the threat of violence to another; identify the potential object of that threat; implement some affirmative act" (Simon, 1992, pp. 126, 127; Michigan Public Act 123, 1989). The duty to warn is a clear exception to the usual rules of confidentiality that govern patient/therapist relationships. In some states, this exception has been extended to persons with AIDS as a means of protecting third parties from exposure to the disease (Reamer, 1991; Simon, 1992). In other states, laws regarding confidentiality related to the results of HIV testing prevent disclosure without the patient's consent.

PROFESSIONAL ROLES: CONFIDENTIALITY

Confidentiality is an important concept in relation to the rights of patients/clients of mental health services. "Confidentiality refers to the right of a patient to have communications spoken or written in confidence not to be disclosed to outside parties without implied or expressed authorization" (Simon, 1992, p. 71). A related concept is testimonial privilege, which refers to rights of patients in regard to rules of evidence presented in judicial proceedings. Another perspective on confidentiality concerns the ethical and legal obligations of mental health professionals in relation to their patients/clients (Smith, 1994; Smith-Bell & Winslade, 1994). The mental health professional needs a thorough understanding of the ethical and legal implications of confidentiality. Extensive discussions of confidentiality can be found in books such as *Psychiatry and Law for Clinicians* (Simon, 1992), *Legal Issues in Mental Health Care* (Weiner & Wettstein, 1993), and *Child Mental Health and the Law* (Nurcombe & Partlett, 1994).

The major sources of protection of patient confidences include state statutes, ethical codes of professional organizations, common law, and constitutional rights of privacy (Simon, 1992; Reamer, 1994; Kagle & Kopels, 1994). Simon (1992) has identified several kinds of information that come under the rules of confidentiality, such as "communications by the client during treatment, observations by the therapist, the results of psychological testing and laboratory testing, diagnosis, and prognosis" (p. 203). The right of the patient to confidentiality is not absolute, however, and may be breached under certain clinical and legal circumstances. For example, confidentiality can be breached : "(1) during an emergency; (2) in acting to civilly commit the client for mental health care; (3) in protecting third parties from the client; (4) in conforming to child abuse reporting requirements; (5) in conforming to other statutory reporting requirements; and (6) in discussing a case with supervisors and collaborators in the case" (Weiner & Wettstein, 1993, p. 203). Although the principle of permissible ethical and legal breaches to confidentiality is well established, the implementation of this principle is not always clear in professional codes or state statutes.

In general, individuals have the right of access to their records, assured by state statute. There may be conditions to this access, however, based on the mental health status of the patient (Weiner & Wettstein, 1993). There are also times when patients are asked or choose to waive confidentiality in order for records to be made available for employment, insurance, and other purposes. Again, caution must be taken so that the individual's rights are not violated once information has been released to other parties.

LEGAL RIGHTS OF CHILDREN

Children and adolescents under 18 years of age do not have the same rights that adults have with regard to mental health services. The rights of children vary considerably by age and other factors, as well as by state of residence. In general, "children are presumed to be incompetent"; that is, they are limited in the kinds of decisions they can make due to age (Weiner & Wettstein, 1993, p. 310). However, the courts in some states are willing to declare an adolescent an "emancipated minor" if the person "is married, is living separately from his parents, or is economically self-supporting" (p. 311). In such cases, the adolescent is viewed as an adult. In other instances, an adolescent may be declared a "mature minor," usually at the age of 14 or over, and permitted to make decisions regarding outpatient mental health treatment without parental consent (Croxton, Churchill, & Fellin, 1988). As already noted in regard to voluntary hospitalization, parents generally have the authority to place children in a hospital for psychiatric care (*Parham v. J.R.*, 442 U.S. 584, 1979). In addition, some states permit a minor to enter a hospital for psychiatric care without parental consent (Weiner & Wettstein, 1993). For the most part, the rights of children with regard to mental health care are similar to those pertaining to medical care, with the principal issues related to whether parental consent is required (Weisz, 1995).

ADVOCACY LAWS

In response to concerns about abuse and neglect of mentally ill persons, in 1986 the U.S. Congress established a program for protection of the rights of these individuals through the Protection and Advocacy for Mentally Ill Individuals Act of 1986 (P.L. 99-319). The Act made the following acknowledgments:

1. Mentally ill individuals are vulnerable to abuse and serious injury;
2. Mentally ill individuals are subject to neglect, including lack of treatment, adequate nutrition, clothing, health care, and adequate discharge planning;
3. State systems for monitoring compliance with respect to the rights of mentally ill individuals vary widely and are frequently inadequate (Sec. 101).

This Act called for states to establish protection and advocacy agencies to investigate and monitor the care of mentally ill persons in institutions. While the goals of these agencies have been supported by voluntary private-sector organizations such as the Alliance for the Mentally Ill, concerns have been raised about the ways in which protection and advocacy boards function (Wilk, 1993). For example, it is claimed that in some programs, funds for education and training are used to promote anti-psychiatric ideology, such as denying the existence of mental illness or opposing the use of medications for treatment. The fact that the Protection and Advocacy agencies provide legal services for the mentally ill is strongly supported by civil libertarians. Yet, this has created concern among mental health professionals that the Protection and Advocacy lawyers "often act contrary to their clients' best interests" (Isaac, 1991). Of special concern to some advocates is the difficulty some states have experienced in implementing the Act of 1986. Obstacles to implementation include the conflicting expectations of interest groups, diversity among disability groups, limited resources, and potential co-optation of advocates (Wilk, 1993).

REVIEW

Some of the major policy issues relative to the rights of mental health consumers are presented in terms of civil commitment, procedural due process, right to treatment, right to refuse treatment, competency and the criminal justice system, professional roles and ethics, legal rights of children, and advocacy laws. It is recognized that the states vary considerably with regard to statutes and legislation pertaining to patient/client rights. The continued tension between mental health professionals, clients, and the legal profession is noted, as well as some of the major changes in rights that have emerged due to the interactions of these groups and the decisions of the courts. These changes are represented in mental health law that has emerged based on federal and state court rulings.

8.
Ethnic Minorities and Mental Health

Ethnic, racial, and social dimensions of mental health and mental illness are significant considerations in mental health service provision and policy making. This is based on the recognition that in addition to membership in a "mainstream" American culture, many individuals possess cultural characteristics associated with a particular ethnic group. For some Americans, ethnic group membership results in negative experiences with the mental health system. The system is not always sensitive to the needs of ethnic groups such as white ethnics and religious groups; however, ethnic minority groups appear to be the least well served.

The major ethnic minority groups in American society have been identified by the Equal Employment Opportunity Commission established by the Civil Rights Act of 1964 (Glazer, 1983). These groups include African-Americans, Asian-Americans, Native Americans, and Hispanic Americans. Since 1978, the U.S. Government has collected and reported statistical data on these groups (Lott, 1993). In this chapter we examine policy and service issues related to the mental health needs of these ethnic minority groups (Comas-Diaz & Greene, 1994; Gaw, 1993; Neighbors, 1985; Neighbors et al., 1992; Rogler, Malgady, & Rodriguez, 1989; Snowden & Cheung, 1990). Our exploration of these issues is based on a conceptual framework developed by Rogler et al. (1989). This framework focuses on five phases of a person's experience with the mental health system. These phases are described as follows:

> Phase One...factors contributing to or associated with the emergence of a mental health problem;
>
> Phase Two...intricate help-seeking efforts which may or may not lead the afflicted person to contact official mental health service providers;
>
> Phase Three...attempts, valid or invalid, by such help providers to evaluate or diagnose the client's psychological conditions;
>
> Phase Four...the mental health provider's attempt to deal with the problem through therapeutic interventions;
>
> Phase Five...termination of treatment...rehabilitation (Rogler et al., 1989, p. 2).

CONCEPTUAL DEFINITIONS

The concepts of ethnicity, culture, race, and minority status are used in ambiguous and overlapping ways (Adebimpe, 1994; Bell, 1994; Davis & Proctor, 1989; Lott, 1993; McAdoo, 1993; Rendon, 1994; Rivera & Erlich, 1992). An ethnic group has traditionally been defined as a "collectivity based on presumed common origin," usually in terms of race, religion, or nationality (Greeley & McCready, 1974, p. 35). Longres (1995) describes ethnic groups in terms of identity as a subcommunity developed through common ancestry by collections of families. The element of common ancestry as a basis for ethnicity is derived from "language, culture, and physical type" (p. 92). Fernando (1991) suggests that "The overriding feature of an ethnic group is the sense of belonging together that the individuals feel; it is basically a psychological matter" (p. 11). The basis for a sense of belonging is often a set of cultural factors that distinguishes one group from another and from the larger society, such as customs, language, history, and identity. Under these formulations, the concept of ethnicity often modifies race as the distinguishing feature of minority groups in American society.

Ethnic groups in the United States may be characterized in several ways, such as white ethnic groups, ethnic minority groups, and religious groups. In the first instance, there is an emphasis on groups historically differentiated in terms of varying European nationalities, such as Polish, Italian, French, and German. These groups are distinguished from ethnic minority groups, wherein race, minority status, and color constitute the major points of reference. In the United States, the term "minority" has come to refer to people of color who are a minority in number within society and have experienced high degrees of discrimination, prejudice, and oppression (Bernal, 1990). The term "ethnic" is combined with "minority group" to refer to people of color, thus assuring recognition of culture as well as minority status.

It is clear that the major categories of ethnic minority groups are not homogeneous in terms of ancestry. For example, there is considerable diversity within and among Native American tribes; among Asian-American groups such as Japanese, Chinese, Filipinos, and Vietnamese; among African-American groups; and among Hispanics of varying origins, such as Mexicans, Spanish, Cubans, Puerto Ricans, Central and South Americans (Orlandi, Weston, & Epstein, 1992). Often this diversity is related to national origin, social class, stage of acculturation and assimilation, as well as other sociocultural factors.

In our exploration of the phases of mental health care, we do not present an elaborate listing of cultural differences for ethnic minority groups. Presentations of such cultural characteristics can be found in the literature, where various groups are described in terms of "the shared values, norms, traditions, customs, arts, history, folklore, and institutions of a group of people" (Orlandi et al., 1992, p. 3). These "traits" are usually viewed as part of culture being passed on from one generation to another. For example, the structure and functioning of family is often used to highlight differences in ethnic minority groups (McAdoo, 1993; McGoldrick, Pearce, & Giordano, 1982; Sue & Morishima, 1982). Other examples of cultural characteristics associated with ethnic groups include food preferences, musical styles, clothes and other dress features, language and other communication patterns, ceremonies, world views, and religious affiliations and practices (Butler, 1992; Green, 1982; Newman, 1989).

The concept of race is often used in relation to ethnicity and culture, usually referring to "biological differences among groups of people" (Longres, 1995, p. 88). However, Green (1982) notes that race is not the same as culture, even though race is often used as a factor in defining cultural and/or ethnic groups. Green recognizes that while race has traditionally referred to physical characteristics and color, currently race is more properly defined as a social concept. From this point of view, race and racism constitute social factors that must be taken into account in terms of their impact on mental health and mental illness. Within American society, people perceived as members of non-white races are subjected to individual prejudice and discrimination, as well as institutional racism. This treatment has negative effects on the mental health of these individuals (Landrum-Brown, 1990). At the same time, members of these groups have strengths from adaptive lifestyles, social-psychological support systems, and ethnocultural values that counteract societal stresses and serve to maintain and enhance mental health (Franklin & Jackson, 1990).

PREVIEW

In this chapter, we examine some important dimensions of mental health policies and services that relate to ethnic minorities, with attention to the phases of a person's contacts with the mental health system. The central question is this: How does ethnic minority status influence what happens to individuals in their experiences with the mental health system? We recognize that ethnic minority status has different meanings for members of various groups within American society and that these meanings are influenced in important ways by gender. Thus, women of color "living as they do in a racist social system that is also patriarchal, are a 'double minority' that involves the dynamics of both racism and sexism" (Comas-Diaz & Greene, 1994, pp. x, xi). Our consideration of ethnic minority groups and mental health in this chapter has not been extended to gender distinctions due to a lack of knowledge about the "interaction of gender and ethnicity in mental health treatment" (p. xvi). There remains a need for further exploration of this topic. An important source of information is the volume edited by Comas-Diaz and Greene (1994) entitled *Women of Color: Integrating Ethnic and Gender Identities in Psychotherapy*. The contributors to this volume provide "a cultural, racial, and gender context for the mental health needs and treatment of women of color" through the presentation of "ethnocultural and clinical issues with specific groups of women of color," including help-seeking behavior, assessment and diagnosis, and treatment (p. 8). The reader may wish to incorporate this knowledge into the framework employed here in examining the phases of a person's experience within the mental health system.

EMERGENCE OF MENTAL HEALTH PROBLEMS

Epidemiological studies provide useful information about the distribution of mental health problems among some ethnic minority groups in the United States (Robins & Regier, 1991). ECA reports are limited in that they make comparisons only between African-Americans, non-Hispanic whites, and Hispanic Americans. For example, the data from one ECA report show that African-Americans have higher rates of lifetime and active disorders than non-Hispanic whites or Hispanics. Hispanics had the second highest rates. Robins and Regier (1991) suggest these differences may be the result of other demographic characteristics, such as lower levels of education and socioeconomic status among the ethnic groups in comparison to the white group.

When ECA data are examined for different age groups, older African-Americans have a higher lifetime rate of disorder than older whites. The rates of specific disorders indicate that the higher overall rate of disorders among African-Americans is due largely to the disorders of older African-Americans and to higher rates of cognitive impairment and somatization (Robins & Regier, 1991). Robins and Regier (1991) suggest that "Since both the disorders more common in blacks than whites are strongly associated with low educational levels, it is likely that the low educational level of the older black population plays a major role in explaining their higher rate of disorder" (p. 352). As noted in Chapter 3, the National Comorbidity Survey (Kessler et al., 1994) indicated somewhat different findings for race, with no significant differences between whites and African-Americans for active or lifetime disorders. Hispanics did not have lower rates of active or lifetime disorders than non-Hispanic whites.

In addition to the ECA studies, other research has given attention to the distribution of mental disorders among ethnic minority groups. Rogler et al. (1989) review research on Hispanics, providing equivocal answers to the question of whether this ethnic group has higher or lower rates of illness than other ethnic groups or the non-Hispanic white majority population. Rogler et al. (1989) recognize that these mixed findings may be attibutable to methodological problems in conducting the research, such as measurement error and sampling. These authors acknowledge the increased sophistication of ECA research methods, but they conclude that "we do not have a comprehensive picture of the relative distributions of DSM-III categories in different ethnic populations" (Rogler et al., 1989, p. 19; Karno et al., 1983).

One of the problems in studying mental health problems among Hispanics involves the diversity among this population in terms of national origin, migration experience, language, age structure, family patterns, and socioeconomic status. The fact that Hispanics are disproportionately located in low socioeconomic levels has led to the inference that such individuals are at higher risk for mental problems. Similar observations have been made in regard to African-Americans. Neighbors et al. (1992) have commented on the association between social conditions, such as socioeconomic status, and mental health problems among African-Americans. These authors suggest that African-Americans at lower socioeconomic levels are likely to use public mental health services, to receive inadequate care, and to be overrepresented in counts of mental illness.

For some ethnic minority groups, especially Hispanics and Asian-Americans, the process of immigration appears to be a major source of stress, placing these individuals at risk for mental disorders. Immigrants have generally entered the economic and social system at the lower rungs of the ladder, and their acculturation experiences have tended to disturb the primary interpersonal relationships of family and kin (Rogler et al., 1989). The "role strains" inherent in these immigration experiences are said to lead to stress associated with psychological disturbance. "An immigrant who is at high risk for the development of psychological distress is one who is inserted into the bottom of the host society's socioeconomic system, has acculturation problems which swing him or her away from an adaptive bicultural identity, and is separated from socially supportive networks by migration. Along with such primary strains, he or she is a person experiencing a high quotient of life-event stresses but is unable to cope effectively with such strains and stresses because of limited intrapsychic and social resources" (Rogler et al., 1989, p. 37).

As suggested here, it is likely to be advantageous for immigrants to remain attached to elements of a native culture, while at the same time assimilating into the host culture. The effects of a moderate level of biculturalism on mental health have been shown to be positive in studies of Cuban-Americans (Gomez, 1990; Szapocznick & Kurtines, 1980). These studies support the idea that "an assessment of an ethnic group member is not complete without an evaluation of the client's level of biculturalism" (Gomez, 1990, p. 387).

HELP-SEEKING BEHAVIOR

A person's response to a mental health problem or crisis may be characterized as help-seeking behavior (Rogler & Cortes, 1993). The concepts of help-seeking and service utilization refer to the process of an individual seeking and receiving services from the mental health system. Need for services is a significant factor in determining whether members of minority groups overutilize or underutilize services. Thus, in order to examine utilization rates, one must be aware of the rates of illness in ethnic minority groups. Low utilization may be a result of low rates of illness. If, however, the rate is the same or greater than that of a comparison group, then there are likely to be other factors that interfere with the help-seeking experience and lead to low utilization. In this regard, a number of researchers have noted that when need for service is controlled, members of ethnic minority groups are less likely than the general population to use mental health services

(Gary, 1987; George, 1987; Neighbors, 1985; Padgett et al., 1994; Rogler et al., 1989).

Economic considerations do not appear to be the main cause of underutilization of mental health services. Such underutilization has been shown to occur among nonpoor, insured ethnic minority populations. A study of a national sample of federal employees by Padgett et al. (1994) showed that African-American and Hispanic employees were less likely than whites to use outpatient mental health services. However, other studies have shown that when use of inpatient mental health services is separated out from overall utilization rates, some ethnic minority groups have higher service use than the majority population. For example, African-Americans and Native Americans are more likely than whites to be hospitalized for mental illness, with Mexican-Americans and Asian-Americans having lower rates of hospitalization than whites (Snowden & Cheung, 1990).

Various explanations have been advanced to account for the underutilization of mental health services by the total population and by specific ethnic minority groups. Rogler et al. (1989) cite two theoretical approaches to understanding utilization of services by Hispanics: alternative resources and barriers. In the first instance, utilization may be low because individuals seek help from family, friends, religious groups, or indigenous natural healers. Rogler et al. (1989) note that the family, the extended family in particular, is often the group to which individuals with mental health problems go for help. Findings in this regard are mixed, with differing behaviors displayed by Puerto Ricans, Mexican-Americans, and other Hispanic groups.

Some of these same resources/barriers associated with utilization among Hispanics have been identified in relation to African-Americans. Thus, Congressional briefings in 1994 (*Hospital and Community Psychiatry*, 1994) recognized that "some unique historical and cultural factors may affect the way African-Americans experience mental illness," such as "a history of discrimination; ongoing economic stresses; informal networks of support, including the church and the extended family; continuing problems of access to health care; symptom expression that is often different from that in the general population; and underrepresentation of minorities among treatment professionals and researchers" (p. 837).

Barriers to mental health care may be due to values, beliefs, and attitudes toward informal care versus formal, professional care. In other instances, barriers may come from the institutional culture of service giving, which interferes with use of services. For example, the primary obstacle for Hispanics is the lack of Spanish-speaking, bicultural professionals in mental health agencies (Rogler et al., 1989). Also, there is often a class difference between the help-seekers and the professionals providing the service. This may generate attitudes on the part of the providers that turn away the ethnic group member.

An important aspect of social class is that the individual may not have sufficient income to use mental health services. Another institutional barrier has been the location of services, often inaccessible to lower class and ethnic minority groups, in terms of transportation, hours of service, and necessity for appointments. What is clear is that the interrelationships of these factors should be examined by the professional in order to understand help-seeking patterns and utilization rates among ethnic minority groups.

MODELS FOR STUDY OF HELP-SEEKING

Although evidence is available regarding utilization rates of mental health services by ethnic minority members, there has been a paucity of research studies that investigate the actual help-seeking behaviors of these individuals. George (1987) has noted that in regard to the general population, "current research suggests that help-seeking depends upon a complex configuration of psychological, social, economic, and environmental factors" (p. 43). The major approaches for explaining help-seeking behaviors contain concepts that have particular salience for ethnic minority groups. For example, psychological determinants of help-seeking are incorporated into health belief models for explaining why individuals seek help for medical or psychiatric problems (George, 1987; Rosenstock, 1966, 1974; Becker, 1974). Health belief models focus on four factors: "belief that one is susceptible to disease; belief that one's symptoms are sufficiently severe to merit attention; belief in the efficacy of medical or psychiatric treatment; belief that the costs of treatment are reasonable..." (George, 1987, p. 32). Another way of viewing these models is in terms of stages of help-seeking: symptom recognition, symptom attribution, cost-benefit analysis, and provider choice. Using this perspective, George (1987) suggests that help-seeking occurs when an individual recognizes the symptom, considers it to be serious, sees the advantage of getting the help, and locates a provider who appears able to provide successful treatment. A framework such as this could be useful in research exploring the help-seeking patterns of ethnic minority individuals.

Andersen and his colleagues (Andersen & Newman, 1973; Andersen & Aday, 1978) use a sociological approach in studying help-seeking. These researchers rely on three types of variables to explain the use of health services: need factors, or the clinical status of the individual;

predisposing factors, such as the person's age, gender, race, education, or beliefs about health services; and enabling factors, such as geographic location, income, and health insurance coverage. This framework includes a number of the social and environmental factors associated with the resources of ethnic minority groups. Both psychological and sociological approaches have particular relevance for ethnic minority groups, especially in regard to definitions of service needs, the role of family and social networks, and the impact, positive or negative, of the mental health system on help-seeking and utilization.

Research into help-seeking and utilization includes studies by Leaf et al. (1985) and by Neighbors (1985). Leaf et al. (1985) have examined data from one of the ECA Project areas, New Haven, Connecticut, analyzing the effects of need, predisposing, and enabling factors on the use of health professionals for treatment of mental and emotional problems. In this study, these authors report that "Consistent with earlier studies, race emerges as a significant factor in utilization once level of symptomatology is taken into account, with whites being more likely to report some mental health related contact than nonwhites" (p. 1134). Neighbors (1985) has reported on the help-seeking behaviors of African-Americans in relation to mental health services. Using a national African-American sample, Neighbors studied the ways in which this group defined their health and mental health problems, and their use of various kinds of help for these problems. He found high use of informal social network helpers (87%), with less than half using professional help (48.7%). Professional help included hospital emergency room (21.9%), physicians (22.3%), ministers (18.9%), social services (8 %), mental health centers (4%), and psychiatrists or psychologists (5%). Thus, most respondents who had a serious personal problem did not seek help within the mental health sector. When African-Americans defined their problem as a severe psychiatric difficulty, i.e., nervous breakdown, then about 55% of this group sought professional help. Of this 55%, only 15% contacted a psychiatrist or psychologist, with 9.4% going to a mental health center.

While Neighbors's study of a range of mental health problems did not reveal the reasons for the low utilization of the mental health service sector, he has suggested that the stigma of having a mental health problem may be an important factor in this finding. Also, the importance of the church to African-American individuals appears to lead them to seek help from ministers. In addition, Neighbors suggests that African-Americans may view mental health services as ineffective or unacceptable, leading to an unmet need among this population group.

EQUALITY AND EQUITY OF SERVICES

Policy makers and planners of mental health services have been concerned with the question of how to provide minority groups with equitable services proportional to their need (Meinhardt & Vega, 1987). Such an approach is based on equity (proportion in need related to proportion in population) rather than parity (assumes equal need for population groups). Tien (1992) has provided a useful framework for determining fair and just allocations of resources and services in regard to ethnic minority groups. Tien distinguishes between the concepts of equality (parity) and equity as standards of fairness. His conceptual framework defines an equal system as one which "assumes that rates of mental illness and needs for treatment are the same for all subgroups of the general population" (p. 1104). On the other hand, "An equitable system assumes that special populations have different rates of mental illness and different treatment needs" (p. 1104). Tien's equal and equitable models of mental health systems include three dimensions: (1) utilization of services (number of services, number of users), (2) funding (allocation, expenditures), (3) access (availability, geographic access, programmatic access, cultural compatibility). When these three dimensions are considered, the equitable system appears to be the most fair for special populations.

Of special interest in regard to service delivery for ethnic minority groups is cultural compatibility. This issue focuses on the extent to which services are helpful and the degree to which the treatment provided is congruent with the cultural beliefs of the ethnic minority group. In an equal system, a basic program of services is offered to all mental health consumers, with the option of adding on cultural features. In an equitable system, alternative programs are developed that more fully meet the needs of ethnic minority groups, such as the use of ethnic factors in service delivery: culture, ethnic consciousness, and mixing/matching of clients along ethnic lines (Jenkins, 1980; Tien, 1992).

ASSESSMENT AND DIAGNOSIS

The diagnostic process is crucial to the well-being of the help-seeker. This process ordinarily includes assessment of the mental health status of the person, a psychosocial history, and the administration of psychological tests. Professional mental health service providers engage in an interview process with the patient/client and use diagnostic frameworks such as DSM-IV in making their clinical judgments about the person's mental health. Numerous concerns have been raised about the evaluation and diagnostic process when the help-seeker is a member of an ethnic minority group. These concerns focus on issues such as the extent to which the professional is sensitive to the culture of the client, the possible language constraints on the process, the possibility of test bias, problems of misdiagnosis (over-diagnosis, under-diagnosis), and whether or not the concept of mental disorder is culturally relative (Kirmayer, 1994; Loring & Powell, 1988; Neighbors et al., 1989; Wakefield, 1994).

Referring to these problems, Rogler et al. (1989) note that "At the apex of the problem is the dilemma of imposing culture-bound definitions of mental illness or psychiatric symptomatology on individuals from diverse ethnic and demographic backgrounds" (p. 90). Ethnic groups often differ in their belief systems about mental illness, subscribing to "various cultural views of mental health, psychological disorder, and illness," including supernatural models, religious explanations, and natural explanations (Cheung & Snowden, 1990, p. 284). The lack of recognition of cultural differences in the expression of symptoms and distress can lead the professional to inaccurate assessment and misdiagnosis (Vega & Murphy, 1990).

Recognizing the need to include increased attention to culture in diagnosis, a Steering Committee of the NIMH-sponsored Group on Culture and Diagnosis provided the DSM-IV Task Force with recommendations for the fourth edition of DSM (Rogler, 1992). These recommendations emphasized the role of culture in assessing psychiatric symptoms, in configuring symptoms into disorders, and the ways in which cultural factors intervene in the diagnostic process (Rogler, 1993). In response to such concerns, DSM-IV cautions the clinician about the use of the manual with individuals from different cultures, and "includes three types of information specifically related to cultural considerations: (1) a discussion in the text of cultural variations in the clinical presentations of those disorders that have been included in the DSM-IV Classification; (2) a description of culture-bound syndromes...; (3) an outline for cultural formulation designed to assist the clinician in systematically evaluating and reporting the impact of the individual's cultural context" (APA, 1994, p. xxiv). Of particular concern is the need for the professional to recognize differences between his or her own values and orientations and those of the client and the need to take account of sociocultural considerations in assessment and diagnosis (Rogler et al., 1989; Westermeyer, 1987).

Rogler et al. (1989) have provided some insights about how the professional helper can acknowledge culture in assessment and diagnosis of Hispanic clients. These authors suggest that one should be aware of some of "the sociocultural dimensions on which Anglo Americans and Hispanic Americans characteristically differ" (p. 89):

> For example, unlike Anglo Americans, Hispanic Americans often display
>
> - a greater concern for immediacy and the "here and now," as opposed to a more futuristic orientation in Anglo American culture;
> - an external locus of control, causality being attributed to factors such as luck, supernatural powers, and God;
> - an extended family support system, rather than a nuclear family;
> - a concrete, tangible approach to life, rather than an abstract, long-term outlook;
> - a unilateral communication pattern with authority figures, such as avoidance of eye contact, deference, and silence as signs of respect;
> - multilingual language behavior, ranging from English to Spanish, to "Spanglish," a hybrid of the two (Rogler et al., 1989, p. 89).

Rogler et al. (1989) warn that while taking into account these cultural "traits," the professional must recognize differences between various Hispanic groups and be aware that individuals may differ greatly along these dimensions. In order to avoid stereotyping, each person's sociocultural background must be viewed in the context of the individual's characteristics and identification with the ethnic minority culture and/or the mainstream American culture.

A central concern in regard to recognition of cultural differences is the possibility of misdiagnosis. Jones and Gray (1986) have identified some major reasons for misdiagnosis of psychiatric conditions among African-Americans, noting that diagnosis in psychiatry relies primarily on signs, symptoms, and behaviors "which may be similar for different illnesses and may be culturally related and thus differ from other ethnic group to another" (p. 62). An example of misdiagnosis for African-Americans has been the over-diagnosis of schizophrenia and underdiagnosis of affective disorders (Fellin, 1989; Jones & Gray, 1986; Neighbors et al., 1989; Lawson et al., 1994). Another example has been the tendency toward overdiagnosis of psychotic disorders among ethnic minority groups as compared to the nonminority population. These types of misdiagnosis have been attributed to bias in psychological testing, bias in the interview situation, gaps in the understanding of the non-English-speaking person, and cultural barriers within the professional-client interaction (Malgady, Rogler, & Costantino, 1987). As

Westermeyer (1987) notes, "Without knowing the norms of the patient's culture, the clinician is limited in assessing the patient's grooming, dress, speech, behavior, and even cognition and affect" (p. 160). "Understanding the sociocultural milieu in which the patient lives and functions is crucial in assessing not only psychopathology but also skills, resources, and coping behavior" (p. 161).

An example of how African-American culture affects the assessment and diagnostic process is found in the work of members of the Maryland Black Psychiatrists Association (Wagner & Gartner, 1994). A number of cultural influences are identified, such as "the expression of language, behavior, coping styles, and religious beliefs" (p. 15). In regard to language, individuals who speak nonstandard dialect may "use the term 'bad nerves' to describe a range of thoughts, feelings, beliefs, psychomotor states, and behavior" and as a "code word for mental illness in general" (p. 15). Thus, failure on the part of the clinician to properly interpret the meaning of terms such as "bad nerves" is likely to lead to misdiagnosis. In regard to African-American families, it is recognized that "there is no one black family type," but that "some characteristics remain from the unique history of African-Americans, including their West African origins and the experience of slavery and racism" (p. 15). Thus, the professional needs to be aware of the "realities" of the African-American family, such as kinship bonds, extended family networks, family member roles, family exchanges and obligations, and family structure (Wagner & Gartner, 1994; McAdoo, 1993). The need for an understanding of the nature of spirituality among members of the African-American community is yet another illustration of the influence of culture on mental health. Emphasis is placed on the importance of exploring the "African-American patient's perspectives on spirituality," which leads the professional to "acknowledge this aspect of the patient's upbringing in therapy, and recognize that spirituality may be a source of strength" (Wagner & Gartner, 1994, p. 16).

MENTAL HEALTH SERVICES: TREATMENT

The central question with regard to members of ethnic minority groups and mental health treatment is whether the treatment is appropriate and effective. Studies of treatment dropout rates consistently show that ethnic minority clients are more likely than non-minority clients to discontinue treatment (Rogler et al., 1989; Sue & Zane, 1987; Sue, 1988). This leads to a number of recommendations on how to make treatment more appropriate and acceptable for ethnic minority members, such as by matching ethnic therapists with ethnic clients, assuring that the therapist is knowledgeable about cultural differences, and providing modifications of therapy that are consistent with the cultural values of the client.

Findings from studies of treatment outcomes comparing ethnic minority clients to non-minority clients have been mixed, leading to unclear conclusions (Sue, 1988). Despite the considerable limitations of research in regard to psychotherapeutic services for ethnic minorities, criticisms of the public mental health service delivery system continue, focused mainly on the need to develop culturally sensitive mental health services. It is therefore useful to examine some of the treatment frameworks that have been developed for providing service to ethnic minority populations. These frameworks have been presented in the mental health literature and implemented in practice, but they still await systematic research study in regard to treatment outcomes.

There are a number of principles established with regard to culturally sensitive mental health practice. As Rogler et al. (1989) note, "At the most specific and practical level of application, culturally sensitive therapy must accord with the needs of the individual client" (p. 102). This principle suggests that while there may be generalized cultural traits associated with various ethnic minority groups, individuals differ with regard to their "fit" with any particular culture. At the same time, the therapist may "hold stereotypes or biases concerning ethnic minority clients. These stereotypes or biases tend to reflect the nature of race or ethnic relations in our society" (Sue, 1988, p. 302). Thus, the therapist is cautioned to recognize the diversity of ethnic groups within the Hispanic population, and to be aware that such individuals can fall anywhere along the spectrum from the "most Hispanic" to the most Anglo. Professionals must consider factors such as the individual client's level and stage of acculturation and assimilation, linguistic abilities and preferences, extent of biculturalism and marginality, and identification with the values of minority-majority cultures. An example of this individualized approach is provided in the work of Gomez (1983), who suggests a cultural assessment based on the extent to which cultural factors are part of the individual and/or environment, are resources and strengths, or are a part of the problem.

Sue and Zane (1987) and Sue (1977) suggest that culturally responsive forms of treatment come from changes in the system of delivery and changes at the client-therapist level. Changes in the system level might include the employment of ethnic minority therapists, ethnic client-therapist matching, use of bilingual/bicultural therapists, and training of all personnel with regard to cultural issues and treatment. A second type of systemic change might come from the development of parallel services that focus mainly on services to ethnic minority clients. Sometimes nonparallel services may need to be developed—services that are distinctively cultural and depart from the traditional services, offering new treatments, new programs, and new settings.

Changes at the therapist-client level occur in a variety of ways. There are many well-developed treatment approaches in the mental health field, such as individual therapy, group therapy, family therapy, and insight-oriented therapy. One approach to the treatment of ethnic minority groups is to select the mode of treatment that best "fits" the individual client vis-à-vis the client's culture. A second major approach is to modify the treatment in keeping with the individual's needs and culture, with the modification incorporating cultural elements into the treatment (Sue & Zane, 1987; Malgady et al., 1987; Rogler et al., 1989).

Importance has been placed on the need for the therapist to gain knowledge about the culture of the individual client. Several cautions have been suggested in regard to the use of cultural knowledge and techniques, such as the need to avoid acting on insufficient knowledge about cultures and to refrain from overgeneralization in a stereotypical fashion. While knowledge of cultures is important, the fact that the therapist has such knowledge may not be sufficient to assure successful treatment outcomes. Sue and Zane (1987) suggest that knowledge about cultures be translated into techniques and conduct of therapy. As a part of such translation, these authors advocate the importance of two dimensions of treatment that are particularly relevant to work with ethnic minority clients: credibility and giving. They note that cultural knowledge alerts the therapist to possible problems in credibility, which is defined as "the client's perception of the therapist as an effective and trustworthy helper" (p. 40). The next step is to move from the general concept of cultural sensitivity to development of skills in the application of credibility and giving to the treatment process. Still another caution concerns the fact that while knowledge of ethnicity/culture may influence treatment outcomes, this is not the only factor in need of attention. Thus, characteristics of the service delivery system, such as the agency offering the service and its organizational character, as well as personal qualities of the therapist and the client, may enter into the definition of the client's problem, the treatment opportunities available, and the actual delivery of service.

COMMUNITY ADJUSTMENT AND REHABILITATION

Consumers of mental health services follow a number of paths in relation to their treatment and their adjustment to the community. Our focus here is on the effects of membership in an ethnic minority group on these paths. One path is characterized by hospitalization and its accompanying modes of medical and psychiatric treatment, followed by a return to the community. For individuals with serious mental illness, treatment continues in the community, often in the form of psychotherapy, medications, and psychosocial rehabilitation. Whether the patient returns to the family, is placed in supervised residential care, or resides in independent living arrangements, a major goal consists of readjustment to community living. Reintegration of patients into family and community is problematic to some extent for all patients, but especially for members of ethnic minority groups. These problems are caused mainly by strains on ethnic minority families of low socioeconomic status that reduce their ability to provide social and emotional support for the patient. There may be a lessening of social supports available from both immediate and extended family members, from friends and neighbors. At the same time, many families still are a part of extensive informal helping networks and have strengths for helping the person discharged from a psychiatric institution.

Since treatment needs do not usually end upon discharge from a hospital, but continue in the community, issues related to accessibility, appropriateness, and cultural sensitivity of formal caregivers need attention during this period. Psychosocial habilitation and rehabilitation services are usually a significant part of aftercare treatment. Thus, concerns about barriers for ethnic minority persons in the initial help-seeking phase of the client's life apply to the range of community-based psychiatric and rehabilitation services. The more general problem of reintegration into the community reasserts itself for these individuals in terms of location of residential options, especially considering the stigma imposed on mental health consumers by the general public. Barriers to the utilization of service may interfere with participation in psychosocial rehabilitation programs such as clubhouse models (Peterson et al., 1990).

Members of ethnic minority groups are less likely than the majority white population to belong to traditional self-help groups (Lieberman & Snowden, 1993; Snowden & Lieberman, 1994). However, when the focus is on mutual aid organizations, there is an increase in ethnic minority participation (Humphreys & Woods, 1993). For example, Neighbors, Elliott, and Gant (1990) contend that African-Americans provide resources for individual empowerment and for community development. These include groups such as mutual aid organizations for economic, political, and social development; neighborhood groups for community development; church-based organizations; self-help groups for coping with physical illness and death; and groups to strengthen black families and youths. These groups provide a variety of opportunities for mental health consumers to integrate or reintegrate into the local community in order to enhance their rehabilitation. Another example from the mutual aid literature is provided by Gutierrez, Ortega, and Suarez (1990) in their discussion of the involvement of members of the Latino community in natural support groups, such as the extended family, folk healers, religious institutions, and social clubs. These authors suggest that participation in these groups is enhanced by the fact that they are organized around the cultural values of the Latino population.

Another path is followed by clients who are seriously mentally ill and are not hospitalized, but receive treatment in the community. Their relationships to family and community are important aspects of their continued treatment. As with deinstitutionalized patients, integration into family and social networks is crucial to remaining in the community. When these social supports are not available, the plight of the ethnic minority client becomes increasingly problematic, sometimes ending in homelessness. Again, the danger is that this group of individuals will not utilize the various psychosocial rehabilitation programs, and hence, not return to customary social roles in the family, the labor force, and the larger community.

POLICIES AND SERVICES FOR NATIVE AMERICANS

Unlike the mental health policies and services that pertain to ethnic minorities discussed up to this point, psychiatric care of Native Americans has been principally located under the auspices of the Indian Health Service, a component of the U.S. Public Health Service. Traditionally, this care has been provided through mental health and alcoholism programs that were not well coordinated or well funded. The mental health needs of Native Americans are great, yet those services that exist are underutilized. A major difficulty in understanding this population group is the fact that extreme diversity in the cultures of Native American populations can make it difficult to generalize about the mental health status of this group (Thompson, Walker, & Silk-Walker, 1993). Important factors related to this diversity and to the distribution of mental illness among Native Americans include geographic patterns of residence, such as reservations, urban areas, and rural areas, and the extent of acculturation and assimilation (Fleming, 1992).

Recognizing the scarcity of available data on mental illness and its treatment among Native Americans, Thompson et al. (1993) provide some information on the unmet needs for psychiatric care in this population. These authors also examine a number of concepts of mental health and mental illness held within the belief systems of Native Americans, and a range of treatments, including folk medicine, Indian traditional medicine, and mainstream psychiatric care. It is noted that the psychopathology of Native Americans is not well understood and that most of the psychiatric literature on this population focuses on alcoholism and affective disorders. This situation highlights the need for further epidemiological and clinical research and for a culture-sensitive approach to mental health assessment and treatment of Native Americans.

Recognizing the high risk for mental disorders among Native Americans, the federal government has initiated special efforts to meet their needs through the Mental Health Programs Branch of the Indian Health Service (Nelson, 1991; Nelson et al., 1992). Native Americans who live on and off reservations in the United States have demonstrated considerable individual and community strength, but at the same time, social and environmental conditions impose unusual burdens on their mental health. As Nelson et al. (1992) note, many Native Americans face difficult life circumstances, including poverty, unemployment, minimal educational opportunities, racial discrimination, geographic isolation, and cultural identity conflicts. "These difficult life circumstances appear to be associated with a higher incidence and greater severity of mental disorders among Native Americans compared with most other ethnic groups" (p. 1049). Native Americans suffer high rates of depression, alcohol and substance abuse and dependency, as well as other mental disorders (SAMHSA, 1993c). Environmental conditions are particularly problematic for the mental health of Native American children and adolescents.

Congress has established through the Indian Health Service a number of avenues for Native American tribes to manage their own health and mental health services, especially the Indian Health Care Improvement Act of 1976 (P.L. 94-437), and subsequent amendments in 1980, 1988, and 1990. This Act and its amendments support the development of mental health services, staff training, community education, and research. These developments are based on the principle that mental health programs for Native Americans should take into account the "great cultural and geographic diversity of Native American communities" (Nelson, 1991, p. 1050). Traditional health and mental health care through native healers continues, and it increasingly is coordinated with formal mental health services.

The fact that the needs of most Native Americans with mental health problems remain unmet has led to the development of a National Plan for Native American Mental Health Services. The plan would affect some 1.2 million Native Americans in the United States. It gives special attention to the need for increased provision of mental health services, particularly for children; for improvement of the quality of services provided; and for "prevention of risk factors, such as child abuse and domestic violence, that contribute to the high incidence of mental illness in Native American communities" (Nelson, 1991, p. 1052). The plan "outlines a program of research that will lead to better understanding of the mental health problems of Native Americans and to more effective interventions" (p. 1053).

One example of federal efforts to improve mental health services for Native Americans is the initiation of six Community Support Program projects that focus on this population. These projects emphasize consumer and family empowerment, carried out through the formation of advocacy boards to advise state mental health authorities. Some examples of project programs include supportive extended family clubhouses, peer counseling programs, statewide training for consumers and advocacy groups, leadership training for grassroots advocacy organizations, and interstate advisory councils (SAMHSA, 1993c). Closely allied to the purposes of these projects was a national conference in Albuquerque, New Mexico, in 1993, with the purpose of creating "a shared vision for an effective, comprehensive service delivery system for Native American people with serious and persistent mental illness" (SAMHSA, 1993c, p. 6). A major focus of the conference was on consumer and family advocacy which would lead to mental health services more "relevant to the cultural traditions and needs of Native Americans" (p. 6). In keeping with the purposes of the conference, one result was the creation of a national organization, National Native American Families for Mental Health.

REVIEW

Mental health policy makers and service providers are giving renewed attention to the special issues involved in providing mental health care to members of ethnic minority groups. A framework developed by Rogler and his colleagues (1989) is used to consider these issues in terms of the emergence of mental health problems, help-seeking behavior, service provider assessment and diagnosis, treatment, and social rehabilitation. Despite the somewhat limited scientific study in all of these areas of concern, available research findings confirm the need for special attention to the cultural dimensions of mental health policy and services.

Major efforts have been devoted to the organization of research findings about ethnic minority groups and the identification of areas in need of further research. For example, Rogler et al. (1989) have summarized research on Hispanics and mental health. Reports from the ECA studies include limited but useful information about mental illness and utilization of services among ethnic minority groups. Articles and books on mental health issues of ethnic minority groups have established a basis for development of the idea of what it means to be a culturally competent professional. For example, chapters in the edited work of Gaw (1993), *Culture, Ethnicity, and Mental Health*, examine the psychiatric care of African-Americans, Native Americans, Alaska natives, Asian-Americans, and Hispanics. Finally, policy makers at the national, state, and local community levels have established goals regarding provision of mental health services to members of ethnic minority groups. For example, special policies and programs have been initiated to meet the mental health needs of Native Americans.

9.
Women and
Mental Health

Spurred on by feminist scholarship as well as concerns over how women fare in the mental health delivery system, mental health professionals have created an agenda for improving mental health services for women (Russo, 1990; Travis, 1988; Walker, 1994; Widiger, Corbitt, & Funtowicz, 1994). Gender issues in mental health care have been documented, and policy changes and service alternatives have been advanced to make the health care system more responsive to the needs of women. In this chapter we examine women's mental health issues in terms of the prevalence of mental health problems among women, help-seeking behaviors, diagnosis, treatment, and rehabilitation.

The traditional mental health system has never fully responded to the needs of women. This situation has been attributed to factors such as the small representation of women in policy-making circles and a lack of recognition of the "ways that sex bias, sex role stereotyping, and devaluation of women affect the nature, diagnosis, and treatment of mental health problems" (Russo, 1984, p. 21). Examination of these factors was undertaken by the President's Commission on Mental Health (1978), which created a subpanel to examine women's issues and mental health. The recommendations of this subpanel have served as a "blueprint for developing mental health policies responsive to women's needs" and as "an organizing platform for women's mental health policy advocates" (Russo, 1984, pp. 22, 36). An important feature of the subpanel's report to the President's Commission was its call for research on the mental health of women in an effort to compensate for past limitations in topics studied, theory development, and research methodology (Eichler & Parron, 1987).

Additional major developments relative to women and mental health include the designation of women as a priority population by the Alcohol, Drug Abuse, and Mental Health Administration Act of 1984 (P.L. 98-509). Also, mental health professionals sponsored by the American Psychological Association and the Women and Health Roundtable have developed an agenda on the mental health needs of women. A report of this group, entitled "A Women's Mental Health Agenda," made the following recommendations:

1. Increase the visibility and participation of women in mental health leadership positions;
2. Increase the knowledge base about women's mental health and ensure that sex bias in research does not detract from the quality of that knowledge base;
3. Integrate the new research on women, particularly with regard to diagnosis and treatment, into mental health education, training, and practice;
4. Examine and improve the impact of current and proposed policies and programs, including financing, on women's mental health research, education, training, and service delivery;
5. Develop prevention efforts that will address the conflicts and dilemmas experienced by women in their families, work settings, and communities (Eichler & Parron, 1987, p. 2).

In another development, the National Institute of Mental Health convened a meeting in 1986 to develop a Women's Mental Health Research Agenda. Participants examined five areas of research that focus mainly on women:

1. Diagnosis and treatment of mental disorders in women;
2. Mental health issues for older women;
3. Causes and mental health effects of violence against women;
4. Stressors affecting the mental health of women: multiple roles;
5. Stressors affecting the mental health of women: poverty (Eichler & Parron, 1987, p. 4).

Russo (1990) provides a summary of research findings on these five topics in an article entitled "Forging Research Priorities for

Women's Mental Health" that appeared in a special issue of the *American Psychologist*. Information from articles in this special issue is incorporated into our discussion of women's mental health. At the same time, the reader may wish to explore the literature in psychiatry, psychology, public health, social work, and nursing with regard to the treatment of women with mental health problems. In addition, recent books in the popular press include discussions of controversial issues concerning the use of medications in the treatment of women, such as Kramer's (1993) presentation of the benefits for women of Prozac and psychotherapy in *Listening to Prozac* and a contrasting view by Breggin (1994) in *Talking Back to Prozac*.

One of the major criticisms in the mental health literature has been that the psychology of women has been based largely on the experiences of white middle-class women. This has led to a lack of understanding of women of different cultures (Comas-Diaz & Greene, 1994). In response, women of color have begun to address issues pertaining to gender, ethnicity, race, and mental health. For example, Padgett et al. (1994) have studied the use of outpatient mental health services by African-American, Hispanic, and non-Hispanic white women. As noted in Chapter 8, contributors to a volume edited by Comas-Diaz and Greene (1994) provide a foundation for understanding the interaction of gender and ethnicity in mental health. The reader can draw from this knowledge to supplement our more general discussion of women and mental health.

THE EMERGENCE AND PREVALENCE OF MENTAL DISORDERS

Two questions guide the examination of the prevalence of mental health problems among women. First, in what ways do women differ from men in rates of mental disorders? Second, what social and personal factors are related to gender differences? In regard to the first question, ECA findings on gender and mental illness are presented in *Psychiatric Disorders in America* (Robins & Regier, 1991). Gender differences in selected disorders are reported for lifetime and for one-year periods. Men are found to be more likely than women to have had a mental disorder during their lifetimes (36% compared to 30%), with no gender differences (20% for men and women) found in overall prevalence of active disorders within the past year. Findings from the National Comorbidity Survey show no differences in lifetime rates for men and women but indicate that women are more likely than men to have active disorders (31.2% compared to 27.7%) (Kessler et al., 1994).

When ECA findings are examined for specific disorders, lifetime rates show that men are more likely than women to suffer from alcohol abuse and antisocial personality, while women have higher rates for somatization disorder, obsessive-compulsive disorder, and major depressive disorders (Robins & Regier, 1991). For disorders during the past year (active disorders), women have higher rates for the following four disorders: somatization disorder, depressive episodes, generalized anxiety, panic and phobia disorders. Men have higher rates of antisocial personality, drug abuse/dependence, and alcohol abuse/dependence. The most dramatic gender differences occur for alcohol abuse/dependence, where men are about five times more likely to have this disorder than women. For panic/phobia disorders and affective disorders, women are about two times more likely than men to have these disorders. Findings from the National Comorbidity Survey indicate that women are more likely than men (14.1 % compared to 8.5%) to have any affective disorder, to have any anxiety disorder (22.6% compared to 11.8%), and less likely to have any substance/dependence disorder (6.6% compared to 16.1%). In regard to comorbidity, this survey found that women are more likely than men to have three or more disorders (Kessler et al., 1994).

These findings provide insights into gender differences in mental illness, showing that women are more susceptible to some illnesses, men to others. The findings lead to a concern about the factors that may be associated with illness and health; specifically, what factors are related to the emergence of mental health problems in women? The Women's Mental Health Research Agenda recommended that research be carried out on some factors, such as "the ordinary and extraordinary events associated with being a woman in this society with respect to multiple roles, poverty, violence, and aging" (Russo, 1990, p. 370). We now summarize research findings regarding these factors.

Multiple Roles and Mental Health

The several roles women carry out within society can be viewed as sources of stress as well as satisfaction. Given the changing roles of women, especially in regard to family, work, and caregiving, the NIMH women's mental health research agenda "emphasized the priority of research on parenting, work-related stress, and the variation in mental health conditions caused by multiple roles, analyzed by education, economic status, marital status, age, and race/ethnicity" (Russo, 1990, p. 370). In regard to parenting, research has focused on the stresses experienced by women in the transition to parenthood (McBride, 1990; Mowbray et al., 1995). This transition appears to involve substantially more change for women than for men, especially for working-class women and women with difficult infants (Russo, 1990; Mowbray et al., 1995). Research findings indicate that parenthood "increases the symptoms of psychological distress for women whether or not they work outside the home" (Russo, 1990, p. 370).

For many mothers of young children, there are additional stresses when these women are employed outside the home, generating effects of multiple roles. Additional stresses may also come from women's caregiving roles in relation to elderly parents and in-laws. Stresses from multiple roles may be conceptualized as role strain, thought to be influenced by "the structure of an individual's social support network, the person's coping style, the centrality of each role to the self, and self-esteem" (McBride, 1990, p. 382). These ideas suggest negative consequences of multiple roles for the mental health of women and their children (Oyserman, Mowbray, & Zemencuk, 1994). At the same time, research studies are needed to ascertain the link between multiple roles and mental health in terms of possible advantages as well as disadvantages.

Poverty and Mental Health

Belle (1990) cites research findings that attest to a positive correlation between poverty and mental illness. Poverty may be viewed as a social stressor that increases vulnerability to mental illness for women (Mowbray et al., 1994). It follows, then, that with an increasing level of poverty among women and children, attention should be given to the relationship between poverty and women's mental health. An analysis of ECA data by Bruce, Takeuchi, and Leaf (1991) indicated that women with economic hardships are at an increased risk for mental or emotional problems. Research on depression among women clearly shows a relationship between this disorder and poverty (Mowbray et al., 1994). Poverty has been found to negatively affect the role performance of women, women's support systems, social networks, and women's coping strategies (Belle, 1990). At the same time, poverty "takes many forms, such as short term vs. persistent poverty, differences in the experience of poverty by ethnic minority women, and the experiences of poor women who remain emotionally healthy" (Belle, 1990, p. 387). In order to develop mental health policies and treatment approaches for poor women, further research is needed on the dynamics of the relationship of socioeconomic status and mental health.

Violence and Mental Health

Violence against women is well documented in recent social science studies. As Koss (1990) indicates, "These data suggest that for women, the U.S. family is a violent institution," as close friends or family members commit a high proportion of the violence against women (p. 375). Moreover, significant negative mental health implications have been associated with the various forms of violence against women. Victimization of women has been shown to be a significant contributor to a range of mental disorders, particularly major depression, alcohol abuse/dependence, drug abuse/dependence, generalized anxiety, obsessive-compulsive disorder, post-traumatic stress disorder, eating disorders, multiple personality, and borderline syndrome (Koss, 1990; Mowbray et al., 1994).

While community agencies provide services for victims of violence, these services generally are limited in scope and volume, uncoordinated, underfunded, and with limited evaluation of effectiveness. Some efforts have been made to assess the impact of clinical treatment for women victims of violence, but there remains a "pressing, immediate need for treatment research on how to mitigate the effects of violence on its victims" (Russo, 1990, p. 371). Given the mental health implications of violence for women, there is a call for policy makers to be cognizant of the need for prevention strategies and for professionals to be alert to victimization-related mental health problems of women clients.

This involvement of professionals is needed in regarded to individuals considered especially vulnerable to violence and its effects, such as poor women, lesbians, chronically mentally ill women, women with physical disabilities, older women, and adolescent mothers (Russo, 1987). An example of an effort to promote such involvement is a 1994 conference sponsored by the Center for Mental Health Services of SAMHSA on the theme "Dare to Vision: Shaping a National Agenda for Women, Abuse and Mental Health Services." Participants in the conference, including consumer advocates and mental health and health professionals, emphasized the lack of responsiveness of the mental health system to the impact of physical and sexual abuse on women's mental health (SAMHSA, 1994d). Speakers at the conference also noted that "the treatment methods used by the mental health establishment almost always serve abuse survivors poorly, no matter what their symptoms or diagnostic labels may be" (p. 9).

Aging and Mental Health

Consideration of the mental health of aging women requires that attention be given to the care arrangments of the older person. Some aging women with mental disorders reside in the homes of relatives, usually including an adult female daughter or daughter-in-law. A large proportion of the mentally ill elderly live in nursing homes, have incomes below the poverty level, and suffer from physical illnesses. This is particularly true for elderly women who belong to ethnic minority groups. The most common mental disorders among the elderly are depression, organic brain syndromes, and dementias (Eichler & Parron, 1987). The use of multiple medications poses a special problem for elderly women in terms of drug interactions, overuse, and adverse side effects. Use of psychotropic medications for nursing home residents has been of particular concern to policy makers and to family members, as these medications are often administered to residents who do not have mental disorders. Such drugs are often used to control troublesome patients. In response to this problem, federal regulations were introduced in 1991 in an effort to curtail abuses in the use of tranquilizers and other drugs for older nursing home residents (Winslow, 1991).

Survey data about the mental health of women in nursing homes have been collected by the U.S. Public Health Service (1990). In a 1987 National Medical Expenditure Survey, women constituted about three-fourths of the 1.5 million residents of U.S. nursing homes, with more than two-thirds of these residents having one or more psychiatric symptoms. According to this survey, "Women were more likely than men to experience multiple symptoms at all ages" (p. 330). Male residents were slightly more likely than females (52% compared to 46%) to have behavior problems, but men were twice as likely as women to hurt others physically (16% compared to 9%). Given the fact that a large proportion of nursing home residents are women, the Nursing Home Reform Amendments of the 1987 Omnibus Budget Reconciliation Act have special significance for aging women. These amendments established procedures entitled Preadmission Screening and Annual Resident Review (PASARR) directed toward keeping people with mental disorders and developmental disabilities out of nursing homes.

Homelessness and Mental Health

As Buckner, Bassuk, and Zima (1993) have noted, "Homeless women comprise a heterogeneous population with diverse psychosocial needs and multiple problems" (p. 385). Severe mental illness and substance abuse are among these problems, sometimes contributing to homelessness and at other times exacerbated by the homeless condition. Estimates of mental illness among the homeless in general are about 30%, with single women more likely than men to have mental disorders. These women often have "past histories of child abuse, family violence, and more recent traumatic events" (p. 388). Studies of alcoholism and drug abuse estimate that about one-fifth of homeless women have a history of alcohol problems, compared to two-fifths of homeless men, while the sexes are similar in regard to drug problems (between 10% and 20%).

Homeless women with dependent children are more likely to have mental disorders than are non-homeless women with dependent children. Single homeless women are more likely to have mental health problems than single non-homeless women. While provision of mental health services is important for homeless women with mental illness, Buckner et al. (1993) maintain that basic needs must be met first, such as shelter, food, safety, and care for acute medical illnesses. Further, they suggest, these programs should be sensitive to differences in needs among subgroups of homeless women, especially in the development of supportive case management services. For example, mentally ill homeless women with children need interventions related to parenting skills and the problems of raising children.

Women with Serious Mental Illness

The mental health policy of deinstitutionalization has had a number of negative effects on severely mentally ill women, including vulnerability to sexual exploitation and violence, homelessness, diversion into the criminal justice system, and stigmatization (Bachrach, 1984; Bachrach & Nadelson, 1988). Mental health policy makers have usually viewed people with serious and persistent mental illness as "genderless," resulting in "a failure to recognize and appropriately treat the special needs of female clients in terms of family/mothering roles, physical health and medications, vocational planning, and victimization" (Mowbray, Herman, & Hazel, 1992, p. 109). As a result of recent epidemiological studies, it has been established that women are more likely than men to suffer from serious mental illnesses such as depression and schizophrenia (Ashbaugh et al., 1983; Myers et al., 1984). Among the seriously mentally ill, women are less likely than men to utilize mental health treatment for such illnesses (Mowbray & Benedek, 1988).

In their review of the literature on women with severe mental illness, Mowbray et al. (1994) have noted that these women tend to live under adverse socioeconomic conditions, to have problems in parenting that have affected their children, to experience more general health problems than men, to suffer more than men from adverse effects of psychotropic medications, and to have been victims of childhood sexual abuse and of adult sexual victimization. Parenting is particularly problematic for seriously mentally ill women, as the research literature "suggests that these women experience multiple risk factors (e.g., lack of prenatal care, medication effects) and a paucity of emotional and economic support during the initial phases of parenthood: pregnancy, childbirth, and the postpartum period" (Mowbray et al., 1995, p. 1). For women who have been deinstitutionalized, the effects have been positive for some, but negative for many. Bachrach (1984) has observed that these women often experience problems in regard to sexual behavior and reproductive control and are in need of special counseling in this area. These women are also "particularly vulnerable to sexual exploitation and violence" (p. 29), to homelessness, and to being diverted into the criminal justice system.

HELP-SEEKING BEHAVIOR

One of the principal findings from the ECA studies has been the underutilization of treatment and other services by all individuals with mental disorders (Regier et al., 1993). Of the non-institutionalized population, "only 19% of household residents with an active disorder in the current year reported either inpatient treatment in the last year or outpatient treatment in the last six months" (Robins et al., 1991, p. 341). Of these residents with active disorders, women were more likely than men (23% compared to 14%) to obtain treatment during these time periods. Most likely to receive treatment were unmarried women with at least a high school education. Other studies of service utilization have shown that women seek treatment for mental disorders and emotional problems at a higher rate than men and actually receive more mental health services. Women use outpatient services to a greater degree than men, while men are more likely to use inpatient care (Hankin, 1990; Wilcox & Yates, 1993). Most studies demonstrate that a variety of factors in addition to gender influence utilization of treatment services, such as age, income, marital status, education, usual source of medical care, psychiatric status, and attitudes toward services (Leaf et al., 1985).

Utilization data from three sites of the ECA studies examined by Shapiro et al. (1984) not only showed higher use of treatment services by women, but also indicated gender differences in regard to where services were obtained. Women were less likely than men to seek help from mental health specialists, in comparison to the general medical sector. In another report from the ECA studies, data were examined from the Yale site only, a site where data were collected to discover the relationship of service utilization to need, predisposing, and enabling factors (Leaf et al., 1985). This analysis showed only slight differences between women and men in service utilization, with factors other than gender exerting greater influence. While there is higher utilization among women, the fact remains that this population group, along with men, underutilizes treatment services, creating a major concern for policy makers.

In a study of federal employees insured by Blue Cross/Blue Shield, Padgett et al. (1994; 1994a) found that women were more likely than men to use outpatient mental health services. This pattern held for non-Hispanic whites, Hispanics, and African-Americans. In a separate analysis of women only, these authors found that whites displayed the highest use, followed by Hispanics, with lowest utilization by African-Americans. With regard to inpatient utilization, some studies indicate that men, including white, Hispanic, and African-American males, are more likely than women to receive inpatient care for serious mental illness.

ASSESSMENT AND DIAGNOSIS

There have been several areas of concern about the use of DSM for the assessment and diagnosis of mental disorders in women (Kass, Spitzer, & Williams, 1993; Travis, 1988; Walker, 1994; Widiger et al., 1994). First, the contention that gender biases were eliminated in the criteria for disorders used in DSM-III and DSM-III-R was challenged by women in mental health, especially in regard to personality disorders (Walker, 1994). Second, there has been continued controversy over proposed inclusion in DSM III-R and DSM-IV of new diagnostic categories that apply mainly or exclusively to women. Third, there has been concern over the use of DSM by male mental health professionals in the assessment and diagnosis of women.

The challenge to the diagnostic criteria for disorders in DSM-III was asserted by Kaplan (1983) in her contention that "masculine-biased assumptions about what behaviors are healthy and what behaviors are crazy are codified in diagnostic criteria; these criteria then influence diagnosis and treatment rates and patterns" (p. 786). Kaplan asserted that "male-centered assumptions...the sunglasses through which we view each other...are causing clinicians to see normal females as abnormal" (p. 791). In their critique of Kaplan's work, Williams and Spitzer (1983) took issue with Kaplan's thesis that "there is a general bias toward diagnosing females as having a mental disorder" (p. 793). These writers contended that Kaplan's position was not supported, since an analysis of data from field trials of DSM-III indicated no "general tendency for all major categories to be given more frequently to women" (p. 793).

New Diagnostic Categories

In the development of DSM-III-R, proposals were made to include three new diagnostic categories that pertain mainly or exclusively to women (Pugliesi, 1992; NASW, 1986). These diagnoses were Self-Defeating Personality Disorder, Premenstrual Dysphoric Mood Disorder, and Paraphilic Coercive Disorder. Objections to including these categories as mental disorders were made by feminist groups, professional organizations such as the National Association of Social Workers, and by other women mental health professionals, particularly women psychiatrists and psychologists.

The category of Self-Defeating Personality Disorder focused on "the transient effects of battering or sexual assault on women's functioning" (Wetzel, 1991, p. 16), and was "a diagnosis for people who stay in abusive relationships" (Kutchins & Kirk, 1989, p. 93). The National Association of Social Workers opposed this new category on the grounds that its features were a "survival strategy," not psychopathology, and that the diagnosis "could be used against women in custody battles, in self-defense murder cases, in sexual harassment litigation" (NASW, 1986). This diagnostic category was not included in DSM-III-R as a mental disorder but was included in the appendix as Proposed Diagnostic Categories Needing Further Study.

In regard to Premenstrual Dysphoric Mood Disorder, the major argument against inclusion was that premenstrual syndrome (PMS) "is primarily a physical disorder with concomitant disturbance of emotion, mood and behavior" and not a psychiatric disorder (NASW, 1986, p. 1). This category was also included in the appendix of DSM-III-R.

Finally, paraphilic rapism was to be included as a paraphilic coercive disorder, making "a psychiatric diagnosis out of rape" (p. 1). In response to women's objections, this category was dropped.

An appendix of DSM-IV includes several proposals for new categories of disorders, including Premenstrual Dysphoric Mood Disorder. This category stipulates that in "most menstrual cycles during the past year, five (or more) of the following symptoms were present for most of the time during the last week of the luteal phase, began to remit within a few days after the onset of the follicular phase, and were absent in the week postmenses" (APA, 1994, p. 717). Classification of this disorder requires one or more of a number of symptoms listed in the appendix, such as markedly depressed mood, marked anxiety, marked affective lability, and decreased interest in activities (p. 716). These symptoms must be severe enough to "markedly interfere with work or school or with usual social activities and relationships with others" (p. 716). The manual specifically notes that "the transient mood changes that many females experience around the time of their period should not be considered a mental disorder" (p. 716).

Developmental Theories

Traditional developmental theories that guide the assessment of women's mental health have been challenged within the women's movement and by feminist scholars for several decades. These challenges have been based on the importance given to clinical theories in "evaluating clients' behavior, for ascertaining their psychological health or illness, and for formulating treatment goals" (Marecek & Kravetz, 1977, p. 324; Brown & Ballou, 1992). There is an extensive literature that attacks psychoanalytic theories, especially Freudian theory, as well as biological theories that have formed the basis for much of the treatment of women with mental disorders (Brown & Ballou, 1992; Marecek & Kravetz, 1977; Gilligan, 1982). Criticisms of these theories focus on the concepts of sex bias and sex-role stereotyping, and the likelihood "that behaviors expressing either extreme conformity or deviance to traditional gender roles will be classified as indicative of mental disorder" (Travis, 1988, p. 182).

Sociocultural explanations for health and illness in women have been emphasized by feminist scholars as explanations of mental stress and illness as well as foundations for treatment (Mowbray, Lanir, & Hulce, 1984). Sociocultural theories focus on socialization patterns of women, on societal forces such as economic, political, and social factors, as well as sexism, discrimination, and oppression of women in society. Some of these factors, such as poverty, multiple roles, and violence, have been discussed earlier in this chapter as social conditions that influence the mental health of women. Currently, much emphasis is placed on the need for recognition of ways in which women's roles have changed—or not changed—in regard to sexuality, employment, sex role requirements (e.g., family), and standards of behavior. Feminist theorists continue to provide important contributions to the understanding of women's psychological and social development (Bernstein & Lenhart, 1993; Travis, 1988). These scholars have given special attention to differences among women with regard to ethnicity, age, marital status, education, sexual orientation, and occupational status.

TREATMENT/REHABILITATION

Mental health treatment for women includes a wide variety of interventions, including various types of treatment: psychotherapy, cognitive behavioral therapy counseling, psychopharmacological treatment, social work, and feminist therapy. The nature of the treatment provided is usually connected to the type of mental health problem diagnosed and to the theoretical orientation of the professional. Since women constitute a diverse population, individuals in special groups may receive differential treatment. Factors considered include age, ethnicity, homelessness, marital status, chronicity of illness, dual diagnoses, sexual orientation, and victimization by violence (Mirkin, 1994).

The traditional mental health interventions provided through the mental health delivery system have been the object of criticism by women professionals (Zukerman, 1979). First, there have long been objections to therapies based on psychoanalytic theories (Penfold & Walker, 1983; Travis, 1988; Guttentag, Salasin, & Belle, 1980). The concern has been that these theories deal with definitions of psychopathology based on a biological model of sex differences, on stereotypes of appropriate male/female roles and behavior, on sex role identity, socialization of children, male definitions and expectations of gender-based behavior, and on goals of adjustment and conformity to these expectations as normal behavior. These theories become problematic for women when they are used as standards of behavior and as a basis for the development of treatment goals (Marecek & Kravetz, 1977; Kiresuk, Schultz, & Baxter, 1980; Bernstein & Lenhart, 1993).

A second major concern about treatment of women has been the increasing use of psychoactive drugs. Numerous studies demonstrate that women are more likely than men to receive psychotropic medication (Eichler & Parron, 1987). Related concerns deal with the side effects of these drugs and the need for research on the effects of these drugs on women. While most attention has been directed to the effects on women with serious mental disorders, concern has also been expressed about the use of medications for "near well" people. For example, the ethical implications of using Prozac with such women have been recognized by Kramer (1993), as medication may be viewed in some instances as "cosmetic psychopharmacology." Thus, some drugs may be used for the "chemical enhancement of a variety of psychological traits...social ease, flexibility, mental agility, affective stability" (p. 273), leading to the question, should drugs be used as "mood brighteners" to "improve normal people's mood"? (p. 215).

A third major concern involves the question of whether many women might benefit more by remaining outside the professional treatment system and using self-help groups, or by combining treatment within the mental system with membership in self-help groups (Gartner, 1985). Other forms of alternative services that might be more beneficial than mental health services for some women include consciousness-raising groups and assertiveness training groups.

Alternative Therapies

In recent years, alternative approaches to mental health treatment have been developed for women. Women scholars have provided alternative formulations for human development that have led to new or modified forms of therapy. In some instances, the reformulations of human development have resulted in modifications of traditional therapy. Two of these types of modifications are nonsexist therapy and feminist therapy (Ballou & Gabalac, 1985; Travis, 1988). Marecek and Kravetz (1977) view these as treatment philosophies, similar but also distinctive, and not as a set of specific strategies for conducting therapy. Thus, the principles of these approaches can be used in various forms of traditional therapy. These authors take the view that "In nonsexist therapy (as in traditional therapies), the focus of treatment is individual change and the modification of personal behavior" (p. 325). On the other hand, "In feminist therapy...the critique of society and social institutions is a central element. Social change is considered the necessary counterpart to personal change" (p. 325).

Ballou and Gabalac (1985) define feminist therapy as an orientation, "a conceptual frame of reference based upon a philosophical-value position." They identify a number of principles of feminism that are common to various forms of feminist therapy, such as the following: "women as a gender...have less social, political and economic power than men," leading to "the inferior status of women"; "women's pathology is fundamentally caused by external, not internal sources"; and "women must attain both economic and psychological autonomy" (pp. 22–25).

Ballou and Gabalac (1985) recognize three approaches in feminist literature in regard to mental health. First, there is a radical perspective that represents early efforts in the women's movement, "challenges the roots of Western thought and the most fundamental concepts of therapy," and "differs strikingly from traditional therapy" (p. 31). Second, there is a "questioning" perspective that comes mainly from scholarship within the mental health professions, is critical of traditional therapy, and proposes alternative treatment forms. Third, there is a set of literature that attempts to integrate feminist philosophy and theories of development into radical, socialist, or liberal practice perspectives.

Feminist therapy clearly challenges the traditional, medically oriented model used in mental health professions, in regard to "the basic understanding of personality, mental illness, and assessment, diagnosis and treatment" (Ballou & Gabalac, 1985, p. 142). This challenge is based on the belief that "The conclusion that traditional mental health services are anti-feminist is inescapable" (p. 163). From this perspective, Ballou and Gabalac (1985) suggest that the traditional mental health system must be changed through a feminist orientation, especially in regard to "knowledge base change, institutional change, personnel change and ideological change" (p. 163). An important aspect of such change would be societal and community environmental changes through social policies involving services that help women, such as day care, self-help groups, women's health care, and so on.

The goals of feminist therapy are different for the three types of feminism: liberal, socialist, and radical (Penfold & Walker, 1983; Travis, 1988). For example, some authors assert that liberal feminists assume that factors such as equal rights, improved social conditions, changing attitudes toward women on the part of professionals, public education, and increasing numbers of women professionals will result in improved mental health status for women. Radical feminists seek sweeping changes in social institutions and the elimination of sexism. Socialist feminists seek change in society along socialist democratic lines (Penfold & Walker, 1983).

Self-Help Groups

Self-help groups that provide social support for women are not usually regarded as forms of mental health treatment; however, such groups are closely related to treatment (Gartner, 1985). In some instances, they may help individuals cope with stressful life events, thereby preventing the need for more formal mental health treatment. Thus, self-help and support groups can be used to "divert many women from traditional one-on-one therapy and provide help to deal with problems at an earlier stage without making them clients of the mental health system" (Michigan Department of Mental Health, 1982, p. V). Problems that can be addressed in self-help and support groups include "crises of childbirth (including teen pregnancy and abortion), single parenting, isolation/displacement from the homemaker role, domestic abuse, and victimization" (p. 3). While the potential benefits of self-help groups for women appear to be substantial, the ECA studies show that women are less likely than men (lifetime rates of 2.2% compared to 3.6%) to take part in these groups. The utilization rates are low despite the fact that women mental health professionals have supported the use of self-help through education, referrals, and sponsorship of self-help groups.

Self-help groups serve important functions for women who are receiving treatment within the mental health system, as well as for individuals who have terminated formal treatment. These women's groups are designed to provide "health education by and to women" and "to aid women in self-fulfillment" (Gartner, 1985, p. 26). Women's self-help groups that focus on mental health problems are similar to other health-related groups in that they may may focus on rehabilitation, behavior change, primary care, or prevention (Gartner, 1985). In regard to prevention, self-help groups provide support for women undergoing various kinds of life stresses that might otherwise lead to mental illness. As Gartner (1985) has noted, "Self-help groups offer two unique preventive features: they provide social support through the creation of a caring community, and they increase members' coping skills through the provision of information and the sharing of experiences and solutions to problems" (p. 29).

Many self-help groups, such as Recovery, Inc., provide support for "ex-patients" as a supplement to professional aftercare services. Among the more recent types of self-help groups for women are some that focus on "private violence...rape, child abuse, wife beating, and incest," on bereavement in widowhood, and on a range of specific persistent and serious mental health problems (Gartner, 1985, p. 30). Women may be members of self-groups that also include men, but in many instances these groups consist of women only.

PROGRESS IN WOMEN'S MENTAL HEALTH

Since the call for research on women's mental health was made in the reports of the President's Commission on Mental Health (1978), there has been an increase in theoretical developments as well as empirical studies relevant to women's mental health issues. These advances in knowledge have been strongly supported by women mental health professionals and by feminist scholarship in academic and professional practice circles. An initial focus on psychotherapy and women has been broadened into an examination of special population groups of women, of social conditions that affect women's mental health, and on alternative modes of treatment and services for women. The collection of this knowledge into a systematic framework remains unfinished business.

New theoretical developments concerning gender, as well as empirical findings on women and mental health, remain scattered throughout the professional literature. Still, a basic foundation of knowledge about women and mental health has been established. The

ECA studies have generated evidence about gender differences in mental illness and in utilization of mental health services. Research demonstrates that women differ from men in relation to some mental disorders and emotional problems and that the identification of these mental health problems is not always the result of the sex biases of mental health professionals (Franks & Rothblum, 1983). Ongoing research on sources of stress for women, such as multiple roles, poverty, violence, aging, and homelessness, has contributed to the understanding of women's mental health and of the types of social intervention necessary to reduce stresses and improve mental health.

Significant involvements and changes have occurred among women with regard to diagnosis and treatment of mental health problems. In most instances, these developments and changes are associated with women who identify with feminism, recognizing that there are various strains of feminist thought. In regard to assessment and diagnosis, women professionals with a feminist perspective have become actively involved in the revision of developmental theories of personality and in changes in the DSM classification system of mental disorders. In regard to treatment, feminist thought has influenced the traditional interpersonal therapies, as well as initiating the development of feminist therapy. In addition, alternatives to traditional therapy have been developed, most noticeably the use of women's groups, such as self-help and mutual aid groups. Throughout these developments there has been an increased concern about the ways in which the mental health system affects women of color.

Finally, there is evidence that there have been positive policy changes in recent years that affect women's mental health. Assessment of policy changes is difficult for several reasons, since so many different types of policies are related to the needs of women. Some policies are directly related to the mental health system, focusing on mental health and mental illness. Other policies pertain to general health care, social welfare, and educational systems, which are topics that have direct or indirect implications for mental health. Still other policies relate to the political and economic systems of the society and of communities and have a more indirect impact on mental health. Individuals promoting the involvement of women in policy making have emphasized that "any public policy that touches women's lives (e.g., housing, energy, criminal justice, health) has an effect on women's mental health" (Stringer & Welton, 1984, p. 43).

Changes in mental health systems that have affected women's mental health are evident at the federal level in legislation of the Congress, decisions of the Supreme Court, and policies of the National Institute of Mental Health. An example of a Supreme Court decision related to women's mental health is found in a 1993 ruling on sexual harassment in the workplace, based on Title VII of the Civil Rights Act of 1964. In this decision, "the court ruled unanimously that workers suing their employers for sexual harassment need not show that they suffered psychological injury" (*The New York Times*, 1993). Opinions by the Supreme Court justices in this case provided elaborations of "discriminatorily abusive work environments," such as Justice O'Connor's assertion that determination of the presence of such an environment "may include the frequency of the discriminatory conduct; its severity; whether it is physically threatening or humiliating, or a mere offensive utterance; and whether it unreasonably interferes with an employee's work performance" (*Harris v. Forklift Systems*, 1993, P.L. 92-1168). Justice O'Connor goes on to say that "The effect on the employee's psychological well-being is, of course, relevant to determining whether the plaintiff actually found the environment abusive. But while psychological harm, like any other relevant factor, may be taken into account, no single factor is required" (*Harris v. Forklift Systems*, 1993, P.L. 92-1168).

Examples of recent federal legislation with implications for women's mental health include the Americans with Disabilities Act of 1990, which outlines the rights of physically and mentally ill persons; the Family and Medical Leave Act of 1993, which allows for leave without pay for care of seriously ill, newborn, or newly adopted members of families; the State Comprehensive Mental Health Services Plan Act of 1986, which focuses on mental health policies and community-based services for chronically mentally ill persons; and the Nursing Home Reform Amendments in the 1987 Omnibus Budget Reconciliation Act, along with subsequent 1990 amendments, which established goals regarding aging mentally ill persons. Pending are possible health and mental health care policies stimulated by the 1994 health reform proposals of the Clinton administration. Health care reform policies clearly have implications for the nature and coverage of mental health care for women, particularly individuals and families who are living in poverty or employed by companies that do not provide health coverage.

REVIEW

Knowledge about women's mental health has increased dramatically over the past two decades. Gender issues, in terms of social policies, programs, and services, have been clarified and advanced through feminist perspectives. Changes in responses to the mental health needs of women have been supported at federal and state governmental levels. Most important has been the establishment of a Women's Mental Health Research Agenda, including a focus on the need for knowledge in relation to women's multiple roles, poverty, violence, and aging. ECA studies have generated new knowledge about gender differences in the prevalence of mental disorders, as well as in the patterns of help-seeking behavior and service utilization rates. Assessment, diagnosis, and treatment of women for mental disorders remain controversial areas in the mental health field. At the same time, these areas have benefited from the scholarly work of women in regard to personality theories, developmental theories, and psychopathology, as well as the development of feminist therapy.

Increased numbers of women professionals in medicine, psychiatry, psychology, social work, and nursing appear to be having a positive impact on the consideration of gender issues in mental health policy making and implementation of treatment and service programs. Continued attention to improvement of women's mental health can be expected as women assume professional and academic positions, are elected to political office, become involved in policy making, take leadership roles in the mental health system, engage in scholarship relevant to women, deliver alternative mental health treatment/services for women, and participate, as consumers, in the mental health system.

10.
Mental Health of Special Population Groups

Several groups in American society have special mental health needs and also face unusual barriers to obtaining services. Policy and service issues related to some of these groups have been discussed in earlier chapters. We have described service needs and utilization patterns of people with severe and persistent mental illness, alcohol and other substance-related disorders, dual diagnosis, and developmental disabilities (Chapter 2), as well as people who are members of ethnic minority groups (Chapter 8) or women (Chapter 9). In this chapter, we explore mental health issues related to children and adolescents, homeless persons, and older adults.

MENTAL HEALTH OF CHILDREN AND ADOLESCENTS

Children and adolescents constitute a special population group within the mental health system, as their needs differ significantly from those of the adult population (18 years and over). While there may be some common elements in definitions of mental health and mental illness for children and adolescents, the reader should keep in mind differences related to other factors such as age, developmental stages, and environmental risk factors (Powers, Hauser, & Kilner, 1989). It has been noted that "Children as a group span a broad developmental range and present with highly variable problems.... Their service needs are complex and change rapidly, relative to the needs of adult populations" (Stroul et al., 1994).

Gaps in scientific knowledge about the mental health status of children and adolescents have been highlighted by Hoagwood and Rupp (1994). These authors assert that "basic questions about the extent of mental health problems among children, the extent of unmet need for care, the types of services currently used by those who are able to access them, and the pathways by which children enter systems of care, cannot now be answered" (p. 52). Still, there is some extant knowledge about this population that can be used in policy planning and service development. For example, central ideas about child and adolescent mental health are presented in two major reports: (1) Research on Children and Adolescents with Mental, Behavioral, and Developmental Disorders (Institute of Medicine, 1989); and (2) National Plan for Research on Child and Adolescent Mental Disorders (NIMH, 1991a). We draw from these reports to identify mental health issues related to children and adolescents. For a more comprehensive review, the reader may wish to consult the extensive literature on the mental health of children and adolescents (Garfinkel, Carlson, & Weller, 1990; Hoagwood & Rupp, 1994; Institute of Medicine, 1989; King & Noshpitz, 1991; Lewis, 1991; NIMH, 1991a; Powers et al., 1989; Stiffman & Davis, 1990; Tuma, 1989; Zeanah, 1993).

The Nature of the Problem

The prevalence of mental disorders among children and adolescents is not as well documented as mental illness in the adult population. Nevertheless, a report by the National Institute of Mental Health (1991a) indicates that approximately 12% of children and youth in the United States have some type of clinical maladjustment, and "of these 7.5 million youngsters, nearly half are presumed to be severely handicapped by their mental disorder and even in less severe cases, a child or adolescent may have difficulty coping with the demands of school, family, and community life" (p. 2). Other epidemiological studies suggest that the prevalence of mental disorders among children and adolescents may be as high as 20% at any given time (Friedman & Kutash, 1992).

Mental disorders in children and youth include problems of "emotional disturbances, such as depression and crippling states of anxiety; behavioral problems characterized by disruptive and antisocial acts; and developmental impairments that limit a child's ability to think, learn, form social attachments, or communicate effectively with others" (Friedman & Kutash, 1992, p. 2). The Center for Mental Health Services of NIMH defines children with serious emotional disturbance as "persons from birth up to age 18 who currently or at any time during the past year have had a diagnosable mental, behavioral, or emotional disorder of sufficient duration to meet diagnostic criteria specified within DSM-III-R that resulted in functional impairment which substantially interferes with or limits the child's role or functioning in family, school, or community activities" (Federal Register, 1993). Functional impairment for children is defined as "difficulties that substantially interfere with or limit a child or adolescent from achieving or maintaining one or more developmentally appropriate social, behavioral, cognitive, communicative, or adaptive skills" (Federal Register, 1993).

The American Psychiatric Association's DSM-IV lists disorders that usually are first diagnosed in infancy, childhood, or adolescence (APA, 1994). These disorders were listed in Chapter 2 under our discussion of developmental disabilities. Children and adolescents may be classified in terms of disorders that are commonly associated with adulthood. The criteria used in defining and classifying emotional, behavioral, or mental disorders among individuals under 18 years of age constitutes an important issue for mental health professionals. Development of this area is needed to assure sound clinical practice, as well as to provide a foundation for epidemiological studies of mental disorders among this group. The NIMH has responded to the need for improved classification and assessment of mental disorders in children and adolescents. To meet this need, NIMH has supported the development of a Diagnostic Interview Schedule for Children and the pilot testing of survey instruments and procedures for measuring impairment, use of services, and risk factors for mental disorders among children and adolescents (NIMH, 1991a). For example, environmental risk factors thought to be associated with mental disorders include poverty and minority status, parental psychopathology, maltreatment, teenage parenting, premature birth/low birth weight, parental divorce, major physical illness, and outpatient pediatrician visits (Tuma, 1989).

Service Delivery Issues

A number of community social systems provide services for children and adolescents with mental health problems. These systems include mental health, public health, education, child welfare, health and social welfare, and juvenile justice (Tuma, 1989). Services are often organized within the field of developmental disabilities, especially with regard to comorbidity of mental retardation and other psychiatric disorders (Campbell & Malone, 1991; Patterson et al., 1995). Children and adolescents are treated by professionals in social work, education, clinical psychology, psychiatry, school guidance, family therapy, nursing, and pediatric and family medicine. Locations for such services are hospitals, schools, mental health clinics, private practice offices, child welfare agencies, juvenile justice facilities, and residential treatment centers (Dulcan, 1992; Johnson, 1993). Over the past several years, there have been advances in knowledge about the major forms of interventions within the mental health system for children and adolescents, such as clinical services in the form of social casework, family counseling, psychotherapy, behavior therapy, cognitive therapy, and medications (Brown & Prout, 1989; King & Noshpitz, 1991; LeCroy, 1992). Models of outreach programs have been employed to provide these kinds of services in schools, particularly for disadvantaged preschoolers (Edlefsen & Baird, 1994).

Fragmentation of care within the public sector, as well as between public and private services, has interfered with effective coordination of systems of care and service delivery (Sawyer & Woodlock, 1994). A community-based system is difficult to create because agencies serving children and adolescents are accustomed to operating independently and competing for community resources (Friedman & Kutash, 1992). There are a number of examples of initiatives for system reform in the mental health care of children and adolescents (Friedman & Kutash, 1992). Among these initiatives are programs funded by the Robert Wood Johnson Foundation, with "a primary focus on expanding the range of services available to support children and families, creating multiagency partnerships, and modifying fiscal policies so that they are more supportive of individualized and home-based care" (p. 132). Another example is the program of the Edna McConnell Clark Foundation, which "focuses on holistic services, use of flexible funds to provide comprehensive and individualized care, and regular data collection on the well-being of children" (p. 132). Still another example is a program of the Annie E. Casey Foundation that focuses on neighborhood-based services for children and families ranging "from prevention to early intervention to treatment" (p. 132). A number of features of the American Health Security Act proposed by President Clinton promise to improve mental health and substance abuse services for children and adolescents. These include extension of services to the uninsured, expansion and availability of a range of service alternatives, reduced fragmentation of services, and improved services for seriously ill children and adolescents (Stroul et al., 1994).

Improvements in service coordination for young people with severe mental disorders were introduced in 1984 through the efforts of the Child and Adolescent Service System Program at NIMH (Friedman & Kutash, 1992). This initiative provided support to a large number of states to coordinate agencies in planning "for systems of care that will better serve youth with serious emotional disturbances" (England & Cole, 1992, p. 630). There are three major dimensions of the CASSP: services, infrastructure, and evaluation. An infrastructure for services is required so as to assure a "comprehensive and integrated service delivery environment at both the state and community levels" (Pensinger et al., 1993, p. 10). Primary program goals are to:

- improve access to and the availability of a continuum of care;
- develop a leadership capability and increase priority in resource allocation for these services;
- improve coordination and collaboration among the child-serving agencies including mental health, education, child welfare, health, substance abuse, and juvenile justice;
- ensure that all systems are able to respond competently to cultural and ethnic differences (p. 10).

Under the NIMH's Comprehensive Community Services Program for Children with Serious Emotional Disturbances, funds are awarded to states and local communities to develop community care for children and adolescents. The goals of the program are directed toward assuring:

- that services are provided collaboratively across child-serving systems;
- that each child or adolescent served through the program receives an individualized service plan developed with the participation of the family (and, where appropriate, the child);
- that each individualized plan designates a case manager to assist the child and family;
- that funding is provided for mental health services required to meet the needs of youngsters in these systems (Pensinger et al., 1993, p. 11).

Following these ideas from NIMH on planning and coordination, the Robert Wood Johnson Foundation developed a Mental Health Services Program for Youth, with grants awarded to eight state-community partnerships to develop systems of care for mentally ill children and adolescents (England & Cole, 1992). These programs focus on care in the family and community by coordinating the services of agencies that serve children, such as mental health, child welfare, public health, education, and juvenile justice in both public and private sectors.

Prevention Services

The coordination of services for children and adolescents is of particular importance in prevention and early intervention programs (Berlin, 1990; Edlefsen & Baird, 1994). The community mental health center movement has promoted prevention, but community mental health centers have been limited in personnel, funding, and policy support for this type of mental health work. Center personnel have been able to collaborate with schools and some social service agencies in programs such as Head Start, special education, and child welfare services, but the role of mental health personnel in community mental health centers requires further development in terms of "primary, secondary, and tertiary prevention for infants, children, and adolescents" (Berlin, 1990, p. 89).

There are opportunities for primary prevention efforts in relation to prenatal care, nutrition, emotional and physical development of infants, special education programs, consultation with teachers, and developmental issues in adolescence. Secondary prevention involves "very early recognition of disturbances or disorders, and prompt and early intervention" (Berlin, 1990, p. 100). For example, parents of a handicapped infant can be provided treatment and education; preschool, school-age children, and adolescents can be helped through programs that focus on developmental tasks. Tertiary prevention involves treatment of mental disorders to "enable functional adaptation in living," and for these services community mental health centers need personnel who have education and experience in treating children and adolescents (p. 102).

The field of infant mental health has encompassed all levels of prevention, especially in response to "at-risk infants." These infants are "usually the children of vulnerable parents such as families in poverty; teenage, single or otherwise isolated parents, psychiatrically or medically at-risk mothers" (Shapiro & Gisynski, 1989, p. 19). As a result, these parents and infants are often seen in settings where social workers are the primary service providers, such as community mental health centers, family and child welfare agencies, hospital social service departments, and child guidance clinics.

Infant Mental Health

While the field of infant mental health includes prevention programs, it includes a number of other areas of interest. This field is closely linked to the mental health of children and adolescents, but has been given separate and special consideration in recent decades, especially in the work of Fraiberg (1959). Zeanah (1993) has identified several dimensions of the field of infant mental health, including "efforts to diagnose and treat disorders in children from birth to 3 (or so); efforts to develop effective prevention strategies; the application of research on infant development to developmental psychopathology; efforts to revise, update, or refute our various theories of infant development; applying knowledge gained from research to a number of social policy issues that affect large numbers of infants" (p. x). The reader will find an in-depth discussion of these dimensions in the *Handbook of Infant Mental Health* (Zeanah, 1993).

Topics covered in Zeanah's *Handbook* illustrate areas of knowledge that overlap with older children and adolescents, as well as topics specifically related to infants. Thus, the context of infant mental health includes models of development and developmental risk, the family context of infant mental health, and the sociocultural context of infant development. Risk conditions and protective factors are studied in terms of poverty and infant development, prematurity and serious medical illness in infancy, adolescent parenthood, parental mental illness and infant development, maternal substance abuse and infant development, and maltreatment and infant development.

Closely related to models of infant development and risk/protective factors is the assessment of infants and their families through various classification systems. This professional activity involves attention to specific infant disorders and to various interventions with infants and parents. Of particular relevance to mental health policies and services are issues surrounding infant day care, infant placement and custody, and infant mental health and social policy. Zigler, Hopper, and Hall (1993) note that "there is a growing discrepancy between the image of the United States as a family-oriented nation and the harsh reality of the failure of our social policies to keep pace with the new realities of family life" (p. 480). Some of these realities include infants in poverty, homelessness, access to health care, child abuse, child care, schools, and parental leave. Identification of these problems provides a context for thinking about the ways in which solutions to social problems might affect the mental health of parents, infants, children, and adolescents.

Research Agendas

Increased attention is being given to research on risk and protective factors related to child and adolescent development (England, 1992; Mrazek & Haggerty, 1994). Studies are needed on biological and social environmental factors associated with the emergence of mental health problems for this population. The National Institute of Mental Health has identified the need for study of the following factors:

- genetic factors, which increase a child's vulnerability to autism, affective and anxiety disorders, Tourette's disorder, and attentional and learning disorders;
- poor prenatal care, which leads to increased risk of premature birth and a host of related problems;
- chronic physical illness, such as leukemia, diabetis mellitus, asthma, cystic fibrosis, epilepsy, and AIDS;
- cognitive impairments, such as those resulting from mental retardation, as well as deficits in sensory perception, including deafness and blindness;
- persistent psychological adversity, such as poverty, disorganized and inadequate schooling, and homelessness;
- parental mental illness, with the potentially dangerous combination of psychologically traumatic disruptions of family life and inconsistent parenting (NIMH, 1991a, pp. 14–15).

The research agenda established by the NIMH in 1991 responded to these major issues concerning the mental health of children and adolescents (NIMH, 1991b). The program announcement for this research included attention to the following major areas:

- the epidemiology of child and adolescent mental disorders and other associated mental health problems;
- the determination of optimal approaches for defining, assessing, and diagnosing mental disorders and related conditions in children and adolescents;
- basic neuroscience and behavioral research that clarifies the developmental origins, dynamics, and characteristics of mental disorders and suggests new avenues for overcoming them;
- the determination of effective treatment techniques and preventive interventions for mental disorders;
- clinical services research and service systems research to evaluate and improve the efficacy, organization, delivery, and accessibility of treatment and prevention services to young people with mental disorders;

- research with special applicability to children, including the impact of developmental factors on mental disorders in children, the joint effects of environment and biology in modulating children's behavior, and comorbidity (NIMH, 1991b, p. 1).

The report of the Committee on the Prevention of Mental Disorders (Mrazek & Haggerty, 1994), sponsored by the NIMH, includes a number of illustrations of preventive intervention research on infants, children, and adolescents. This research includes studies on (1) interventions with infants: "physical health interventions with applications to mental health (prenatal and perinatal care, immunization)...; programs aimed at improving parenting and reducing risks for infants" (pp. 223–241); (2) interventions for young children: "programs aimed at improving parenting and enhancing child development...; programs aimed at enhancing social competence" (pp. 241–249); (3) interventions for elementary-age children: "programs aimed at enhancing parenting skills and family functioning...; family preservation services; programs aimed at enhancing academic achievement..." (pp. 249–261); (4) interventions for adolescents: "programs aimed at enhancing academic achievement and school behavior...; programs aimed at preventing substance abuse...; programs aimed at preventing conduct disorder; programs altering school organization and social environments; programs aimed at violence prevention" (pp. 261–275). The studies cited in this review of prevention research on infants, children, and adolescents represent "a range of promising program approaches to achieving diverse prevention goals" (p. 215).

Treatment and Utilization of Services

Three features of utilization of mental health services by children and adolescents are especially noteworthy.

First, the National Plan for Research on Child and Adolescent Mental Disorders (NIMH, 1991a) estimates that among young people with mental disorders "less than one-fifth of the afflicted children now receive appropriate treatment, and many of those treated—even by the best clinicians—fail to recover because their disorders are not adequately understood" (p. iv). According to studies of the practices of pediatricians, these physicians "diagnose only about one-half of the mental illness episodes in their practices" (Bromet & Schulberg, 1989, p. 75). Of these cases, only about 50% were referred to psychiatric specialists. A report by the Mental Health Association on "Invisible Children" indicates that children who do receive treatment may not be treated appropriately, especially ethnic minority children and adolescents (Rovner, 1989).

Second, ethnic minority children and adolescents constitute a group at risk for mental health problems and in need of culturally sensitive mental health services. In this regard, Stiffman and Davis (1990) highlight the need to examine the relationship of ethnicity to adolescent mental health, that is, "the effect of social and environmental conditions as causes of mental health problems and the necessity for understanding ethnic values and attitudes in developing appropriate helping strategies" (p. 12). Recommendations for basic research on the problems of minority children and adolescents are included in the National Plan (NIMH, 1991a), especially in regard to "the validity of various behavioral tests and assessment instruments for minority groups," and "mental health problems associated with childhood disorders in various minority groups" (p. 50). Service system research is recommended in regard to these questions: "How effective and culturally appropriate are various mental health services used by minority children and adolescents and their families? What barriers deter their service use?" (NIMH, 1991b, p. 14).

Third, selection of the appropriate location for treatment is controversial; there is disagreement regarding the advantages of community-based programs (including family care) versus hospital or other institutional (treatment center) care. Given the dramatic increase in the numbers of children and adolescents receiving mental health care in private hospitals during the 1980s and early 1990s, there are claims that psychiatric units in general hospitals have been overutilized by these groups. For example, in one study of 27,000 children in such hospital units, it was found that "two-thirds of the children were admitted for 'relatively non-serious' problems," and there was "no evidence that inpatient is more effective than good quality outpatient care" (Rovner, 1989, p. 1). This study suggested that financial considerations often determine the use of hospitals rather than community-based care; however, such contentions have been rejected by the American Psychiatric Association (Rovner, 1989; Schwartz, 1989).

The American Academy of Child and Adolescent Psychiatry has developed guidelines for child and adolescent psychiatric hospitalization, maintaining that both outpatient and inpatient services need to be available choices for treatment (Schowalter, 1989). Still, there remains some concern regarding overutilization of hospital care for adolescents, especially in relation to the effects of advertising on parental decisions to seek mental health care for their children. In this regard, a study by Greer and Greenbaum (1992) examined the effects of aggressive marketing by hospitals through newspaper advertising. These researchers found a correlation between fear ratings created by advertising and the number of parents seeking hospital services for their children.

Advertisements were found to create fears in mothers, especially in relation to children least in need of mental health services.

Education and Mental Health Services

Social workers are involved in the mental health treatment of children and youth in most settings serving these age groups. In recognition of this involvement, special efforts have been initiated by NIMH to strengthen the education of social workers for practice with this patient population. One major project has involved the development of curricula for professional education in child mental health (Johnson, 1993). This project recognized a number of recent developments in the child mental health field, such as the parent advocacy movement, NIMH support for education and training, new technological advances, and a focus on "empowerment practice." The project also emphasized the need for education in the areas of ethnocultural practice, etiologies of mental and emotional disorders in children and adolescents, biological factors, child physical, sexual, and emotional abuse, and a range of practice interventions (psychosocial, family, and psychopharmacological). Another framework for education of social workers who deliver mental health services to children has been developed by LeCroy (1992). This approach focuses on knowledge about assessment, treatment, and service delivery that is considered necessary to inform competent social work practice with children and youth.

In the field of medicine, child and adolescent psychiatry has developed as an independent speciality. The elements of an educational curriculum are illustrated in a comprehensive textbook, *Childhood and Adolescent Psychiatry* (Lewis, 1991). This text includes chapters on the following topics: normal development, development of symptoms, overview of etiological influences, nosology and classification, diagnostic assessment, syndromes, treatment, allied professions, and training and research. The mental health professional will also benefit from discussions of psychopathology in childhood and child psychiatric diagnosis in *Pathways of Growth: Essentials of Child Psychiatry* (King & Noshpitz, 1991).

Summary

The mental health needs of children and adolescents have been recognized by a number of federal legislative acts, including the 1963 Community Mental Health Centers Act (P.L. 88-164), the 1975 amendments to this act, and the Education for All Handicapped Children Act of 1977 (P.L. 94-142). This legislation called for the provision of specialized services for children and adolescents by community mental health centers, related mental health agencies, and schools. Epidemiological studies suggest that 12% to 20% of children and youth have some type of mental disorder. Professionals have given increased attention to improving systems of classification and assessment of the mental health of young people. A continuing service delivery problem involves the need for coordination of community services provided through the mental health, education, health and social welfare, and juvenile justice systems. Problems with service coordination contribute to the underutilization of mental health services for a high proportion of children and youth with mental disorders, especially members of ethnic minority groups. National reports have highlighted the need for research studies on biological and social environmental factors associated with the mental health of children and youth, as well as research on preventive interventions.

MENTAL HEALTH OF HOMELESS PERSONS

During the 1980s and early 1990s, increased public and professional attention has been given to the treatment and service needs of homeless mentally ill persons. These individuals usually suffer from some mixture of social problems, including poverty, mental illness, and substance abuse. The presence of the mentally ill among the homeless population has been attributed to numerous causes, but especially to deinstitutionalization (Lamb, 1992). There is some consensus among mental health professionals that deinstitutionalization has been only one of several major factors leading to homelessness for some mentally ill persons (Bachrach, 1992a; Jencks, 1994). Other significant factors include poverty, lack of affordable housing, fragmentation and service integration problems, community resistance and discrimination, lack of prevention efforts, lack of social supports, and general resource limitations (Leshner, 1992).

Prevalence of Mental Illness

It is generally acknowledged that at least one-third of the homeless population suffer from a mental disorder (Leshner, 1992). Variations in the size estimates of this group are associated with inconsistent definitions of mental illness and homelessness. Still, it appears that a substantial proportion of these individuals are severely and persistently mentally ill (U.S. Dept. of Health and Human Services, 1991; Goldfinger, 1990; Koegel, Burnham, & Farr, 1988). At least one-half of this group have a concurrent substance use disorder (Fischer &

Breakey, 1991). Diversity in the homeless population is reflected in special population groups that include homeless women (Milburn & D'Ercole, 1991), homeless men (Giamo, 1989), homeless families, children, and adolescents (Bassuk & Rubin, 1987), homeless racial and ethnic minorities (Martin, 1986), homeless people in the criminal justice system (Belcher, 1988), and homeless people with alcohol and drug disorders (Fischer & Breakey, 1991). Among these homeless groups, the mentally ill have the greatest need for housing, health, mental health, and social services and are the most underserved (Institute of Medicine, 1989; Leshner, 1992).

Mental Health Policies

Policy directions related to the homeless mentally ill come from several sources. In recognition of the special problems of the homeless mentally ill, a 1984 Task Force of the American Psychiatric Association "called for a comprehensive and integrated system of mental health care," that was to include "high-quality psychiatric and medical services; an adequate number and range of supervised, supportive housing settings; a well-functioning system of clinically oriented case management; adequate, comprehensive, and accessible crisis intervention capabilities, both in the community and in hospitals; less restrictive laws governing involuntary treatment; ongoing rehabilitative services; and consultation to community agencies and organizations that provide other essential services to homeless populations" (Lamb, Bachrach, & Kass, 1992, pp. 1, 2). While this somewhat idealistic proposal has not been achieved, it highlights the numerous elements needed to administer an integrated system of care among this population.

Federal, state, and local community governmental units have developed policies and programs that respond to the needs of the homeless mentally ill. For example, the Stewart B. McKinney Homeless Assistance Act of 1987 (P.L. 100-77) includes policies related to the mentally ill homeless, including a block grant program for services to homeless individuals who are chronically mentally ill, and Community Mental Health Services Demonstration projects for homeless individuals who are chronically mentally ill (Levine & Haggard, 1989). The Homeless Assistance Act made possible a number of state and community projects for the development of comprehensive mental health service systems. These projects were funded through the National Institute of Mental Health and followed a Community Support Program model. NIMH has assisted a number of communities in development of community support systems that include specialized services to the homeless mentally ill.

The State Comprehensive Mental Health Services Plan Act of 1986 (P.L. 99-660) is an example of another federal policy that includes a focus on the mentally ill homeless, requiring that state plans "provide for the establishment and implementation of a program of outreach to, and services for, chronically mentally ill individuals who are homeless" (Title V, Sec. 1920c). Most states have made use of federal funds for the provision of services in local communities. In the private sector, the Robert Wood Johnson Foundation's nine-cities project has developed innovative approaches to serving this group of mentally ill persons (Dennis et al., 1991; Goldman et al., 1990). Both governmental and private-sector program efforts have demonstrated ways of successfully meeting the mental health and social service needs of this population. Still, the type of mental health system recommended by the 1984 American Psychiatric Association (APA) Task Force has not been developed. As a result, a 1992 APA report urged the implementation of the 1984 recommendations through the granting of high priority to the "care, treatment, and rehabilitation of chronically mentally ill individuals… including chronic mentally ill persons who are homeless or at risk for becoming homeless" (Lamb et al., 1992, p. 5).

Attention was given to the needs of the homeless mentally ill by a 1990 task force composed of members of federal departments. This task force, created by the Secretary of Housing and Urban Development and the Secretary of Health and Human Services, developed a national strategy "designed to end homelessness among people with severe mental illness" (Leshner, 1992, p. iv). The report of this task force, entitled *Outcasts on Main Street*, proposed a plan that involved the participation of all levels of government, as well as private and voluntary sectors of health and welfare services. The national strategy focused on a goal of an integrated service system for homeless people with severe mental illness. The elements proposed for an integrated system of care included assertive outreach and integrated care management; safe havens and housing options; legal protections in clinical care; consumer and family involvement; rehabilitation, vocational training, and employment assistance; income support and benefits; health care; alcohol and/or other drug abuse treatment; and treatment of mental illnesses (Leshner, 1992).

Help-Seeking Patterns

The help-seeking patterns of homeless mentally ill persons are quite different from those of other mental health patient/client groups. A large proportion of this population is disaffiliated, isolated, and alienated from society, community, friends, and family, with limited social networks and social supports (Rossi, 1989; Chafetz, 1990; Levine & Haggard, 1989). As a consequence, many homeless mentally ill persons avoid contact with the mental health system, as well as with social services and health care. These individuals have been labeled "treatment- and service-resistant clients."

Research findings on the attitudes of homeless people, including mentally ill persons, have been mixed. On the one hand, there is some evidence that homeless mentally ill persons "have become detached from community mental health centers" (Sosin, Colson, & Grossman, 1988, p. 372), and that "many of the homeless mentally ill have made it clear that they prefer life on the streets to life in an institution" (Johnson, 1990, p. 154). For those who do not seek services, Rog (1988) has identified a number of factors that may influence this decision, such as fears of involuntary hospitalization, the stigma of being labeled mentally ill, and the nature of the mental health system.

On the other hand, Levine and Haggard (1989) review research results indicating that "homeless mentally ill persons are usually willing to accept assistance" (p. 288). Martin (1990) has noted that "Individuals with severe, persistent and disabling mental illness who have become homeless almost always want help. All of the research efforts supported by NIMH found this to be true" (p. 441). These individuals may place high priority on social services and housing needs, however, while mental health providers often emphasize mental health interventions (Sargent, 1989).

Martin's (1986) review of research findings from NIMH projects involving ethnic and racial minorities found that differences in perceptions of needs and services by professionals and members of ethnic minorities lead to a service delivery system that is not responsive. A similar argument has been made with regard to homeless women, with Koegel (1987) suggesting that treatment resistance among this group is a myth. In her review of help-seeking efforts on the part of homeless women, Koegel found that "setting and service provider related characteristics...were every bit as important as client-related characteristics" in influencing the use of services (p. 43).

Treatment and Utilization of Services

The question of whether homeless mentally ill persons should be treated in the community or in an institution remains controversial (Kaufman, 1988). Usually the guidelines for involuntary civil commitment of the mentally ill, based on criteria of illness, dangerousness, and disability, are followed in regard to the homeless. These criteria are thought to assure protection of homeless persons' civil liberties.

However, these guidelines leave a number of homeless mentally ill individuals in the community without appropriate services and treatment. Some professionals suggest a "need-for-treatment" standard for involuntary commitment of homeless people (Armat & Peele, 1992). One of the arguments against involuntary treatment has been that treatment is not effective with such individuals. However, there is research evidence that supports treatment effectiveness with involuntary patients, leading to the argument that involuntary commitment is an avenue for the right to treatment for homeless mentally ill patients (Armat & Peele, 1992).

Traditional and customary outpatient clinical psychiatric treatment in community mental health centers appears not to be effective in reaching homeless mentally ill people (Kuhlman, 1994). As a consequence, the dominant feature of service delivery in the community for homeless mentally ill people is some form of modified case management (Levine & Rog, 1990; Tessler & Dennis, 1989; Swayze, 1992). Several versions of case management have been developed to serve homeless mentally ill persons in outreach street teams, drop-in centers, shelters, and community centers (Ridgway, 1986; Bond et al., 1991; Morse et al., 1992). Case management with the homeless mentally ill includes variations for different client groups, such as individuals with mental illness and drug/alcohol disorders, families and children, young adults, and ethnic minority groups.

As a service model for service to homeless persons with mental illness, case management has become "intensive case management." This model involves "a comprehensive, aggressive approach to accessing and securing basic health and mental health services for seriously mentally ill individuals who are most in need" (Rog et al., 1987, p. 8). Intensive case management includes the core functions of case management but places an emphasis on assertive outreach, on "advocacy for clients' needs as well as rights, on provision of services in vivo (shelters, streets, day drop-in centers) and in accord with the client's wishes" (p. 8). This approach gives priority to housing needs and clinical treatment, with services delivered in a "non-time-bound" manner, not restricted by appointment schedules but extended over a long period of time, with continued follow-up (Rog et al., 1987). One of the major features of intensive case management involves the attempt to overcome service resistance. As Rog (1988) has noted, it is an intervention that seeks to "engage homeless persons with mental illness into treatment" and to utilize other existing services (p. 1).

Ideally, intensive case management becomes one part of an integrated service system. The Task Force on Homelessness and Severe Mental Illness (Leshner, 1992) has emphasized the need for a systems approach to servicing the homeless mentally ill. The case management component of the service system is referred to by the Task Force as "integrated care management," with the goals of "enhancing continuity of care, access to services, and efficiency and accountability of service provision and integration" (p. 37). A key feature of integrated care management is its focus on helping the client negotiate access to and utilization of a range of services, benefits, and entitlements.

Research Studies

A number of research studies have demonstrated effectiveness in reaching client service goals with homeless mentally ill persons. Studies of case management show attainment of the following service goals: improved occupational functioning, increased income, reduced social isolation, improved interpersonal adjustment, more independent living, continuing engagement in treatment, reduction of psychiatric symptoms, and an increase in use of community services (Toomey et al., 1989; Rife et al., 1991; First, Rife, & Kraus, 1990; Goering et al., 1992; Morse et al., 1992; Barrow et al., 1989).

Approaches to serving homeless mentally ill persons have been studied in five federal demonstration projects. These projects provided clients with "a comprehensive set of mental health treatment, housing, and support services" (Psychiatric Services, 1995, p. 301). Preliminary findings show that homeless persons "can be reached by the service system, will accept and benefit from mental health services, and can remain in community-based housing with appropriate help" (p. 301). Findings are of special import for mental health policy making, as they suggest "the need to integrate mental health services with substance abuse treatment, social services, and the criminal justice system; the need to include substance abuse treatment as part of mental health services to prevent recurrent homelessness; the need to offer clients a range of housing options; and the need for preventive health care and education" (p. 301).

Homeless adults with a dual diagnosis of severe mental illness and substance abuse have been particularly difficult to serve. Insights into the effectiveness of residential programs for this population have emerged from a study by Blankertz and Cnaan (1994). These researchers used a quasi-experimental design to evaluate two programs, one "a hybridized psychosocial rehabilitation model" and the other "a modified therapeutic community model" (p. 537). "The experimental program focused on psychosocial rehabilitation based on individualized client needs," with "24-hour staffing, individual counseling by staff, skills teaching, psychoeducational and peer support groups, and intensive case management," as well as traditional substance abuse treatment both on- and off-site (p. 539).

A comparison program by a drug and alcohol agency followed a modified, but traditional, substance abuse therapeutic community model that stressed the role of group pressure and used traditional case management. While the psychosocial rehabilitation program was more successful than the comparison program (29% compared to 7.9% successful), most clients did not have successful outcomes. Success was measured in terms of maintaining "sobriety, no hospitalization, and permanent residency status for a period of at least 3 months after exiting the program" (p. 551). Studies such as this demonstrate the difficulties in serving homeless people with a dual diagnosis, while supporting the usefulness of a psychosocial rehabilitation approach for some clients.

Summary

A significant proportion of homeless people suffer from mental illness, especially severe and persistent illness. Federal, state, and local levels of government have developed policies and programs for this population, but their special needs remain largely unmet. Part of the social problem of the homeless mentally ill is attributed to deinstitutionalization and the service delivery patterns of the mental health and other service systems. Another cause is the help-seeking patterns of homeless mentally ill persons, with a high proportion resisting treatment and services. Case management approaches, when modified to meet the special needs of the homeless, appear to be effective in meeting some treatment and service goals; however, the lack of community support systems in many communities prevents adequate mental health care for the homeless. As illustrated by the policies and programs related to homeless mentally ill persons in New York City, challenges to deinstitutionalization by local governments result in difficulties in implementing new policies and programs. As discussed in Chapter 7, the case of Joyce Brown in New York City demonstrates the complex issues facing the mental health and legal systems when efforts are made to remove mentally ill persons from the "streets" and into hospitals for evaluation and treatment (Rochefort, 1993).

MENTAL HEALTH OF OLDER ADULTS

Attention to the mental health of older adults, as indicated by policies, programs, services, and research, has increased dramatically since about 1975. Older adults have been the target of new mental health legislation, especially in regard to health and mental health financing arrangements. There has been an increase in mental health programs for the mentally ill elderly provided by psychiatrists, psychologists, social workers, and other mental health professionals. The complexity of mental health programs and services for older adults is apparent in the publication *Handbook of Mental Health and Aging* (Birren, Sloane, & Cohen, 1992), in special journals on mental health and aging, and in general mental health journals, such as *Hospital and Community Psychiatry*.

While there is some disagreement as to the age at which older adulthood begins, various studies use ages of 55, 60, or 65. National and international reports on aging indicate that the older adult population is increasing in size, and there is a consensus that a substantial number of these individuals have some type of mental disorder. As Lebowitz and Niederehe (1992) have noted, "The mental disorders of late life are widespread and serious and have pervasive effects on older persons and those who are close to them" (p. 4). Still, these authors highlight the fact that the presence of mental disorders is not disproportionately high among older adults, nor necessarily due to aging effects. It is clear that many older adults with mental disorders do not receive treatment and other services in relation to their needs, even though numerous effective treatments are now available. Many of these treatments are grounded in the perspective that mental disorders among the elderly are "bio-psycho-social phenomena...and their understanding requires the integration of biological, psychological, social, and environmental perspectives and factors" (Lebowitz & Niederehe, 1992, p. 6). This perspective is highlighted by Lebowitz and Niederehe (1992) in relation to themes for understanding mental health and aging:

- *the gerontological revolution:* many people lead long, healthy lives for the most part, "until risk factors accumulate to the point of disease and disability" (p. 10);
- *the geriatric revolution:* extension of life for individuals who have had disease or disability from birth or early childhood;
- *senescence:* age-related changes in biological, psychological, cognitive, and behavioral systems;
- *comorbidity:* simultaneous occurrence of physical illnesses and mental disorders, which increases the complexity of diagnosis and treatment.

Prevalence of Mental Illness

Epidemiological studies provide basic information about the prevalence of mental disorders among various age groups. Data from the ECA studies provide basic information for persons who are 65 and over, indicating that approximately 21% have lifetime disorders and 13% have active disorders. Major sources for these data include the *Handbook of Mental Health and Aging* (Birren et al., 1992) and *Psychiatric Disorders in America* (Robins & Regier, 1991). These volumes present data in a variety of ways, both in terms of overall rates of mental illness among various age groups and rates of specific disorders. In some instances the data are not presented for the total group in the age range of 65 and over, but in terms of men and women by age group. Most data are presented in terms of lifetime and annual prevalence (Robins & Regier, 1991; Anthony & Aboraya, 1992).

As the ECA studies indicate, onset of new mental disorders is unusual in old age. Onset usually occurs when individuals are young, with about 90% of the population having experienced their first symptoms by age 38. Cognitive impairment is most frequent among older adults. With the exception of cognitive impairment (severe and mild), data on the prevalence of any mental disorder among age groups show that people 65 and older have the lowest rates (percentages) of both lifetime and active cases. It is unclear why overall lifetime rates would not be higher for the group over 65, but the findings do not seem to be related to research methodology or artifacts (Robins & Regier, 1991).

An examination of the relationship of rates of lifetime disorders to age, gender, and ethnicity shows that in the age group of 65 and over, the rates for non-Hispanic white men (21%) and women (19%) differ from those of African-American men (39%) and women (30%) and from those of Hispanic men (30%) and women (18%) (Robins & Regier, 1991, p. 335). In regard to specific disorders, ECA data indicate that active rates are highest for cognitive impairment and phobic disorders, and lowest for panic disorders. For lifetime rates, the most prevalent disorders are cognitive impairment, alcohol abuse/dependence (for men), and phobic disorders (for women), with panic disorders displaying the lowest rates. Women have higher rates for affective disorders, panic and phobic disorders, and obsessive-compulsive disorders, while men have higher rates for substance abuse/dependence and alcohol abuse/dependence.

Service Utilization Patterns

Not unlike other age groups, there is a wide gap between the mental health needs of older adults and the availability and accessibility of treatment and services (Lebowitz, 1988). For example, "Most older adults with psychiatric disorders are in the community, yet only about half of them receive mental health services" (George, 1992, p. 808). In particular, community mental health centers show a low utilization of services for older people with mental disorders (Flemming et al., 1986). Centers that do provide appropriate services are associated with trained personnel in special service units for older adults, and have interorganizational relationships with other agencies that serve the older population (Lebowitz, Light, & Bailey, 1987). For long-term care, families provide some services, but the major location for care of mentally ill elderly is nursing homes. Elderly persons in the community usually seek care from family physicians, rather than from mental health professionals (Goldstein, 1994).

Barriers to the utilization of psychiatric services include fragmentation of services within the mental health system, problems with financing of mental health care, and public attitudes involving ageism and stigma associated with mental illness (Goldstein, 1994; George, 1992). Older adults with mental disorders who are members of ethnic minority groups have particularly low utilization rates, usually due to one or more of the following factors: limited income; language barriers; problems with availability, accessibility, acceptability of services; transportation difficulties; and lack of sensitivity to cultural differences (Fellin & Powell, 1988).

Assessment and Treatment

Assessment and diagnosis of mental disorders among older adults is a complex process. Three major frameworks provide a basis for assessment. Neuropsychiatric assessment gives attention to the effects of aging on people, especially in terms of biological, psychological, and social processes (Caine & Grossman, 1992). Neuropsychological assessment gives attention to cognitive function and emotional status, with an aim of understanding "the role of brain processes in such complex activities as learning, communicating, and thinking" (LaRue, Yang, & Osato, 1992, p. 644). Functional assessment focuses on "the person's ability to look after himself or herself and to function in various environments," commonly referred to as activities of daily living (Kemp & Mitchell 1992, p. 672). These frameworks may be incorporated into a multidisciplinary assessment, especially with the use of clinical methods as well as structured techniques (Gurland & Borne, 1989).

Major forms of treatment for older adults include behavioral and psychotherapeutic interventions (Newton & Lazarus, 1992), psychopharmacological treatments (Salzman & Nevis-Olesen, 1992), and environmental interventions (Regnier & Pynoos, 1992). Within the last decade, there has been a renewed interest in modifying traditional behavioral and psychotherapeutic approaches in order to treat older adults. Psychopharmacological treatments now recognize the critical role of the aging process in choosing drugs in terms of their effects on older adult patients (Salzman & Nevis-Olesen, 1992). Environmental interventions focus principally on housing and the physical environment, with attention to environment-behavior principles such as privacy, social interaction, control/choice/autonomy, orientation and wayfinding, safety and security, accessibility and functioning, stimulation and challenge, sensory aspects, familiarity, aesthetics and appearance, personalization, and adaptability (Regnier and Pynoos, 1992).

Treatments for mental disorders in older adults are provided within the medical and mental health service delivery systems. Most older adult recipients of mental health services are in the community, in home care, nursing homes, or other residential facilities (George, 1992). Community-based treatment includes a range of services, including treatment by primary care physicians or by mental health professionals, including psychiatrists, psychologists, social workers, and nurses. The community locations for services may be in outpatient treatment settings, day treatment and partial hospitalization, emergency programs, home and respite care, inpatient treatment, supervised housing, and hospice care. Most often, this continuum of care is not available to older adults in their communities, and older adults with mental illness are often excluded from such services for financial reasons (George, 1992).

A major treatment concern is the fact that older adults are not likely to receive treatment from mental health professionals but from the general health care sector, where a major treatment is psychotropic drugs (George, 1992). In particular, residents of nursing homes appear very likely to receive drug treatment even if they have no psychiatric disorder. Some studies have shown that about one-half of nursing home residents who were receiving tranquilizer drugs did not have a clinical reason for such use (Winslow, 1991). In response to this problem, the federal government established regulations in 1990 to prohibit prescription of drugs specific to mental disorders to individuals not so diagnosed. Another major concern is the fact that assistance to older adults with mental disorders frequently is provided mainly by family and friends in the community, resulting in caregiver burdens and fragmented relationships between informal care and formal mental health services.

Nursing Home Care

Nursing home care is a major service for older mentally ill persons, as a range of studies suggest that at least one-third of nursing home residents have a mental disorder (Liptzen, 1992; Linn & Stein, 1989). Data from a 1987 National Medical Expenditure Survey indicated that of the more than 1.5 million nursing home residents, more than two-thirds had one or more psychiatric symptoms (U.S. Public Health Service, 1990). Deinstitutionalization of patients from state and county mental hospitals and other facilities has been supported by Medicaid and Medicare financing policies. These policies moved fiscal responsibilities from the state to the federal government and led to nursing homes replacing hospitals as a locus of care for the elderly mentally ill (Liptzen, 1992).

Concern over the lack of mental health services for nursing home residents led to the enactment of the Nursing Home Reform Act of 1987 (P.L. 100-203). This legislative act requires states to establish processes for assuring that persons with mental illness and developmental disabilities are screened for treatment needs (skilled nursing care/mental health care) prior to admission to, or while already residing in, a Medicare- or Medicaid-certified facility (Gottlieb, 1992). Five dispositional categories were created, based on the nature of the person's disorder and need for care. These categories are as follows: (1) discharge or not admit; (2) choose current facility or elsewhere, needs active treatment; (3) stay, no need for active treatment; (4) stay, needs active treatment; (5) stay, needs mental health care (Eichmann et al., 1992). Based on data from a National Nursing Home Survey of residents of nursing homes, Eichmann et al. (1992) examined the possible impact of this legislation on the nursing home industry. They estimated that "nursing homes can be expected to have a more homogeneous sample of elderly residents with senile dementia and serious nonpsychiatric disabilities...and that these facilities also will be required to provide more intensive mental health services than they do currently" (p. 788).

Summary

Federal and state legislation has included policies promoting the provision of mental health services to older adults. With the exception of cognitive impairment, the prevalence of mental disorders among this population is lower than that of younger age groups. Still, the active rates for persons 65 and older are 13%, with lifetime rates of 21%. Data on specific disorders for older adults reveal some differences between men and women and between the various disorders. There remains a wide gap between the mental health needs of this population and the availability and accessibility of treatment and services. Major barriers to services include financing difficulties as well as problems associated with membership in an ethnic minority group. Nursing home care is a major service for older adults, along with care in family homes. Finally, the need for research on the occurrence and treatment of psychiatric problems among older adults is a major concern among professionals serving this group (Cohen, 1992).

11.
Future Mental Health Policies, Programs, and Services

Mental illness and its associated personal and social costs are not likely to be eradicated in the foreseeable future. Nevertheless, the response of policy makers and the public mental health system to this social problem remains uncertain, especially given the failure of the U.S. Congress to pass any major health reform measures during 1994 and 1995. Still, the American people look to public mental health policy makers and service providers to fulfill "government's responsibility to continue to improve its efforts to enhance the well-being and functioning of mentally ill persons" (Rochefort, 1989, p. xvi). In this light, our discussion of past and current trends and issues provides a basis for making judgments about government policies and programs for the future. Most often, these judgments involve establishing priorities within the wide range of mental health programs and services (Callahan, 1994). Specific issues for debate are presented in this chapter to stimulate the reader's examination of what might occur in the field of mental health in the decades to come. We conclude this chapter by looking at the role of advocacy in promoting changes and improvements in the mental health system of the United States.

MENTAL HEALTH POLICY MAKING

Public mental health policies in the United States are generated and implemented at the national, state, and local levels of government through legislation, the courts, administrative rules, and day-to-day professional practice. These policies focus on goals for the improvement of the mental health status of the total population. Because of the fluctuating politics involved in policy making, the responsibility for public mental health care shifts back and forth between various levels of government. Given ongoing changes in federal and state funding arrangements, and renewed attention to health care reform, a major policy question involves the future role of the federal government vis-à-vis the states in mental health policy making and service delivery.

The role of the federal government in relation to that of the states was discussed in connection with the 1994 National Health Care Reform policies proposed by the Clinton administration (Mechanic, 1993). For example, a coalition of 33 national organizations, including advocacy organizations, state systems, professional associations, provider agencies, families, and consumers, made recommendations concerning the roles of the states and the federal government (Koyanagi et al., 1993). This coalition emphasized the need for continued involvement of the states in mental health care issues such as establishing and monitoring standards for mental health professionals; developing and financing state plans for services to special groups, such as persons with severe mental illness and children with major disabilities; and financing services for institutionalized populations (Koyanagi et al., 1993). This coalition recommended that the federal government respond to the need for mental health promotion and prevention; for collection of data related to needs assessment, quality assurance, and services and systems research; and for support of states in the development of innovative approaches to mental health service delivery. These recommendations emphasize the fact that both state and federal governments need to be actively involved in a complementary way in regard to mental health policies and services. At the same time, they confirm the need for national leadership and responsibility for mental health care.

Past and current national leadership for mental health care is illustrated by numerous mental health–related acts, as well as activities within the National Institutes of Health (National Institute of Mental Health, National Institute on Drug Abuse, National Institute on Alcoholism and Alcohol Abuse) and the Substance Abuse and Mental Health Services Administration. These mental health policies and activities represent a "macro level of broad etiological theories, program structures, and the general content of public policies" (Rochefort, 1993, p. 116). At the same time, "bottom up" policy changes occur at "the micro level of the actual services delivered to patients who enter the mental health system," especially when professionals make policy within their day-to-day practice (p. 116). As Rochefort (1993) has observed, the policy-making cycles in mental health show changes in policies and services originating from both macro and micro levels of policy and practice.

Mental health professionals continue to assert that the United States needs, but does not have, a national mental health policy. The mental health policies that exist are fragmented and highly influenced by changes in the presidency, the congress, the judiciary, and the various states (Marshall, 1992). Health care reform proposals sponsored within Congress and the Clinton administration have stimulated discussion of the weaknesses of the mental health system and the need for new national health care policies. Passage of any major health reform proposal in the future could more clearly establish a national mental health policy.

A major issue in mental health policy making is the separation of public policies from those of the private sector, a separation that results in a "two-class" system for delivery of mental health services. The privatization of mental health service delivery, whereby public funding is used to purchase private-sector services, has led to the creation of quasi-public agencies and the blurring of public/private responsibilities for mental health care (Hollingsworth, 1994). The 1994 Clinton administration proposal for health care reform would replace this blurring with a "move from the traditional two-tier structure for separate public and private mental health and substance abuse services" to an "integrated, comprehensive managed system of care" (American Health Security Act of 1993, Sec. 27). This policy goal speaks to the problems inherent in first- and second-class mental health services by focusing on a managed competition approach within a public/private systems framework. Such a framework would also need to respond to the fact that services to persons with mental illness are influenced by public policies of a number of provider systems, including health, mental health, social services, and justice systems. The policy question in this regard concerns the extent to which coordination can be developed between these systems in order to minimize fragmentation of services and improve care for mental health consumers.

Issues for Debate

1. Health care reform in the 1990s and beyond will/should result in a national health care policy that includes mental health care, with provision of mental health services including inpatient and residential treatment, intensive non-residential treatment, psychotherapeutic medications, and a range of social services.

2. Private- and public-sector mental health care will/should be merged into a "one-class" system under an overall national mental health policy.
3. A national mental health policy will/should be closely integrated with state and local community mental health policies in terms of who gets what, how treatment and services are delivered, and how they are financed.

DEFINING MENTAL HEALTH AND MENTAL ILLNESS

Mental health and mental illness are defined somewhat differently by professionals, individuals and families, and members of the community at large. Professionals rely on definitions of mental illness located in state mental health codes and in the DSM of the American Psychiatric Association (APA, 1994). A key question about these definitions concerns whether mental health/illness should be defined in terms of exclusive categories or on a continuum of well-being (Praeger & Scallet, 1992). One possible resolution of this issue is to differentiate between mental disorders that are severe and persistent and others that are less serious, with less functional impairment and shorter duration. For example, in recent years young adults with severe and persistent illnesses have placed a strain on the mental health system, both in the use of hospitalization and community-based services, in part because the system has not viewed this patient group as in need of long-term, continuing care (Grob, 1994).

Committees under the sponsorship of the American Psychiatric Association have continued over a period of several years to revise the DSM so that there is now a general use among mental health professionals of this classification system. However, there remains a major concern over whether DSM is too inclusive, that is, defines too many conditions as disorders, especially those not well grounded in science (Kirk & Kutchins, 1994). While the DSM provides a sophisticated system for classification of mental disorders, it does not deal with explanations of the causes of mental illness. As noted in our discussion of the nature of mental health and mental illness, there are a number of theories of causation in the biological, social, and behavioral sciences. Proponents of the various theoretical models appear to agree on the need for further scientific evidence in relation to the causes of mental disorders.

Some of the specific challenges to the DSM system have been identified in our discussions of the mental health of ethnic minorities and of women. Issues of classification center around the creation of new diagnostic categories that pertain mostly to women, and to the need for more culturally relevant criteria for classifying disorders among ethnic minority groups. Another important emerging definitional issue is related to the increase in comorbidity, especially in terms of dual diagnosis of a mental disorder along with a substance abuse disorder. This issue involves how to overcome problems in defining these interrelated disorders and in providing treatment for them (Sabshin, 1991).

The fact that the mental health system's diagnostic classifications label people as mentally ill continues to be experienced in a negative way by some people. Many consumers of mental health services and their family members believe that psychiatric labels stigmatize, in contrast to the classification and labels associated with other disabilities (Caras, 1994; Lefley, 1992). The principal issue here concerns how the individuals seeking help can avoid and/or overcome the stigmatizing effects of being labeled by and receiving services from the mental health system. Stigma continues to be generated by the mass media (e.g., newspaper and television reporting, movies, comic strips), mental health professionals, and the service system in general. While public education and changes in public attitudes about the nature of mental health and mental illness are helpful, stigma attached to people with mental illness remains. At the same time, the inclusion of psychiatric impairments along with physical disabilities within legislation such as the Americans with Disabilities Act of 1990 may help reduce this stigma.

Issues for Debate

1. The stigmatizing effects of mental illness will/should be reduced, so that mental disorders will be viewed in a manner similar to physical disorders.
2. Research on the nature of mental illness and its causes will/should result in improved linkages between assessment, diagnosis, and treatment.
3. Definitions of mental disorders will/should highlight distinctions between individuals with acute mental health problems and those with severe and persistent illness.
4. Members of ethnic minorities will/should benefit from the inclusion of cultural considerations in the DSM-IV classification system.

EPIDEMIOLOGY OF MENTAL DISORDERS

A number of factors influence mental health policies with regard to the allocation of resources, such as political idealism and pragmatism, implementation expertise, and research findings (Regier, 1986). A comprehensive research data base regarding mental health and illness has been established through the ECA studies of the NIMH (Robins & Regier, 1991) and the ongoing National Comorbidity Study (Kessler et al., 1994). The NIMH now has the methodology for estimating the distribution of mental disorders among the U.S. population and for understanding help-seeking patterns. Of particular interest to policy makers and service providers is the knowledge generated about associations between group membership and mental disorders. Data on differences in disorders by age, social class, gender, and ethnicity have implications for service provision. Data on service utilization suggest the following policy question: What can be done in response to the fact that only a small proportion of people with mental disorders actually seek and/or receive help? Given the findings regarding utilization among the several service sectors, including specialty mental health, general medical, human services, and voluntary support networks, should efforts be made to increase the utilization by one group or another? Should research studies be directed to achieve better understanding of barriers to utilization of service by various population groups, such as ethnic minorities, homeless persons, and older adults?

One of the major purposes of collecting ECA data was to provide a scientific foundation for policy making, especially in regard to information on health service needs, finances, and personnel needs. Data on mental disorders within the general population are especially helpful in guiding the activities of the NIMH and other federal departments within the Department of Health and Human Services. It remains to be seen what use mental health professionals in states and local communities will make of the epidemiological findings of the ECA program and the National Comorbidity Study for policy making and allocation of resources for mental health.

Issues for Debate

1. The federal government will/should continue to sponsor ECA studies.
2. ECA research findings will/should be used to formulate mental health policies and to develop mental health services.
3. ECA study findings will/should be used to developed services for underserved population groups, including ethnic minorities and older adults.

MENTAL HEALTH PROGRAMS AND
SERVICE DELIVERY

The public mental health system has primary responsibility for the provision of psychological and medical treatments, but often takes responsibility for delivery and/or coordination of services that focus on social, economic, housing, and other needs of mental health consumers. Policies of deinstitutionalization have led to changes in the delivery of these treatments and services, such as dramatic decreases in state hospital care, increases in psychiatric care in general hospitals, and the emergence of community-based care as the dominant mode and location of mental health service delivery. An important policy question in this regard has been raised by Lamb (1992a): "Is it time for a moratorium on deinstitutionalization?" (p. 669). Lamb contends that in the light of inadequate social and economic resources for seriously mentally ill individuals, further reductions in hospital care should cease until such resources are made available, so that "each patient in the community can be adequately housed and treated" (p. 669).

Effective community care programs require community resources that include a variety of professional and nonprofessional staff. State and local community mental health programs continue to be criticized for their inadequate staff levels for the delivery of psychiatric treatment and social services. The representation of mental health professionals in these programs is often below appropriate levels. There is a strong dependence on nurses, social workers, and other counselors for professional services for mentally ill persons in the community, especially for people with serious and persistent illness. Social workers provide the majority of services in community mental health center and residential aftercare programs. Nonprofessional personnel serve in a variety of community programs, such as residential care, neighborhood services and recreation, and volunteer programs of social agencies and religious organizations. Case management has become well established in community mental health centers and in psychosocial rehabilitation programs. The roles of professionals are crucial for case management in relation to the delivery of both treatment and social services, especially in assertive community treatment programs, outreach programs for homeless mentally ill persons, and linkages to social welfare benefits (Cain, 1993).

The involvement of psychiatrists, psychologists, social workers, nurses, and counselors in public community-based mental health programs is essential for meeting the needs of mentally ill people, yet there continues to be a lack of interest by these professionals in the public mental health system. In response to this personnel problem, Mechanic (1989b) has proposed an expansion in the roles played by nurses in community mental health programs. Since nurses are generally perceived to be associated with general medical care, rather than with psychiatry, they are in a position to be effective "boundary practitioners" linking service-resistant clients to psychiatric services. Nurses could add to their skills and knowledge by obtaining training in some of the traditional social work areas of expertise, such as use of community social services, social welfare entitlements, and socio-emotional supports. With such a development, the pool of case managers for serving mentally ill persons would include increased numbers of nurses and a refocus on the medical model of treatment. A major concern about such a development would be over the possibility that social treatments and services would be diminished, to the detriment of persistent and seriously mentally ill persons.

Several important policy questions about mental health programs and the service system remain, such as the following:

- *What is the future role of the state mental hospital within the mental health system?* There are several choices for states in regard to the role of public mental hospitals: close all state hospitals and fund care in community general and psychiatric hospitals; close all state hospitals and create new, small, public hospital units affiliated with universities, with a focus on quality care and research; reduce state hospitals to a small number that focus on long-term care for severely ill persons; reduce the number and size of state hospitals and use these facilities for acute care only.

- *Will national policies promote the further development of community support programs in the states and local communities?* The answer to this question depends in large part on the extent to which the Congress is willing to support the activities of NIMH, and the funding of mental health services at the state and local levels. Without federal funding and support, state governments may be unwilling or unable to provide for local community support systems.

- *Will state and local governments support psychosocial rehabilitation programs for the serious mentally ill?* Currently, there is a serious underfunding of these programs by state and community mental health funds. These programs depend in large part on funding from local community organizations. Psychosocial rehabilitation programs are not usually given as high a priority for funding as are the clinical services provided in community mental health programs.

- *What kind of preventive services will be provided in local communities?* Local community mental health boards and center administrations now give priority to clinical services, not allowing attainment of the original goals of the community mental health movement for prevention programs. For example, chronically mentally ill adults at risk for HIV/AIDS have been identified as in "urgent need for HIV prevention programs" (Kalichman et al., 1994, p. 221).
- *Will the public mental health system continue a trend toward privatization of services, with increased involvement of the private mental health sector in the delivery of publicly funded mental health services?* Privatization offers an opportunity for improvement of the quality of services, but it may have an adverse effect on utilization.
- *Will the mental health system be able to adequately respond to the mental health needs of special populations, such as members of ethnic minority groups, women, children and adolescents, older adults, the homeless, and people with AIDS?* There are a number of choices open to the mental health system for meeting the needs of special populations, including development of special programs directed toward these population groups; retraining of personnel with a focus on cultural competence; support of personnel engaged in educational programs that focus on these populations; and funding of pilot programs to encourage innovative services.

Some of the choices vis-à-vis these questions depend in large part on funding patterns and coordination of services. Coordination has been one of the major goals of community mental health centers, an objective still unfulfilled (Rochefort, 1993). A major issue centers around how the mental health system can prevent individuals in need of mental health care from "falling through the cracks." This problem is usually referred to as fragmentation, or lack of coordination and integration of services. It involves "gaps and discontinuities in care as patients move between hospital, outpatient treatment, and rehabilitation programs; and in the inability of any one agency to ensure continuity of care across catchment areas" (Rosenberger, 1990, p. 1171).

Responses to the need for coordination have been made through national legislation, such as the State Comprehensive Mental Health Services Act of 1986 and the Stewart B. McKinney Homeless Assistance Act of 1987. Some responses have been directed toward clients, such as the mandate for case management or multidisciplinary treatment teams as service modalities. Others have focused on the organization or system, such as community support systems, integrated services programs, assertive community treatment programs, or mental health authorities and other funding innovations (Rochefort, 1993; Mechanic, 1991). In recent years, central mental health authorities have been created in selected communities through funds from the Robert Wood Johnson Foundation. Evaluations of these programs in nine cities have identified some of the problems in developing comprehensive systems of care for patients with severe mental illness (Goldman et al., 1990).

Issues for Debate

1. The public mental health system will/should provide for a continuum of care, including state hospital care and a range of community-based treatment and services.
2. The original goals of the community mental health movement will/should be achieved, especially through promotion of community support programs and psychosocial rehabilitation services for meeting the needs of mentally ill persons in local communities.
3. Mental health policies will/should require the further development of linkages of the mental health sector with social support services in the community, including an emphasis on delivery of prevention services and coordination with self-help groups.
4. Community mental health agencies will/should become major providers of services for people with HIV/AIDS and for homeless persons with severe mental disorders
5. Increased mental health services will/should be extended to people living in rural areas.

FINANCING

The question of what levels of government and what service systems should take responsibility for mental health programs involves both service delivery and fiscal policy concerns. While the mental health system has accepted some responsibility for providing both treatment and selected social and community services, funding is still a policy issue, since psychiatric care, social services, and income maintenance programs are delivered by various health and social welfare systems. These systems compete for funds and may lack consensus on whose domain includes serving mentally ill persons. A related policy issue concerns how public and private funding for mental health services is to be coordinated, such as payment for mental health services under federal Medicaid and Medicare programs and through private employment-based insurance (Mechanic, 1993).

A classic example of financing vis-à-vis coordination of institutional and community-based care is found in the case of Sylvia Frumkin, described at the close of Chapter 2. As noted by Moran et al. (1984), the journey of Sylvia "dramatically illustrates the fragmentation of responsibility and care for chronic mental patients, the comprehensive range of community support services needed...," with a conservative estimate of costs of her direct care at about $636,000 (p. 887). Sheehan's (1995) account of "The Last Days of Sylvia Frumkin" indicates that these patterns of care and high costs continued from the early 1980s until Sylvia's death in November 1994 at the age of 46. For example, the cost of her care for a 15-month period in Bellevue Hospital during 1991 and 1992 was $381,625, paid by Medicaid and Medicare.

The cost of mental health care affects the availability and utilization of services. The interrelationship between mental health services and financing is highlighted in current funding variations of mental health benefits. The interconnections between funding and mental health benefits are apparent in privatization of services, funding of mental health services under Medicare and Medicaid, and managed care and reimbursement of the costs of care through HMOs, capitation plans, and DRGs. The major policy issues inherent in these approaches to mental health care financing have emerged in debates over proposals in 1994 for national health care reform. These policy issues included the sources of funds for care (e.g., employers, self-pay, third-party insurers, governmental units); single-payer vs. multiple-payer; tax credit deductions; restrictions in benefits coverage; and restrictions on payments to service providers. A central theme of the Clinton administration's health care reform plan involved managed competition, whereby "employers and public sponsors would have the function of negotiating benefit packages, supervising the enrollment process, and determining 'risk-adjusted' payments for different health plans" (Rochefort, 1993).

Even if an overall health care political stance were established that all citizens should be insured, a policy issue would remain in regard to who would be covered by private-sector financing and who would be covered by public funds. Since some restrictions are likely to be imposed on benefits, an important issue concerns whether or not mental health services will be treated in the same way as general medical benefits. Payments to medical service providers have been imposed by the federal government through DRG classifications. There is a question as to whether or not DRG approaches for cost control can be applied to mental health treatment. Related to this issue is the question of whether both acute and long-term care can be incorporated under the same financing system. Current systems of financing mental health care are problematic for individuals who have severe and persistent mental illness, due to the disabilities connected with these illnesses. Another policy question concerns whether or not financing plans will cover preventive mental health services, such as screening for mental health problems and counseling for high-risk individuals and families.

Perhaps the primary issue in mental health care financing is cost containment. Is more money the answer to the need for treatment and services? Consumers and advocates say "yes," highlighting the unmet needs of mentally ill persons. Policy makers and taxpayers say "no," emphasizing the high level of current funding provided through a number of offices, administrations, and departments within the federal government, such as the Departments of Education, Labor, Transportation, Housing and Urban Development, and Justice. Some states make substantial budget allocations to mental health care, while others provide limited support for their mental health systems. Differences between states in financial support of mental health care raises the policy question of whether the federal government should provide additional funding for states that do not have the capacity to provide adequate levels of funding for mental health services.

A principal issue in the allocation of funds by state mental health systems is related to the amount of money spent on institutional care vs. community-based care. Over the past several years most states have reduced the number of mentally ill persons in institutions but have continued to assign a large amount of funding for institutional care. The funding of public community mental health agencies and other service programs by the states and federal government is not considered by professional experts and consumer advocacy groups to adequately meet the needs of patients/clients living in the community. This circumstance is sometimes attributed to the fact that allocations for mental health care are a part of the overall political process, leaving the mental health budget to compete with budgets for other citizen needs, such as education, criminal and juvenile justice, public health, and social welfare.

Issues for Debate

    1.   Health policies established by the Congress will/should assure universal insurance benefits for mental health care on a par with benefits for physical illness.

2. Mental health authorities and managed care organizations will/should be the customary modes of monitoring the financing and delivery of mental health care services.
3. States with limited resources will/should benefit from federal funding for the development and delivery of mental health care.
4. Funding for mental health care will/should shift from institutional care to community-based care.
5. Privatization, the use of public funds to purchase services from the private sector, will/should become the dominant mode of providing and financing mental health care.

POLICIES ON RECIPIENT RIGHTS

Consumers of mental health services have well-established rights, including due process vis-à-vis civil commitment, personal and civil rights, the right to treatment, and the right to refuse treatment. These rights are well articulated in mental health law (legislative and judicial decisions), in administrative rules and regulations, and in codes of professional ethics. Yet there continues to be tension between the legal profession and the mental health profession, between consumer advocates and mental health professionals. These tensions arise in a variety of ways as courts hear conflicting opinions about the presence or absence of mental illness and dangerousness. As a result, mental health professionals assert that some individuals in need of treatment do not receive it. On the other hand, lawyers and other patient/client advocates contend that the liberty interests of the individual are violated by unnecessary involuntary commitment to institutions (Mosher, 1994; Schwartz & Sibert, 1994).

Once confined to a psychiatric care facility, patients have the right to treatment. Complicating matters is the fact that there appears to be no consistent definition of what constitutes appropriate treatment. Even when criteria are established, such as a humane psychological and physical environment, qualified staff, and individual treatment plans, the implementation of these criteria may be lacking (Reisner & Slobogin, 1990). For consumers of mental health services provided outside of institutions, there are few, if any, legal interpretations concerning what appropriate treatment might be or whether or not an individual has a right to treatment in the community.

The other side of the treatment coin is the right to refuse treatment. This right is usually related to care in a hospital setting on an involuntary basis. While the right of refusal generally exists for individuals with mental disorders, there are issues over the conditions under which this right is qualified (such as in emergencies), who (mental health professional, judge) can grant an exception to the rule, and what procedures should be followed in determining if a person is capable of making the decision. Generally, patients must be able to give informed consent to decisions about treatment, and their advocates emphasize the need for implementation of this right, especially in light of potential adverse affects of some treatments, such as electroconvulsive therapy and medications.

Most consumers of public mental health services receive these services in the community, rather than in a hospital setting. While many states have provisions allowing judges to require that individuals accept treatment in the community, such outpatient civil commitment is not common. More usual is the assurance of patient rights in the community, such as civil rights, treatment rights, and personal rights. Implementation of these rights often depends on grievance systems and patients' rights representatives in hospitals and community mental health agencies, and there is concern as to whether or not rights officers, as employees of the mental health system, can appropriately represent the users of the system. Questions of rights and due process continue to be debated among mental health professionals, members of the legal profession, mental health consumers, their family members, and members of advocacy groups.

Issues for Debate

1. The patient's right to treatment will/should be strengthened, and the patient's right to refuse treatment will be modified for individuals with serious and persistent illness.
2. The tensions between the mental health profession and the legal profession will/should be lessened as "due process" procedures are increasingly honored and professional judgments about mental illness become more consistent.
3. New definitions of dangerousness and severe mental illness will/should permit an increase in involuntary admission to hospital care.
4. Outpatient commitment to treatment and services in the community will/should be more widely used to promote alternatives to institutional care.

SPECIAL POPULATIONS

Ethnic minorities, women, children and adolescents, homeless mentally ill persons, and older adults have been given special attention in policies established through federal legislation and national task force reports. For example, severely mentally ill homeless persons are specified as target groups in the State Comprehensive Mental Health Services Plans Act of 1986. A report of a task force sponsored by the American Psychiatric Association, entitled *Treating the Homeless Mentally Ill* (Lamb et al., 1992), declares that "the care, treatment, and rehabilitation of chronic mentally ill individuals, including those who are homeless or at risk of becoming homeless, must be given the highest priority in public mental health and receive first priority for public funding" (p. 5). Further attention to services for homeless mentally ill persons is found in a report of a federal task force, entitled *Outcasts on Main Street* (Leshner, 1992).

Older adults are given special attention in the Nursing Home Reform Amendments of the 1987 Omnibus Budget Reconciliation Act (OBRA) legislation in regard to screening for specialized mental health treatment. Amendments to the Community Mental Health Centers Act in 1975 (P.L. 94-63) called for specialized services for children and the elderly. In regard to women and mental health, this population group was designated as a priority for services by the Alcohol, Drug Abuse and Mental Health Administration in 1984 (P.L. 98-509), by a 1984 NIMH task force on a Women's Mental Health Agenda, and by the SAMHSA in 1994. While continued policy development with regard to special population groups has been of benefit to them, enactment of policies through funding and program initiatives has not been in keeping with their mental health service and treatment needs.

As a result of the ECA studies, there has been an increase in epidemiological data on some ethnic minority groups, such as African-American and Hispanic populations, on male/female differences and similarities in the distribution of mental disorders, and on age groups, including older adults. In addition, ECA studies have provided information on the help-seeking behaviors of these population groups. These data have established a foundation for the development of policies and services that respond to the underutilization of services, to the need for culturally sensitive services, and the need for research on factors leading to illness among these groups. The policy question concerns whether an already overburdened mental health system is willing and/or able to meet the needs of special population groups for psychiatric treatment and social services.

A number of major issues have been raised about the assessment and diagnostic process in relation to ethnic minorities, women, children and adolescents, homeless mentally ill persons, and older adults. In regard to ethnic minorities, one important issue centers around the lack of attention to the role of culture in the classification of mental disorders, leading to possible misdiagnosis. Another question focuses on the lack of knowledge and understanding by non-minority professionals of ethnic minority cultures and the effect this factor has on assessment and diagnosis.

Assessment and diagnostic issues regarding women center around masculine-based biases in the following areas: theoretical explanations of mental disorders among women and men; the DSM classification system; the inclusion of diagnostic categories that pertain almost exclusively to women; and the assessment and diagnosis of women by male professionals. In regard to assessment of children and adolescents, there is a consensus among professionals of the need for research on biological and social environmental factors associated with mental disorders among this group. While the DSM system includes criteria for disorders among children and adolescents, the major research need is in the area of factors that lead to mental health problems for this population.

A somewhat different situation prevails in regard to homeless mentally ill persons and older adults. Social conditions of homelessness are intertwined with psychological factors, making assessment of mental disorders more complicated. This is especially true when the assessment is carried out in the streets, shelters, food kitchens, or daytime drop-in centers. For older adults, there are complications with the assessment and diagnosis of mental disorders since the process involves neuropsychiatric and neuropsychological assessment, as well as functional assessment based on activities of daily living.

There are several common elements in the mental health treatment and service needs of these special population groups. One element is the need for social services beyond the traditional therapies. A second element is the need for these services to be coordinated. A third element is the need for modification in the ways in which treatment and services are delivered. Many of the individuals from special at-risk populations are unlikely to receive appropriate psychiatric treatment and related services. For homeless mentally ill people, a major problem has centered around the delivery of treatment and services. This is due in part to a treatment-resistant population, to a lack of responsiveness of professionals to the needs of the homeless, and to the need for methods of intervention that engage this population. One response to these issues has been the development of special forms of case management for coordinating treatment and services to homeless mentally ill persons. Major impediments to successful intervention with this population have been the lack of community-based health and social welfare services, together with fragmentation of services for these individuals.

For older adults, the major treatment issues concern the type of treatment and location of treatment. Older adults with mental disorders are more likely than other groups to be treated with medications and less likely to receive treatment from mental health professionals. Nursing homes, not hospitals, are a primary location for treatment of mentally ill older adults, and mental health care is often lacking in this type of residential care. One response to this problem has been federal legislation that requires screening of older adults before and during nursing home care.

The mental health needs of individuals with HIV/AIDS require a range of services, such as prevention, treatment and counseling, social services, and rehabilitation services (Kalichman et al., 1994). SAMHSA has recognized this group of individuals as a special population by establishing an Office on AIDS and by taking leadership in developing policies and programs for persons at risk or infected with HIV/AIDS. For example, community outreach programs have been funded to serve people with substance abuse and mental disorders who are at risk for HIV infection. The Center for Substance Abuse Treatment within SAMHSA supports community-based demonstration programs for substance abusers at risk for HIV/AIDS (SAMHSA, 1994a). Community mental health centers have been identified as appropriate locations for HIV/AIDS-related services, but these centers have not been able to provide comprehensive services due to lack of funding, lack of staff training, and lack of program development (Knox, Davis, & Friedrich, 1994).

Issues for Debate

1. Federal mental health policies will/should continue to highlight the special needs of ethnic minorities, women, children and adolescents, older adults, persons with dual diagnosis, and homeless mentally ill persons.
2. Treatment and social services will/should be modified so as to assure accessibility, availability, and acceptability of services for these special populations.
3. A newly emerging special population group in need of mental health interventions will/should consist of persons who have, or are at risk of contracting, HIV/AIDS.

ADVOCACY

In our presentation of "Issues for Debate," we have raised questions regarding "what should be" the future of mental health policies and services. An important element in determining "what should be" is the role of advocacy. Stakeholders in the mental health system invest a considerable amount of time and effort in advocating for change on behalf of mentally ill persons. These stakeholders include patients/ clients/consumers and their family members, state protection and advocacy programs, advocate groups such as the Alliance for the Mentally Ill, self-help groups that take on advocacy roles, mental health professionals, political representatives, the media, and members of the general public.

These stakeholders may differ in regard to the targets of their advocacy efforts. For patients and their families, and self-help groups, advocacy may be directed toward persons who wield political power, mental health professionals, the media, and the general public. These advocates seek changes in policies, service programs, and public attitudes and support. Professionals in direct practice are called upon to influence administrators and policy makers in mental health systems, as well as the media and the general public. Members of the news media increasingly play an advocacy role, sometimes positively and sometimes negatively, as they seek to influence mental health professionals, politicians, and/or the general public. Mental health professionals, client advocacy groups, and politicians are often influenced by public opinion to advocate changes in the financing and delivery of mental health services.

Examples of changes achieved through advocacy appear throughout this chapter, including influences on the development of overall policies and service programs, classification and epidemiology of mental disorders, financing of mental health programs, recipient rights, and policies and programs for special populations. More often than not, the various advocacy groups have not acted in concert with other groups. Increasingly it appears that for the creation of a new "cycle of reform" in mental health care, it will be necessary for all of the advocacy and professional groups to join together in promoting common goals. The challenge to mental health professionals for such cooperation and coordination is well stated in "A Call to Advocacy" by DeFries (1993):

> Adopting an advocacy role means vigorously challenging the status quo. It means not accepting the unrealistic limitations that government agencies place on resources for the poor and other vulnerable segments of society. It means rejecting political expediency that might lead to short-term financial gain. It means convincing the power establishment that preventive services are cost-effective. And it means challenging quiescent peers to join in advocacy efforts (p. 101).

Historical accounts of changes in mental health policies and pro-grams during various cycles of reform attest to the influence of advo-cacy groups and professionals on behalf of mentally ill persons. In general, however, as of the early 1990s, "mental health advocacy con-tinues to be fragmented and weak" (Mechanic & Rochefort, 1990, p. 324). State protection and advocacy programs continue to face obstacles in implementing the objectives of the Protection and Advocacy for Mentally Ill Individuals Act of 1986. This is partially caused by divi-sions in the advocacy and professional groups, especially with regard to "diagnostic categories, advocates for children and adults, emphasis on varying priorities such as prevention versus care, and on medical-legal issues such as civil commitment policy" (p. 324). Advocacy roles remind us of the political and competitive nature of policy making and program development, and the necessity of participation in the political process as a means of improving the mental health system. We hope this book will increase the reader's level of knowledge about mental health and mental illness and related policies and programs. This knowledge should provide an informed context for professional practice, including advocacy roles that support the improvement of the quality of life for individuals in need of mental health treatment and services.

References

Adebimpe, V. R. (1994). Race or ethnicity: In reply. *Hospital and Community Psychiatry, 45*(5).

Albee, G. W., & Ryan-Finn, K. D. (1994). Is primary prevention the best use of funds allocated for mental health intervention? In S. A. Kirk & S. D. Einbinder (Eds.), *Controversial issues in mental health.* Boston: Allyn and Bacon.

Alcohol, Drug Abuse, and Mental Health Administration (ADAMHA). (1992). ADAMHA reorganizes to become SAMHSA. *ADAMHA News, 18*(4).

Allen-Meares, P. (1995). *Social work with children and adolescents.* White Plains, NY: Longman.

Alliance for the Mentally Ill (A.M.I.). (1993). *Mental illness is everybody's business.* Flint, MI: A.M.I.

American Health Security Act of 1993. Washington, DC: Bureau of National Affairs.

American Psychiatric Association. (1987). *Diagnostic and statistical manual of mental disorders* (3rd ed., revised). Washington, DC: American Psychiatric Association.

American Psychiatric Association. (1994). *Diagnostic and statistical manual of mental disorders* ed (4th ed.). Washington, DC: American Psychiatric Association.

Andersen, R., & Aday, L. (1978). Access to medical care in the United States. *Medical Care, 16*(1).

Andersen, R., & Newman, J. (1973). Societal and individual determinants of medical care utilization in the United States. *Millbank Memorial Fund Quarterly, 51.*

Andrulis, D. P., & Mazade, N. A. (1983). American mental health policy: Changing directions in the 80's. *Hospital and Community Psychiatry, 34*(7).

Anthony, J. C., & Aboraya, A. (1992). Epidemiology of selected disorders. In J. E. Birren, R. B. Sloane, & G. D. Cohen (Eds.), *Handbook of mental health and aging* (2nd ed.). New York: Academic Press.

Anthony, W. A. (1992). Psychiatric rehabilitation: Key issues and future policy. *Health Affairs, 11*(2).

Anthony, W. A., Cohen, M. D., & Farkas, M. D. (1990). *Psychiatric rehabilitation.* Boston: Boston University.

Armat, V. C., & Peele, R. (1992). The need-for-treatment standard in involuntary civil commitment. In H. R. Lamb, L. L. Bachrach, & F. I. Kass (Eds.), *Treating the homeless mentally ill.* Washington, DC: American Psychiatric Association.

Armour, P. K. (1989). Mental health policymaking in the U.S.: Patterns, process, and structures. In D. A. Rochefort, *Handbook on mental health policy in the United States.* New York: Greenwood Press.

Arons, B. S., & Buck, J. A. (1994). Mental health and substance abuse benefits under national health care reform. In R. W. Manderscheid & M. A. Sonnenschein (Eds.), *Mental health, U.S., 1994.* DHHS Pub. No. (SMA) 94-3000. Washington, DC: Supt. of Docs., U.S. Government Printing Office.

Arons, B. S., Frank, R. G., Goldman, H. H., McGuire, T. G., & Stephens, S. (1994). Mental health and substance abuse coverage under health reform. *Health Affairs, 13*(1).

Ashbaugh, J. W., Leav, P. J., Manderscheid, R.W., Eaton, W. (1983). Estimates of the size and selected characteristics of the adult chronically mentally ill population living in U.S. households. *Research in Community and Mental Health, 3.*

Aviram, U. (1990). Community care of the seriously mentally ill: Continuing problems and current issues. *Community Mental Health Journal, 26*(1).

Bachrach, L. L. (1984). Deinstitutionalization and women. *American Psychologist, 39*(10).

Bachrach, L. L. (1985). *Slogans and euphemisms: The functions of semantics in mental health and mental retardation care.* Austin, TX: Hogg Foundation.

Bachrach, L. L. (1986). The future of the state mental hospital. *Hospital and Community Psychiatry, 37*(5).

Bachrach, L. L. (1988). Defining chronic mental illness: A concept paper. *Hospital and Community Psychiatry, 39*(4).

Bachrach, L. L. (1992). Psychosocial rehabilitation and psychiatry in the care of long-term patients. *American Journal of Psychiatry, 149*(1).

Bachrach, L. L. (1992a). What we know about homelessness among mentally ill persons: An analytical review and commentary. In H. R. Lamb, L. L. Bachrach, & F. I. Kass (Eds.), *Treating the homeless mentally ill.* Washington, DC: American Psychiatric Association.

Bachrach, L. L., & Nadelson, C. C. (Eds.) (1988). *Treating chronically mentally ill women.* Washington, DC: American Psychiatric Press.

Ballou, M., & Gabalac, N. W. (1985). *A feminist position on mental health.* Springfield, IL: Charles C. Thomas.

Barbanel, J. (1987, November 13). New York court frees a woman taken off the street. *The New York Times.*

Barrow, S. M., Hellman, F., Lovell, A. M., Plapinger, J. D., & Struening, E. L. (1989). *Effectiveness of programs for the mentally ill homeless.* New York: New York State Psychiatric Institute.

Bassuk, E., & Rubin, L. (1987). Homeless children: A neglected population. *American Journal of Orthopsychiatry, 57*(2).

Baxter, E., & Hopper, K. (1981). *Private lives/public spaces: Homeless adults on the streets of New York City.* New York: Community Service Society, Institute for Social Welfare Research.

Beard, J. H. (1978). The rehabilitation services of Fountain House. In L. I. Stein & M. A. Test (Eds.), *Alternatives to mental hospital treatment.* New York: Plenum.

Beard, J. H. (1982). The Fountain House model of psychiatric rehabilitation. *Psychosocial Rehabilitation Journal, 5*(1).

Becker, F. W. (1993). The politics of closing state mental hospitals: A case of increasing policy gridlock. *Community Mental Health Journal, 29*(2).

Becker, M. (1974). The health belief model and sick role behavior. *Health Education Monograph, 2.*

Beers, C. (1908). *A mind that found itself.* New York: Longmans, Green.

Belcher, J. R. (1988). Are jails replacing the mental health system for the homeless mentally ill? *Community Mental Health Journal, 24*(3).

Belcher, J. R., & Bentley, K. J. (1994). Is community-based mental health care destined to fail? In H. J. Karger & J. Midgley (Eds.), *Controversial issues in social policy.* Boston: Allyn and Bacon.

Bell, C. C. (1994). Race or ethnicity: In reply. *Hospital and Community Psychiatry, 45*(5).

Bell, L. V. (1989). From the asylum to the community in U.S. mental health care: A historical overview. In D. A. Rochefort, *Handbook on mental health policy in the United States.* New York: Greenwood Press.

Belle, D. (1990). Poverty and women's mental health. *American Psychologist, 45*(3).

Bentley, K. J. (1993). The right of psychiatric patients to refuse medication: Where should social workers stand? *Social Work, 38*(1).

Berlin, I. N. (1990). The role of the community mental health center in prevention of infant, child and adolescent disorders: Retrospect and prospect. *Community Mental Health Journal, 26*(1).

Bernal, M. E. (1990). Ethnic minority mental health training: Trends and issues. In F. C. Serafica et al. (Eds.), *Mental health of ethnic minorities.* New York: Praeger.

Bernstein, A. E., & Lenhart, S. A. (1993). *The psychodynamic treatment of women.* Washington, D.C.: American Psychiatric Association.

Birren, J. E., Sloane, R. B., & Cohen, G. D. (Eds.). (1992). *Handbook of mental health and aging* (2nd ed.). New York: Academic Press.

Blankertz, L. E., & Cnaan, R. A. (1994). Assessing the impact of two residential programs for dually diagnosed homeless individuals. *Social Service Review, 68*(4).

Bloom, B. L. (1984). *Community mental health: A general introduction* (2nd ed.). Monterey, CA: Brooks/Cole.

Blumberg, I. (1988). Taking issue: Mental health and mental illness. *Hospital and Community Psychiatry, 39*(3).

Bond, D. A., Pensec, M., Dietzen, L., McCaggerty, D., Giemza, R., & Sipple, H. W. (1991). Intensive case management for frequent users of psychiatric hospitals in a large city: A comparison of team and individual caseloads. *Psychosocial Rehabilitation Journal, 15* (1).

Borinstein, A. M. (1992). Public attitudes toward persons with mental illness. *Health Affairs, 11*(3).

Bourdon, K. H., Rae, D. S., Narrow, W. E., Manderscheid, R. W., & Regier, D. A. (1994). National prevalence and treatment of mental and addictive disorders. In R. W. Manderscheid & M. A. Sonnenscheid (Eds.), *Mental Health, U.S., 1994.* DHHS Pub. No. (SMA) 94-3000. Washington, DC: Supt. of Docs., U.S. Government Printing Office.

Breggin, P. (1994). *Talking back to Prozac.* New York: St. Martin's Press.

Bromet, E. J., & Schulberg, H. C. (1989). Special problem populations: The chronically mentally ill, elderly, children, minorities, and substance abusers. In D. A. Rochefort (Ed.), *Handbook of mental health policy in the United States.* New York: Greenwood Press.

Brooks, A. D. (1979). The impact of law on psychiatric hospitalization: Onslaught or imperative reform? *New Directions for Mental Health Services, 4.*

Brooks, A. D. (1988). Law and the chronically mentally ill. In J. Bowker (Ed.), *Services for the chronically mentally ill.* Washington, DC: Council on Social Work Education.

Broskowski, A. (1991). Current mental health care environments: Why managed care is necessary. *Professional Psychology, Research and Practice, 22*(1).

Brown, D. T., & Prout, H. T. (Eds.). (1989). *Counseling and psychotherapy with children and adolescents* (2nd ed.). Brandon, VT: Clinical Psychology Publishing Company.

Brown, L. S., & Ballou, M. (1992). *Personality and psychopathology: Feminist reappraisals.* New York: Guilford Press.

Brown, P. (Ed.). (1985). *Mental health care and social policy.* Boston: Routledge and Kegan Paul.

Bruce, M. L., Takeuchi, D. T., & Leaf, P. J. (1991). Poverty and psychiatric status. *Archives of General Psychiatry, 48*(5).

Buck, J. A., & Koyanagi, C. (1994). The Medicaid program and the Clinton plan: Implications for mental health services. *Hospital and Community Psychiatry, 45*(9).

Buckner, J. C., Bassuk, E. L., & Zima, B. (1993). Mental health issues affecting homeless women: Implications for intervention. *American Journal of Orthopsychiatry, 63*(3).

Butler, J. P. (1992). Of kindred minds: The ties that bind. In M. A. Orlandi, R. Weston, & L. G. Epstein (Eds.), *Cultural competence for evaluators.* Washington, DC: DHHS Pub. No. (ADM) 92-1884.

Cain, L. P. (1993). Obtaining social welfare benefits for persons with serious mental illness. *Hospital and Community Psychiatry, 44*(10).

Caine, E. D., & Grossman, H. T. (1992). Neuropsychiatric assessment. In J. E. Birren, R. B. Sloane, & G. D. Cohen (Eds.), *Handbook of mental health and aging* (2nd ed.). New York: Academic Press.

California Welfare and Institutional Code. (1980). Div. 5, Ch. 2, Pt. 1. St. Paul: West Publishing Company.

Callahan, D. (1994). Setting mental health priorities: Problems and possibilities. *The Milbank Quarterly, 72*(3).

Cameron, J. M. (1989). A national community mental health program: Policy initiation and progress. In D. A. Rochefort (Ed.), *Handbook on mental health policy in the United States.* New York: Greenwood Press.

Campbell, M., & Malone, R. P. (1991). Mental retardation and psychiatric disorders. *Hospital and Community Psychiatry, 42*(4).

Caras, S. (1994). Disabled: One more label. *Hospital and Community Psychiatry, 45*(4).

Chafetz, L. (1990). Withdrawal from the homeless mentally ill. *Community Mental Health Journal, 26*(5).

Cheung, F. K., & Snowden, L. R. (1990). Community mental health and ethnic minority populations. *Community Mental Health Journal, 26*(3).

Cocozzelli, C., & Hudson, C. G. (1989). Recent advances in alcoholism diagnosis and treatment assessment research: Implications for practice. *Social Service Review, 63*(4).

Cohen, D. (1988). Social work and psychotropic drug treatments. *Social Service Review, 62*(4).

Cohen, G. D. (1992). The future of mental health and aging. In J. E. Birren, R. B. Sloane, & G. D. Cohen (Eds.), *Handbook of mental health and aging* (2nd ed.). New York: Academic Press.

Coie, J. D., Watt, N. F., West, S. G., Hawkins, J. D., Asarnow, J. R., Markman, H. J., Ramey, S. L., Shure, M. B., & Long, B. (1993). The science of prevention. *American Psychologist, 48*(10).

Comas-Diaz, L., & Greene, B. (Eds.). (1994). *Women of color: Integrating ethnic and gender identities in psychotherapy.* New York: Guilford Press.

Congressional Record. (1991). Thursday, March 14, 1991. No. 44, Vol. 137.

Coryell, W. (1991). Genetics and dual diagnosis. In M. S. Gold & A. E. Slaby (Eds.), *Dual diagnosis in substance abuse.* New York: Marcel Dekker.

Cournos, F. (1989). Involuntary medication and the case of Joyce Brown. *Hospital and Community Psychiatry, 40*(7).

Croxton, T. A., Churchill, S. A., Fellin, P. A. (1988). Counseling minors without parental consent. *Child Welfare, 47*(1).

Cutler, C. E. (1991). Deconstructing the DSM-III. *Social Work, 36*(2).

Dain, N. (1994). Reflections on antipsychiatry and stigma in the history of American psychiatry. *Hospital and Community Psychiatry, 45*(10).

Davidson, G. C., & Neale, J. M. (1994). *Abnormal psychology.* New York: John Wiley.

Davis, L. E., & Proctor, E. K. (1989). *Race, gender and class.* Englewood Cliffs, NJ: Prentice-Hall.

Davis, S. (1991). An overview: Are mentally ill people really more dangerous? *Social Work, 36*(2).

DeFries, Z. (1993). A call to advocacy. *Hospital and Community Psychiatry, 44*(2).

DeLeon, P. H., VandenBos, G. R., Bulatao, E. Q. (1991). Managed mental health care: A history of the federal policy initiative. *Professional Psychology, Research and Practice, 22*(1).

Dembling, B. (1995). Colonial family care. *Psychiatric Services, 46*(2).

Dennis, D. L. (Ed.). (1987). Research methodologies concerning homeless persons with serious mental illness and/or substance abuse disorders. *Proceedings.* Albany, NY: New York State Office of Mental Health.

Dennis, D. L., Buckner, J. C., Lipton, F. R., & Levine, I. S. (1991). A decade of research and services for homeless mentally ill persons. *American Psychologist, 46*(11).

Dial, T. H., Tebbutt, R., Pion, G., Kohout, J., VandenBos, G., Johnson, M., Schervish, P., Whiting, L., Fox, J., & Merwin, E. (1990). Human resources in mental health. In R. W. Manderscheid & M. A. Sonnenschein (Eds.), *Mental Health, United States, 1990.* DHHS Pub. No. (ADM) 90-1708. Washington, DC: Supt. of Docs., U.S. Government Printing Office.

Dobelstein, A. W. (1990). Social welfare: Policy and analysis. Chicago: Nelson-Hall.

Dorwart, R. A. (1990). Managed mental health care: Myths and realities in the 1990s. *Hospital and Community Psychiatry, 41*(10).

Dorwart, R. A., & Epstein, S. S. (1993). *Privatization and mental health care.* Westport, CT: Auburn House.

Dorwart, R. A., & Schlesinger, M. (1988). Privatization of psychiatric services. *American Journal of Psychiatry 145*(5).

Dowell, D. A., & Ciarlo, J. A. (1989). An evaluative overview of the community mental health centers program. In D. A. Rochefort (Ed.), *Handbook on mental health policy in the United States.* New York: Greenwood Press.

Drake, R. E., Osher, F. C., & Wallach, M. A. (1991). Homelessness and dual diagnosis. *American Psychologist, 46*(11).

Dubin, W. R., & Fink, P. J. (1992). Effects of stigma on psychiatric treatment. In P. J. Fink & A. Tasman, *Stigma and mental illness.* Washington, DC: American Psychiatric Association.

Dulcan, M. K. (1992). Providing mental health care for children and adolescents. *Hospital and Community Psychiatry, 43*(12).

Eaton, W. W., Holzer, C. E., VonKorff, M., Anthony, J. C., Helzer, J. E., & George, L., Burnam, M. A., Boyd, J. H., Kessler, L. G., & Locke, B. Z. (1984). The design of the Epidemiologic Catchment Area Surveys. *Archives of General Psychiatry, 41*(10).

Edlefsen, M., & Baird, M. (1994). Making it work: Preventive mental health care for disadvantaged preschoolers. *Social Work, 39*(5).

Eichler, A., & Parron, D. L. (1987). *Women's mental health: Agenda for research.* Washington, DC: U.S. Dept of Health and Human Services, National Institute of Mental Health.

Eichmann, M. A., Griffin, B. P., Lyons, J. S., Larson, D. B., & Finkel, S. (1992). An estimation of the impact of OBRA-87 on nursing home care in the United States. *Hospital and Community Psychiatry, 43*(8).

Elpers, J. R. (1986). Dividing the mental health dollar: The ethics of managing scarce resources. *Hospital and Community Psychiatry, 37*(7).

England, M. J. (1992). Research must guide services for children and adolescents. *Hospital and Community Psychiatry, 43*(10).

England, M. J., & Cole, R. F. (1992). Building systems of care for youth with serious mental illness. *Hospital and Community Psychiatry, 43*(6).

Eth, S. (1990). Psychiatric ethics: Entering the 1990's. *Hospital and Community Psychiatry, 41*(4).

Fairweather, G. W. (Ed.). (1964). *Social psychology in treating mental illness: An experimental approach.* New York: John Wiley.

Fairweather, G. W. (1980). *The Fairweather lodge: A twenty-five-year retrospective.* San Francisco: Jossey-Bass.

Farr, R., Koegel, P. L., & Burnham, A. (1986). *A study of homelessness and mental illness in the skid row of Los Angeles.* Los Angeles: County Department of Mental Health.

Federal Register. (1993). May 20, 1991.

Fellin, P. (1989). Perspectives on depression among black Americans. *Health and Social Work, 14*(4).

Fellin, P., & Powell, T. (1988). Mental health services and older adult minorities: An assessment. *The Gerontologist, 28*(4).

Fernando, S. (1991). *Mental health, race, and culture.* New York: St. Martin's Press.

Fink, P. J., & Tasman, A. (1992). *Stigma and mental illness.* Washington, DC: American Psychiatric Press.

First, R. J., Rife, J. C., & Kraus, S. (1990). Case management with people who are homeless and mentally ill: Preliminary findings from an NIMH demonstration project. *Psychosocial Rehabilitation Journal, 14*(2).

Fischer, P. J., & Breakey, W. R. (1991). The epidemiology of alcohol, drug, and mental disorders among homeless persons. *American Psychologist, 46*(11).

Fleming, C. M. (1992). American Indians and Alaska natives: Changing societies past and present. In M. A. Orlandi, R. Weston, & L. G. Epstein (Eds.), *Cultural competence for evaluators.* Washington, DC: DHHS Pub. No. (ADM) 92-1884.

Flemming, A. S., Buchanan, J. G., Santos, J. F., & West, P. R. (1986). *Mental health services for the elderly. Action committee to implement the mental health recommendations of the 1981 White House conference on aging. Vol. III.* Washington, DC: American Psychological Association.

Fletcher, R. J., & Dosen, A. (Eds.). (1993). *Mental health aspects of mental retardation.* New York: Macmillan.

Flynn, J. P. (1992). *Social agency policy.* Chicago: Nelson-Hall.

Fraiberg, S. (1959). *The magic years.* New York: Scribner.

Francell, E. G. (1994). What mental illness needs: Public education and a new name. *Hospital and Community Psychiatry, 45*(5).

Frank, R.G., & McGuire, T. G. (1994). Health care reform and financing of mental health services: Distributional consequences. In R. W. Manderscheid & M. A. Sonnenschein (Eds.), *Mental Health, U.S., 1994.* DHHS Pub. No. (SMA) 94-3000. Washington, DC: Supt. of Docs., U.S. Government Printing Office.

Franklin, A. J., & Jackson, J. S. (1990). Factors contributing to positive mental health among Black Americans. In D. Ruiz (Ed.), *Handbook of mental health and mental disorder among Black Americans.* New York: Greenwood Press.

Franks, V., & Rothblum, E. D. (1983). *The stereotyping of women: Its effects on mental health.* New York: Springer.

Freedman, D. X. (1984). Psychiatric epidemiology counts. *Archives of General Psychiatry, 41*(10).

Friedman, R. M., & Kutash, K. (1992). Challenges for child and adolescent mental health. *Health Affairs, 11*(2).

Gabbard, G. O., & Gabbard, K. (1992). Cinematic stereotypes contributing to the stigmatization of psychiatrists. In P. J. Fink & A. Tasman (Eds.), *Stigma and mental illness.* Washington, DC: American Psychiatric Press.

Garfinkel, B. D., Carlson, G. A., & Weller, E. B. (1990). Psychiatric disorders in childhood and adolescence. Philadelphia: Saunders.

Gartner, A. (1985). A typology of women's self-help groups. *Social Policy 16*(3).

Gary, L. E. (1987). Attitudes of black adults toward community mental health centers. *Hospital and Community Psychiatry, 38*(10).

Gaw, A. C. (Ed.). (1993). *Culture, ethnicity, and mental illness.* Washington, DC: American Psychiatric Press.

Geller, J. L. (1990). Clinical guidelines for the use of involuntary outpatient treatment. *Hospital and Community Psychiatry, 41*(7).

George, L. K. (1987). Psychological and social determinants of help-seeking. In *Perspectives on depressive disorders: A review of recent research*. Washington, DC: U.S. Department of Health and Human Services, NIMH, D/ART Program.

George, L. K. (1989). Definition, classification, and measurement of mental health services. In C. A. Taube, D. Mechanic, & A. A. Hohmann (Eds.), *The future of mental health services research*. DHHS Pub. No. (ADM) 89-1600. Washington, DC: Supt. of Docs., U.S. Government Printing Office.

George, L. K. (1992). Community and home care for mentally ill older adults. In J. E. Birren, R. B. Sloane, & G. D. Cohen (Eds.), *Handbook of mental health and aging* (2nd ed.). New York: Academic Press.

Gerhart, U. C. (1990). *Caring for the chronically mentally ill*. Itasca, IL: Peacock.

Giamo, B. (1989). *On the Bowery: Confronting homelessness in American society*. Iowa City: University of Iowa Press.

Gilbert, N., & Specht, H. (1986). *Dimensions of social welfare policy*. Englewood Cliffs, NJ: Prentice-Hall.

Gilligan, C. (1982). *In a different voice: Psychological theory and women's development*. Cambridge, MA: Harvard University Press.

Glazer, N. (1983). *Ethnic dilemmas*. Cambridge, MA: Harvard University Press.

Glover, R., & Petrila, J. (1994). Can state mental health agencies survive health care reform? *Hospital and Community Psychiatry, 45*(9).

Goering, P. N., Wasylenki, D, St. Onge, M., Paduchak, D., & Lancee, W. (1992). Gender differences among clients of a case management program for the homeless. *Hospital and Community Psychiatry, 43*(2).

Goffman, E. (1961). *Asylums: Essays on the social situation of mental patients and other inmates*. Garden City, NY: Doubleday.

Goldfinger, S. M. (1990). Introduction: Perspectives on the homeless mentally ill. *Community Mental Health Journal, 26*(5).

Goldman, H. H., Morrissey, J. P., & Ridgely, S. (1990). The Robert Wood Johnson Foundation Program on chronic mental illness. *Hospital and Community Psychiatry, 41*(11).

Goldman, H. H., Pincus, H. A.,Taube, C. A., & Regier, D. A. (1984). Prospective payment for psychiatric hospitalization: Questions and issues. *Hospital and Community Psychiatry, 35*(5).

Goldman, H. H., & Sharfstein, S. S. (1987). Are specialized psychiatric services worth the higher cost? *American Journal of Psychiatry, 144*(5).

Goldstein, M. Z. (1994). Taking another look at the older patient and the mental health system. *Hospital and Community Psychiatry, 45*(2).

Gomez, E. (1983). The San Antonio model: A culture-oriented approach. In G. Gibson (Ed.), *Our kingdom stands on brittle glass.* Silver Springs, MD: NASW.

Gomez, M.R. (1990). Biculturalism and subjective mental health among Cuban Americans. *Social Service Review, 64*(3).

Gordon, R. (1983). An operational classification of disease prevention. *Public Health, 98*(1).

Gottlieb, G. L. (1992). Economic issues and geriatric mental health care. In J. E. Birren, R. B. Sloane, & G. D. Cohen (Eds.), *Handbook of mental health and aging* (2nd ed.). New York: Academic Press.

Gralnick, A. (1985). Build a better State Hospital: Deinstitutionalization has failed. *Hospital and Community Psychiatry, 36*(7).

Greeley, A. M., & McCready, W. C. (1974). *Ethnicity in the United States.* New York: John Wiley.

Green, J. W. (1982). *Cultural awareness in the human services.* Englewood Cliffs, NJ: Prentice-Hall.

Greer, M. A., & Greenbaum, P. (1992). Fear-based advertising and the increase in psychiatric hospitalization of adolescents. *Hospital and Community Psychiatry, 43*(10).

Grob, G. N. (1987). The forging of mental health policy in America: World War II to New Frontier. *Journal of History of Medicine and Allied Sciences, 42.*

Grob, G. N. (1991). *From asylum to community: Mental health policy in modern America.* Princeton, NJ: Princeton University Press.

Grob, G. N. (1992). Mental health policy in America: Myths and realities. *Health Affairs, 11*(3).

Grob, G. N. (1994). *The mad among us.* New York: Free Press.

Grob, G. N. (1994a). Government and mental health policy: A structural analysis. *The Milbank Quarterly, 72*(3).

Gurland, B. J., & Borne, J. E. (1989). Mental health assessment. *Danish Medical Bulletin, 7.*

Gutierrez, L., Ortega, R. M., & Suarez, Z. E. (1990). Self-help and the Latino community. In T. J. Powell (Ed.), *Working with self-help.* Silver Spring, MD: NASW.

Guttentag, M., Salasin, S., & Belle, D. (1980). *The mental health of women.* New York: Academic Press.

Haimowitz, S. (1991). Americans with disabilities act of 1990: Its significance for persons with mental illness. *Hospital and Community Psychiatry, 42*(1).

Hankin, J. (1990). Gender and mental illness. *Research in Community and Mental Health, 6*(1).

Harris v. Forklift Systems (1993), No. 92-1168.

Hasenfeld, Y. (1986). Community mental health centers as human service organizations. In W. R. Scott & B. L. Black (Eds.), *The organization of mental health services*. New York: Sage.

Hasenfeld, Y., & Gidron, B. (1993). Self-help groups and human service organizations: An interorganizational perspective. *Social Service Review, 67*(2).

Hatfield, A. B. (1991). The national alliance for the mentally ill: A decade later. *Community Mental Health Journal, 27*(2).

Hatfield, A. B., & Lefley, H. P. (1993). *Surviving mental illness*. New York: Guilford Press.

Helzer, J. E., Burnam, A., & McEvoy, L. T. (1991). Alcohol abuse and dependence. In L. N. Robins & D. A. Regier, *Psychiatric Disorders in America*. New York: Free Press.

Hillard, J. R. (1994). The past and future of psychiatric emergency services in the United States. *Hospital and Community Psychiatry, 45*(6).

Hoagwood, K., & Rupp, A. (1994). Mental health service needs, use, and costs for children and adolescents with mental disorders and their families: Preliminary evidence. In R. W. Manderscheid & M. A. Sonnenschein (Eds.), *Mental health, U.S., 1994*. DHHS Pub. No. (SMA) 94-3000. Washington, DC: Supt. of Docs., U.S. Government Printing Office.

Hoge, M. A., Davidson, L., Griffith, E. E. H., Sledge, W. H., & Howenstine, R. A. (1994). Defining managed care in public-sector psychiatry. *Hospital and Community Psychiatry, 45*(11).

Hollingsworth, E. J. (1994). Falling through the cracks: Care of the chronically mentally ill in the United States. In J. R. Hollingsworth & E. J. Hollingsworth (Eds.), *Care of the chronically and severely ill*. New York: Aldine De Gruyter.

Hospital and Community Psychiatry. (1994). News and Notes, *45*(8).

Hough, R. L., Landsverk, J. A., Karno, M., Burnam, M. A., Timbers, D. M., Escobar, J. I., & Regier, D. A. (1987). Utilization of health and mental health services by Los Angeles Mexican Americans and non-Hispanic whites. *Archives of General Psychiatry, 44*(8).

Housing and Urban Development, Department of. (1992). Understanding the Shelter Plus Care Program. Office of Special Needs Assistance Programs, Washington, DC: U.S. Government Printing Office.

Howland, R. H. (1990). Barriers to community treatment of patients with dual diagnoses. *Hospital and Community Psychiatry, 41*(10).

Human, J., & Wasem, C. (1991). Rural mental health in America. *American Psychologist, 46*(3).

Humphreys, K., & Woods, M. D. (1993). Researching mutual help group participation in a segregated society. *The Journal of Applied Behavioral Science, 29*(2).

Hyler, S. E., Gabbard, G. O., & Schneider, I. (1991). Homicidal maniacs and narcissistic parasites: Stigmatization of mentally ill persons in the movies. *Hospital and Community Psychiatry, 42*(10).

Institute of Medicine. (1989). Research on children and adolescents with mental, behavioral, and developmental disorders. Washington, DC: National Academy Press.

Isaac, R. J. (1991, May 7). Protect the mentally ill from their advocates. *The Wall Street Journal.*

Ivanoff, A., Blythe, B. J., & Tripodi, T. (1994). *Involuntary clients in social work practice.* New York: Aldine De Gruyter.

Jansson, B. S. (1993). *The reluctant welfare state.* Pacific Grove, CA: Brooks/Cole.

Jencks, C. (1994). *The homeless.* Cambridge, MA: Harvard University Press.

Jencks, S. F., Goldman, H. H., & McGuire, T. G. (1985). Challenges in bringing exempt psychiatric services under prospective payment system. *Hospital and Community Psychiatry, 36*(7).

Jenkins, S. (1980). The ethnic agency defined. *Social Service Review, 54*(2).

Johnson, A. B. (1990). *Out of bedlam: The truth about deinstitutionalization.* New York: Basic Books.

Johnson, A. B. (1994). Has deinstitutionalization failed? In S. A. Kirk & S. D. Einbinder (Eds.), *Controversial issues in mental health.* Boston: Allyn and Bacon.

Johnson, D. L. (1989). Schizophrenia as a brain disease. *American Psychologist, 44*(3).

Johnson, H. C. (Ed.). (1993). *Child mental health in the 1990's.* Washington, DC: U.S. Dept. of Health and Human Services (Center for Mental Health Services).

Johnson, H. W. (1995). *The social services* (4th ed.). Itasca, IL: Peacock.

Joint Commission on Mental Illness and Health. (1961). *Action for mental health.* New York: Basic Books.

Jones, B. E., & Gray, B. A. (1986). Problems in diagnosing schizophrenia and affective disorders among blacks. *Hospital and Community Psychiatry, 37*(1).

Jones, S. L., Roth, D., & Jones, P. K. (1995). Effect of demographic and behavioral variables on burden of caregivers of chronic mentally ill persons. *Psychiatric Services, 46*(2).

Kagle, J. D., & Kopels, S. (1994). Confidentiality after Tarasoff. *Health and Social Work, 19*(3).

Kalichman, S. C., Kelly, J. A., Johnson, J. R., & Bulto, M. (1994). Factors associated with risk of HIV infection among chronically mentally ill adults. *American Journal of Psychiatry, 151*(2).

Kaplan, M. (1983). The issue of sex bias in DSM-III. *American Psychologist, 38*(7).

Kapp, M. R. (1994). Treatment and refusal rights in mental health: Therapeutic justice and clinical accommodation. *American Journal of Orthopsychiatry, 64*(2).

Karno, M., Burnam, M. A., Escobar, J. I., Hough, R. L., & Eaton, W. W. (1983). Development of the Spanish-language version of the NIMH Diagnostic Interview Schedule. *Archives of General Psychiatry, 40*(11).

Kass, F., Spitzer, R. L., & Williams, J. B. W. (1993). An empirical study of the issue of sex bias in the diagnostic criteria of DSM-III Axis II Personality Disorders. *American Psychologist, 48*(7).

Kaufman, M. S. (1988). "Crazy" until proven innocent? Civil commitment of the mentally ill homeless. *Columbia Human Rights Law Review, 19*(2).

Keilitz, I. (1989). Legal issues in mental health care: Current perspectives. In D. A. Rochefort (Ed.), *Handbook on mental health policy in the United States.* New York: Greenwood Press.

Keilitz, I. (1990). Empirical studies of involuntary outpatient civil commitment: Is it working? *Mental and Physical Disability Law Reporter, 14*(4).

Keith, S. J., & Matthews, S. M. (1993). The value of psychiatric treatment: Its efficacy in severe mental disorders. Introduction. *Psychopharmacology Bulletin, 29*(4).

Kemp, B. J., & Mitchell, J. (1992). Functional assessment in geriatric mental health. In J. E. Birren, R. B. Sloane, & G. D. Cohen (Eds.), *Handbook of mental health and aging* (2nd ed.). New York: Academic Press.

Kessler, L. G., Burns, B. J., Shapiro, S., Tischler, G. L., George, L. K., Hough, R. L., Bodison, D., & Hiller, R. H. (1987). Psychiatric diagnoses of medical service users: Evidence from the E.C.A. Program. *American Journal of Public Health, 77*(1).

Kessler, R. C., McGonagle, K. A., Zhao, S., Nelson, C. B., Hughes, M., Eshleman, S., Wittchen, H., Kendler, K. S. (1994). Lifetime and 12-month prevalence of DSM-III-R psychiatric disorders in the United States. *Archives of General Psychiatry, 51*(1).

Kiesler, C. A. (1980). Mental health policy as a field of inquiry for psychology. *American Psychologist, 35*(12).

Kiesler, C. A. (1992). U.S. mental health policy: Doomed to fail. *American Psychologist, 47*(9).

Kiesler, C. A., & Sibulkin, A. E. (1987). *Mental hospitalization: Myths and facts about a national crisis.* Beverly Hills: Sage.

King, R. A., & Noshpitz, J. D. (1991). Pathways of growth. *Essentials of child psychiatry. Vol. 2: Psychopathology.* New York: John Wiley.

Kiresuk, T. J., Schultz, S. K., & Baxter, J. W. (1980). Tailoring evaluation to measure the accountability of mental health services to women. In M. Guttentag, S. Salasin, & D. Belle (Eds.), *The mental health of women.* New York: Academic Press.

Kirk, S. A., & Einbinder, S. D. (Eds.). (1994). *Controversial issues in mental health.* Boston: Allyn and Bacon.

Kirk, S. A., & Kutchins, H. (1988). Deliberate misdiagnosis in mental health practice. *Social Service Review, 62*(2).

Kirk, S. A., & Kutchins, H. (1992). *The selling of DSM: The rhetoric of science in psychiatry.* New York: Aldine De Gruyter.

Kirk, S. A., & Kutchins, H. (1994, June 20). Is bad writing a mental disorder? *The New York Times.*

Kirmayer, L. J. (1994). Is the concept of mental disorder culturally relative? In S. A. Kirk & S. D. Einbinder (Eds.), *Controversial issues in mental health.* Boston: Allyn and Bacon.

Klerman, G. L. (1986). Scientific and public policy perspectives on the NIMH epidemiologic catchment area program. In J. E. Barrett & R. M. Rose (Eds.), *Mental disorders in the community: Progress and challenge.* New York: Guilford Press.

Knox, M. D., Davis, M., & Friedrich, M. A. (1994). The HIV mental health spectrum. *Community Mental Health Journal, 30*(1).

Koegel, P. (1987). *Ethnographic perspectives on homeless and homeless mentally ill women.* Los Angeles: University of California.

Koegel, P., Burnham, M. A., & Farr, R. K. (1988). The prevalence of specific psychiatric disorders among homeless individuals in the inner city of Los Angeles. *Archives of General Psychiatry, 45*(12).

Kopels, S., & Kagle, J. D. (1993). Do social workers have a duty to warn? *Social Service Review, 67*(1).

Koss, M. P. (1990). The women's mental health research agenda. *American Psychologist, 45*(3).

Koyanagi, C., Manes, J., Surles, R., & Goldman, H. H. (1993). On being very smart: The mental health community's response in the health care reform debate. *Hospital and Community Psychiatry, 44*(6).

Krajeski, J. P. (1993). Cultural considerations in the psychiatric care of gay men and lesbians. In A. C. Gaw (Ed.), *Culture, ethnicity, and mental illness.* Washington, DC: American Psychiatric Press.

Kramer, P. D. (1993). *Listening to Prozac.* New York: Viking.

Kuhlman, T. L. (1994). *Psychology on the streets: Mental health practice with homeless persons.* New York: John Wiley.

Kutchins, H., & Kirk, S. A. (1987). DSM-III and social work mal-practice. *Social Work, 32*(3).

Kutchins, H., & Kirk, S. A. (1989). DSM III-R: The conflict over new psychiatric diagnoses. *Health and Social Work, 33*(3).

LaFond, J. Q. (1994). Law and the delivery of involuntary mental health services. *American Journal of Orthopsychiatry, 64*(2).

Lamb, H. R. (1992). Deinstitutionalization in the nineties. In H. R. Lamb, L. L. Bachrach, & F. I. Kass, *Treating the homeless mentally ill.* Washington, DC: American Psychiatric Association.

Lamb, H. R. (1992a). Is it time for a moratorium on deinstitutionali-zation? *Hospital and Community Psychiatry, 43*(7).

Lamb, H. R. (1994). A century and a half of psychiatric rehabilitation in the United States. *Hospital and Community Psychiatry, 45*(10).

Lamb, H. R., Bachrach, L. L., & Kass, F. I. (1992). *Treating the homeless mentally ill.* Washington, DC: American Psychiatric Association.

Lamb, H. R., & Mills, M. J. (1986). Needed changes in law and proce-dure for the chronically mentally ill. *Hospital and Community Psychiatry, 37*(5).

Landrum-Brown, J. (1990). Black mental health and racial oppres-sion. In D. S. Ruiz (Ed.), *Handbook of mental health and mental disorder among Black Americans.* New York: Greenwood Press.

LaRue, A., Yang, J., & Osato, S. (1992). Neuropsychological assess-ment. In J. E. Birren, R. B. Sloane, & G. D. Cohen (Eds.), *Handbook of mental health and aging* (2nd ed.). New York: Academic Press.

Lasswell, H. D. (1936). *Politics: Who gets what, where, how.* New York: McGraw-Hill.

Lawson, W. B., Hepler, N., Holladay, J., & Cuffel, B. (1994). Race as a factor in inpatient and outpatient admissions and diagnosis. *Hospital and Community Psychiatry, 45*(1).

Leaf, P. J., Livingston, M. M., Tischler, G. L., Weissman, M. M., Holzer, C. E., & Myers, J. K. (1985). Contact with health profes-sionals for the treatment of psychiatric and emotional problems. *Medical Care, 23*(12).

Lebowitz, B. D. (1988). Mental health services. In G. L. Maddox (Ed.), *Encyclopedia of aging.* NY: Springer.

Lebowitz, B. D., Light, D., & Bailey, F. (1987). Mental health center services for the elderly. *The Gerontologist, 27*(6).

Lebowitz, B. D., & Niederehe, G. (1992). Concepts and issues in mental health and aging. In J. E. Birren, R. B. Sloane, & G. D. Cohen (Eds.), *Handbook of mental health and aging* (2nd ed.). New York: Academic Press.

LeCroy, C. W. (1992). Enhancing the delivery of effective mental health services to children. *Social Work, 37*(3).

Lefley, H. P. (1992). The stigmatized family. In P. J. Fink & A. Tasman, *Stigma and mental illness*. Washington, DC: American Psychiatric Press.

Lehman, A. F. (1987). Capitation payment and mental health care: A review of the opportunities and risks. *Hospital and Community Psychiatry, 38*(1).

Lehman, A. F. (1988). A quality of life interview for the chronically mentally ill. *Evaluation and Program Planning, 11*.

Lehman, A. F., Myers, C. P., & Corty, E. (1989). Assessment and classification of patients with psychiatric and substance abuse syndromes. *Hospital and Community Psychiatry, 40*(10).

Leshner, A. I. (Ed.). (1992). *Outcasts on main street*. Washington, DC: Interagency Council on the Homeless, (ADM) 92-1904.

Levine, I. S., & Haggard, L. K. (1989). Homelessness as a public mental health problem. In D. A. Rochefort (Ed.), *Mental health policy in the United States*. New York: Greenwood Press.

Levine, I. S., & Rog, D. J. (1990). Mental health services for homeless mentally ill persons. *American Psychologist, 45*(8).

Lewis, M. (Ed.). (1991.) *Child and adolescent psychiatry*. Baltimore: Williams and Wilkins.

Lieberman, M. A., & Snowden, L. R. (1993). Problems in assessment prevalence and membership characteristics of self-help group participants. *The Journal of Applied Behavioral Science, 29*(2).

Link, B. G. (1987). Understanding labeling effects in the area of mental disorders: An assessment of the effects of expectations of rejection. *American Sociological Review, 52*(1).

Link, B. G., Cullen, F. T., Frank, J., & Wozniak, J. F. (1987). The social rejection of former mental patients: Understanding why labels matter. *American Journal of Sociology, 92*(6).

Linn, M. W., & Stein, S. (1989). Nursing homes as community mental health facilities. In D. A. Rochefort (Ed.), *Handbook on mental health policy in the United States*. New York: Greenwood Press.

Liptzen, B. (1992). Nursing home care. In J. E. Birren, R. B. Sloane, & G. D. Cohen (Eds.), *Handbook of mental health and aging* (2nd ed.). New York: Academic Press.

Longres, J. F. (1995). *Human behavior in the social environment* (2nd ed.). Itasca, IL: Peacock.

Loring, M., & Powell, B. (1988). Gender, race and DSM-III: A study of the objectivity of psychiatric diagnostic behavior. *Journal of Health and Social Behavior, 29*(1).

Lorion, R. P., & Allen, L. (1989). Preventive services in mental health. In D. A. Rochefort (Ed.), *Handbook on mental health policy in the United States*. New York: Greenwood Press.

Lott, J. T. (1993). Policy purposes of race and ethnicity: An assessment of federal racial and ethnic categories. *Ethnicity and Disease, 3*(3).

Lutterman, T. C. (1994). The state mental health agency profile system. In R. W. Manderscheid & M. A. Sonnenschein, *Mental health, U.S., 1994.* DHHS Pub. No. (SMA) 94-3000. Washington, DC: Supt. of Docs., U.S. Government Printing Office.

Malgady, R.G., Rogler, L. H., & Costantino, G. (1987). Ethnocultural and linguistic bias in mental health evaluation of Hispanics. *American Psychologist, 42*(3).

Marecek, J., & Kravetz, D. (1977). Women and mental health: A review of feminist change efforts. *Psychiatry, 40*(4).

Marmor, T. R., & Gill, K. C. (1989). The political and economic context of mental health care in the United States. *Journal of Health Politics, Policy and Law, 14*(1).

Marshall, P. E. (1992). The case for a national mental health policy. *Health and Community Psychiatry, 43*(11).

Martin, G. T. (1990). *Social policy in the welfare state.* Englewood Cliffs, NJ: Prentice-Hall.

Martin, M. A. (1986). *The implications of NIMH-supported research for homeless mentally ill racial and ethnic minority persons.* New York: Hunter College School of Social Work.

Matson, J. L., & Barrett, R. P. (Eds.) (1993). *Psychopathology in the mentally retarded* (2nd ed.). Boston: Allyn and Bacon.

Mayer, A., & Barry, D. D. (1992). Working with the media to destigmatize mental illness. *Hospital and Community Psychiatry, 43*(1).

Mayer, R. R. (1985). *Policy and program planning.* Englewood Cliffs, NJ: Prentice-Hall.

Mayer, R. R., & Greenwood, E. (1980). *The design of social policy research.* Englewood Cliffs, NJ: Prentice-Hall.

McAdoo, H. P. (Ed.). (1993). *Family ethnicity.* Newbury Park: Sage.

McBride, A. B. (1990). Mental health effects of women's multiple roles. *American Psychologist, 45*(3).

McCafferty, G., & Dooley, J. (1990). Involuntary outpatient commitment: An update. *Mental and Physical Disability Law Review, 14*(3).

McGoldrick, M., Pearce, J. K., & Giordano, J. (Eds.). (1982). *Ethnicity and family therapy.* New York: Guilford Press.

McNiel, D. E., & Binder, R. L. (1987). Predictive validity of judgments of dangerousness in emergency civil commitment. *American Journal of Psychiatry, 144*(2).

Mechanic, D. (1986). *From advocacy to allocation: The evolving American health care system.* New York: Free Press.

Mechanic, D. (1989.) *Mental health and social policy* (3rd ed.). Englewood Cliffs, NJ: Prentice-Hall.

Mechanic, D. (1989b). Toward the year 2000 in U.S. mental health policymaking and administration. In D. A. Rochefort (Ed.), *Handbook on mental health policy in the United States*. New York: Greenwood Press.

Mechanic, D. (1991). Strategies for integrating public mental health services. *Hospital and Community Psychiatry, 42*(8).

Mechanic, D. (1993). Mental health services in the context of health insurance reform. *The Milbank Quarterly, 71*(3).

Mechanic, D. (1994). Establishing mental health priorities. *The Milbank Quarterly, 72*(3).

Mechanic, D., & Rochefort, D. A. (1990). Deinstitutionalization: An appraisal of reform. *Annual Review of Sociology, 16*(1).

Mechanic, D., Schlesinger, M., & McAlpine, D. E. (1995). Management of mental health and substance abuse services: State of the art and early results. *The Milbank Quarterly, 73*(1).

Meinhardt, K., & Vega, W. (1987). A method for estimating under-utilization of mental health services by ethnic groups. *Hospital and Community Psychiatry, 38*(11).

Michigan Department of Mental Health (MDMH). (1982). *For better or worse? Women and the mental health system*. Lansing, MI: Michigan Department of Mental Health.

Michigan Public Act No. 123. (1989). H.B. No. 4237, Mental Health—Patient's threats to others—Duty to warn.

Milburn, N., & D'Ercole, A. (1991). Homeless women. *American Psychologist, 46*(11).

Miller, N. S. (1993). Comorbidity of psychiatric and alcohol/drug disorders: Interactions and independent status. In N. S. Miller & B. Stimmel (Eds.), *Comorbidity of addictive and psychiatric disorders*. New York: Haworth Press.

Miller, N. S., & Stimmel, B. (Eds.). (1993). *Comorbidity of addictive and psychiatric disorders*. New York: Haworth Press.

Miller, R. D. (1992). An update on involuntary civil commitment to outpatient treatment. *Hospital and Community Psychiatry, 43*(1).

Millett, K. (1990). *The loony bin trip*. New York: Simon and Schuster.

Minkoff, K., & Drake, R. (Eds.). (1991). *Dual diagnosis of major mental illness and substance disorder*. San Francisco: Jossey-Bass.

Mirkin, M. P. (Ed.). (1994). *Women in context: Toward a feminist reconstruction of psychotherapy*. New York: Guilford Press.

Monahan, J. (1992). Mental disorder and violent behavior. *American Psychologist, 47*(4).

Moran, A. E., Freedman, R. I., & Sharfstein, S. S. (1984). The journey of Sylvia Frumkin: A case study for policymakers. *Hospital and Community Psychiatry, 35*(9).

Morrissey, J. P. (1989). Commentary. In C. A. Taube, D. Mechanic, & A. A. Hohmann (Eds.), *The future of mental health services research.* DHHS Pub. No. (ADM) 89-1600. Washington, DC: Supt. of Docs., U.S. Government Printing Office.

Morrissey, J. P., & Levine, I. S. (1987). Researchers discuss latest findings, examine needs of homeless mentally ill persons. *Hospital and Community Psychiatry, 38*(8).

Morse, G. A., Calsyn, R. J., Allen, G., Tempelhoff, B., & Smith, R. (1992). Experimental comparison of the effects of three treatment programs for homeless mentally ill people. *Hospital and Community Psychiatry, 43*(10).

Mosher, L. R. (1994). Should it be easier to commit people involuntarily to treatment? In S. A. Kirk & S. D. Einbinder (Eds.), *Controversial issues in mental health.* Boston: Allyn and Bacon.

Mowbray, C. T., & Benedek, E. P. (1988). *Women's mental health research agenda: Services and treatment of mental disorders in women.* (Women's Mental Health Occupational Paper Series). Rockville, MD: NIMH.

Mowbray, C. T., Chamberlain, P., Jennings, M., & Reed, C. (1988). Consumer-run mental health services: Results from five demonstration projects. *Community Mental Health Journal, 24*(2).

Mowbray, C. T., Herman, S. E., & Hazel, K. L. (1992). Gender and serious mental illness. *Psychology of Women Quarterly, 16*(1).

Mowbray, C. T., Lanir, S., & Hulce, M. (Eds.). (1984). *Women and mental health.* New York: Haworth Press.

Mowbray, C. T., Oyserman, D., Lutz, C., & Purnell, R. (1994). *Women: The ignored majority.* Ann Arbor: University of Michigan School of Social Work.

Mowbray, C. T., Oyserman, D., Zemencuk, J. K., & Ross, S. R. (1995). Motherhood for women with serious mental illness. *American Journal of Orthopsychiatry, 65*(1).

Mrazek, P. J., & Haggerty, R. J. (Eds.). (1994). *Reducing risks for mental disorders.* Washington, DC: National Academy Press.

Mulvey, E. P. (1994). Assessing the evidence of a link between mental illness and violence. *Hospital and Community Psychiatry, 45*(7).

Munetz, M. R., & Geller, J. L. (1993). The least restrictive alternative in the postinstitutional era. *Hospital and Community Psychiatry, 44*(10).

Myers, J. K., Weissman, M. M., Tischler, G. L., Holzer, C. E., Leaf, P. J., Orvaschel, H., Anthony, J. C., Boyd, J. H., Burke, J. D., Kramer, M., & Stoltzman, R. (1984). Six-month prevalence of psychiatric disorders in three communities. *Archives of General Psychiatry, 41*(10).

Nam, C. B., & Powers, M. G. (1965). Variations in socioeconomic structure by race, residence, and life cycle. *American Sociological Review, 30*(1).

Narrow, W. E., Regier, D. A., Rae, D. S., Manderscheid, R.W., & Locke, B. Z. (1993). Use of services by persons with mental and addictive disorders. *Archives of General Psychiatry, 50*(2).

National Association of Social Workers. (1986). *Position Statement on DSM-III-R*. Alexandria, VA: NASW.

National Institute of Mental Health. (1982). *A Network for Caring.* DHHS Pub. No. (ADM) 81-1063. Washington, DC: U.S. Government Printing Office.

National Institute of Mental Health. (1991). *Caring for people with severe mental disorders: A national plan of research to improve services.* DHHS Pub. No. (ADM) 91-1762. Washington, DC: Supt. of Docs., U.S. Government Printing Office.

National Institute of Mental Health. (1991a). *National plan for research on child and adolescent mental disorders.* Washington, DC: U.S. Dept. of Health and Human Services, NIMH.

National Institute of Mental Health. (1991b). *Implementation of the national plan for research on child and adolescent mental disorders.* Washington, DC: U.S. Dept. of Health and Human Services, NIMH.

National Mental Health Association Quarterly Prevention Newsletter. (1993). 4(3).

Neighbors, H. W. (1985). Seeking professional help for personal problems: Black Americans' use of health and mental health services. *Community Mental Health Journal, 21*(3).

Neighbors, H. W., Bashshur, R., Price, R., Selig, S., Donabedian, A., & Shannon, G. (1992). Ethnic minority mental health service delivery: A review of the literature. *Research in Community and Mental Health, 7*(1).

Neighbors, H. W., Elliott, K. A., & Gant, L. M. (1990). Self-help and black Americans: A strategy for empowerment. In T. Powell (Ed.), *Working with self-help.* Silver Spring, MD: NASW.

Neighbors, H. W., Jackson, J. S., Campbell, L., & Williams, D. (1989). The influence of racial factors on psychiatric diagnosis: A review and suggestions for research. *Community Mental Health Journal, 25*(4).

Nelson, S. H. (1991). A national program supporting mental health services for Native Americans. *Hospital and Community Psychiatry, 42*(10).

Nelson, S. H., McCoy, G. F., Stetter, M., Vanderwagen, W. C. (1992). An overview of mental health services for American Indians and

Alaska natives in the 1990's. *Hospital and Community Psychiatry, 43*(3).

Nevid, J. S., Rathus, S. A., Greene, B. (1994). *Abnormal psychology.* Englewood Cliffs, NJ: Prentice-Hall.

The New York Times. (1993, November 11). Excerpts from Supreme Court ruling on sexual harassment in the workplace.

Newman, K. S. (1989). *Culture and structure in the truly disadvantaged: An anthropological perspective.* New York: Columbia University (mimeograph).

Newton, N. A., & Lazarus, L. W. (1992). Behavioral and psycho-therapeutic interventions. In J. E. Birren, R. B. Sloane, & G. D. Cohen (Eds.), *Handbook of mental health and aging* (2nd ed.). New York: Academic Press.

Nurcombe, B., & Partlett, D. F. (1994). *Child mental health and the law.* New York: Free Press.

Olfson, M. (1990). Assertive community treatment: An evaluation of the experimental evidence. *Hospital and Community Psychiatry, 41*(6).

Orlandi, M. A. (1992). The challenge of evaluating community-based prevention programs: A cross-cultural perspective. In M. S. Orlandi, R. Weston, & L. G. Epstein (Eds.), *Cultural competence for evaluators.* Washington, DC: DHHS Pub. No. (ADM) 92-1884.

Orlandi, M. A., Weston, R., & Epstein, L. G. (1992). *Cultural competence for evaluators.* DHHS Pub. No. (ADM) 92-1884. U.S. Government Printing Office.

Osher, F. C., & Kofoed, L. L. (1989). Treatment of patients with psychiatric and psychoactive substance abuse disorders. *Hospital and Community Psychiatry, 40*(10).

Oyserman, D., Mowbray, C. T., Zemencuk, J. K. (1994). *Mentally ill mothers: Contextual issues.* Detroit: Wayne State University.

Padgett, D. K., Patrick, C., Burns, B. J., & Schlesinger, H. J. (1994). Ethnicity and the use of outpatient mental health services in a national insured population. *American Journal of Public Health, 84*(2).

Padgett, D. K., Patrick, C., Burns, B. J., & Schlesinger, H. J. (1994a). Women and outpatient mental health services: Use by black, Hispanic, and white women in a national insured population. *The Journal of Mental Health Administration, 21*(4).

Pardes, H. (1986). Implementation of service programs suggested by research findings: The view from within NIMH. In J. E. Barrett, & R. M. Rose (Eds.), *Mental disorders in the community: Progress and challenge.* New York: Guilford Press.

Parry, J. (Ed.). (1994). *Mental disabilities and the Americans with Disabilities Act: A practitioner's guide to employment, insurance, treatment, public access, and housing.* Washington, DC: American Bar Association.

Patterson, T., Higgins, M., & Dyck, D. G. (1995). A collaborative approach to reduce hospitalization of developmentally disabled clients with mental illness. *Psychiatric Services, 46*(3).

Penfold, P. S., & Walker, G. A. (1983). *Women and the psychiatric paradox.* Montreal: Eden Press.

Pensinger, T., Sondheimer, D., Katz-Leavy, J. (1993). *CMHS sponsors initiative for children with mental disorders.* Washington, DC: Substance Abuse and Mental Health Services Administration.

Perlin, M. L. (1994). Law and the delivery of mental health services in the community. *American Journal of Orthopsychiatry, 64*(2).

Peterson, C. L., Patrick, S. L., & Rissmeyer, D. J. (1990). Social work's contribution to psychosocial rehabilitation. *Social Work, 35*(5).

Piliavin, I., Westerfelt, A., Wong, Y-L. I., & Afflerbach, A. (1994). Health status and health-care utilization among the homeless. *Social Service Review, 68*(2).

Plaut, T. F. A., & Arons, B. S. (1994). President Clinton's proposal for health care reform: Key provisions and issues. *Hospital and Community Psychiatry, 45*(9).

Popple, P. R., & Leighninger, L. (1993). *Social work, social welfare, and American society.* Boston: Allyn and Bacon.

Powell, T. J. (1987). *Self-help organizations and professional practice.* Silver Spring, MD: NASW.

Powell, T. J. (1993). Self-help research and policy issues. *The Journal of Applied Behavioral Science, 29*(2).

Powell, T. J. (Ed.). (1994). *Understanding the self-help organization.* Thousand Oaks, CA: Sage Publications.

Powers, S. I., Hauser, S. T., & Kilner, L. A. (1989). Adolescent mental health. *American Psychologist, 44*(2).

Praeger, D. J., & Scallet, L. J. (1992). Promoting and sustaining the health of the mind. *Health Affairs, 11*(2).

President's Commission on Mental Health. (1978). *Report to the President.* Washington, DC: Supt. of Docs., U.S. Government Printing Office.

Psychiatric Services. (1995). Data from five federal demonstration projects indicate homeless mentally ill can be helped. *Psychiatric Services, 46*(3).

Pugliesi, K. (1992). Women and mental health: Two traditions of feminist research. *Women and Health, 19*(2/3).

Pulver, G. (1988). Building a comprehensive rural economic development policy. *Northwest Report: A Newsletter of Northwest Area Foundation, 5.*

Quen, J. M. (1994). Law and psychiatry in America over the past 150 years. *Hospital and Community Psychiatry, 45*(10).

Raider, M. C. (1982). Protecting the rights of clients: Michigan sets a model for other states. *Social Work, 27*(2).

Reamer, F. G. (1989). The contemporary mental health system: Facilities, services, personnel, and finances. In D. A. Rochefort (Ed.), *Handbook on mental health policy in the United States*. New York: Greenwood Press.

Reamer, F. G. (1991). AIDS, social work, and the "duty to protect." *Social Work, 36*(1).

Reamer, F.G. (1994). *Social work malpractice and liability*. New York: Columbia University Press.

Redlick, R.W., Witkin, M. J., Atay, J. E., Manderscheid, R. W. (1994). Highlights of organized mental health services in 1990 and major national and state trends. In R. W. Manderscheid & M. A. Sonnenschein (Eds.), *Mental health, U.S., 1994*. DHHS Pub. No. (SMA) 94-3000. Washington, DC: Supt. of Docs., U.S. Government Printing Office.

Regier, D. A. (1986). Mental health service policy implications of epdiemiologic data. In J. E. Barrett & R. M. Rose (Eds.), *Mental disorders in the community: Progress and challenge*. New York: Guilford Press.

Regier, D. A., Farmer, M. E., Rae, D. S., Locke, B. Z., & Keith, S. J. (1990). Comorbidity of mental disorders with alcohol and other drug abuse. *Journal of the American Medical Association, 264*(19).

Regier, D. A., Hirschfeld, M. A., Goodwin, F. K., Burke, J. D., Lazar, J. B., & Judd, L. L. (1988). The NIMH depression awareness, recognition, and treatment program. *American Journal of Psychiatry, 145*(11).

Regier, D. A., Myers, S. K., Kramer, M., Robins, L. N., Blazer, D. G., Hough, R. L., Eaton, W. W., & Locke, B. Z. (1984). The NIMH epidemiologic catchment area program. *Archives of General Psychiatry, 41*(10).

Regier, D. A., Narrow, W. E., Rae, D. S., Manderscheid, R. W., Locke, B. Z., & Goodwin, F. K. (1993). The de facto U.S. mental and addictive disorders service system. *Archives of General Psychiatry, 50*(2).

Regnier, V., & Pynoos, J. (1992). Environmental interventions for cognitively impaired older persons. In J. E. Birren, R. B. Sloane, & G. D. Cohen (Eds.), *Handbook of mental health and aging* (2nd ed.). New York: Academic Press.

Reid, W. (1992). *Task strategies*. New York: Columbia University Press.

Reisner, R., & Slobogin, C. (1990). *Law and the mental health system* (2nd ed.). St. Paul: West Publishing.

Rendon, M. (1994). Race or ethnicity. *Hospital and Community Psychiatry, 45*(5).

Rice, D. P., Kelman, S., & Miller, L. S. (1992). The economic burden of mental illness. *Hospital and Community Psychiatry, 43*(12).

Ridgely, M. S., & Goldman, H. H. (1989). Mental health insurance. In D. A. Rochefort (Ed.), *Handbook on mental health policy in the U.S.* New York: Greenwood Press.

Ridgway, P. (1986). *Case management services for persons who are homeless and mentally ill: Report from an NIMH workshop.* Boston: Center for Psychiatric Rehabilitation, Boston University.

Rife, J. C., First, R. J., Greenlee, R. W., Miller, L. D., & Feichter, M. A. (1991). Case management with homeless mentally ill people. *Health and Social Work, 16*(1).

Rivera, F. G., Erlich, J. L.(Eds.). (1992). *Community organizing in a diverse society.* Boston: Allyn and Bacon.

Robins, L. N., Helzer, J. E., Weissman, M.Y., Orvaschel, H., Gruenberg, E., Burke, J. D., & Regier, D. A. (1984). Lifetime prevalence of specific psychiatric disorders in three sites. *Archives of General Psychiatry, 41*(10).

Robins, L. N., Locke, B. Z., & Regier, D. A. (1991). An overview of psychiatric disorders in America. In L. N. Robins & D. A. Regier (Eds.), *Psychiatric disorders in America.* New York: Free Press.

Robins, L. N., & Regier, D. A. (1991). *Psychiatric disorders in America.* New York: Free Press.

Rochefort, D. A. (Ed.). (1989). *Handbook on mental health policy in the United States.* New York: Greenwood Press.

Rochefort, D. A. (1993). *From poorhouses to homelessness: Policy analysis and mental health care.* Westport, CT: Auburn House.

Rochefort, D. A., & Logan, B. M. (1989). The alcohol, drug abuse, and mental health block grant: Origins, design, and impact. In D. A. Rochefort (Ed.), *Handbook on mental health policy in the United States.* New York: Greenwood Press.

Rofman, E. S., Askinazi, C., & Fant, E. (1980). The prediction of dangerous behavior in emergency civil commitment. *American Journal of Psychiatry, 137*(9).

Rog, D. J. (1988). *Engaging homeless persons with mental illnesses into treatment.* Alexandria, VA: National Mental Health Association.

Rog, D. J., Andranovich, G. D., & Rosenblum, S. (1987). *Intensive case management for persons who are homeless and mentally ill.* Washington, DC: COSMOS Corporation.

Rogler, L. H. (1992). The role of culture in mental health diagnosis: The need for programmatic research. *The Journal of Nervous and Mental Disease, 180*(1).

Rogler, L. H. (1993). Culture in psychiatric diagnosis: An issue of scientific accuracy. *Psychiatry, 56*(4).

Rogler, L. H., & Cortes, D. E. (1993). Help-seeking pathways: A unifying concept in mental health care. *American Journal of Psychiatry, 150*(4).

Rogler, L. H., Malgady, R. G., & Rodriguez, O. (1989). *Hispanics and mental health: A framework for research.* Malabar, FL: Krieger.

Rootes, L. E., & Aanes, D. L. (1992). A conceptual framework for understanding self-help groups. *Hospital and Community Psychiatry, 43*(4).

Rose, S. M. (1992). *Case management and social work practice.* New York: Longman.

Rosenberger, J. W. (1990). Central mental health authorities: Politically flawed? *Hospital and Community Psychiatry, 41*(11).

Rosenfield, S. (1989). Psychiatric epidemiology: An overview of methods and findings. In D. A. Rochefort (Ed.), *Handbook on mental health policy in the United States.* New York: Greenwood Press.

Rosenfield, S., & Neese-Todd, N. (1993). Elements of a psychosocial clubhouse program associated with a satisfying quality of life. *Hospital and Community Psychiatry, 44*(1).

Rosenson, M. K. (1993). Social work and the right of psychiatric patients to refuse medication: A family advocate's response. *Social Work, 38*(1).

Rosenstein, M. J., Milazzo-Sayre, L. J., & Manderscheid, R. W. (1990). Characteristics of persons using specialty inpatient, outpatent, and partial care programs in 1986. In R. W. Manderscheid & M. S. Sonnenschein (Eds.), *Mental health, United States, 1990.* NIMH. DHHS Pub. No. (ADM) 90-1708. Washington, DC: Supt. of Docs., U.S. Government Printing Office.

Rosenstock, I. (1966). Why people use health services. *Milbank Memorial Fund Quarterly, 44.*

Rosenstock, I. (1974). The health belief model and preventive health behavior. *Health Education Monographs, 2.*

Rossi, P. H. (1989). *Down and out in America.* Chicago: University of Chicago Press.

Rothman, D. J. (1971). *The discovery of the asylum.* Boston: Little, Brown.

Rothman, D. J. (1980). *Conscience and convenience: The asylum and its alternatives in progressive America.* Boston: Little, Brown.

Rothman, J. (1992). *Guidelines for case management.* Itasca, IL: Peacock.

Rothman, J. (1994). *Practice with highly vulnerable clients: Case management and community-based service.* Englewood Cliffs, NJ: Prentice-Hall.

Roueche, B. (1984, June 4). The hoofbeats of a Zebra. *The New Yorker.*

Rovner, S. (1989, June 13). When mentally ill children are overlooked. *The Washington Post.*

Russo, N. F. (1984). Women in the mental health delivery system: Implications for research and public policy. In L. E. Walker (Ed.), *Women and mental health policy.* Beverly Hills: Sage.

Russo, N. F. (1987). Position paper. In A. Eichler & D. L. Parron (Eds.), *Women's mental health: Agenda for research.* Washington, DC: U.S. Dept. of Health and Human Services, NIMH.

Russo, N. F. (1990). Overview: Forging research priorities for women's mental health. *American Psychologist, 45*(3).

Sabshin, M. (1991). Comorbidity: A central concern of psychiatry in the 1990's. *Hospital and Community Psychiatry, 42*(4).

Sales, B. D., & Shuman, D. W. (1994). Mental health law and mental health care: Introduction. *American Journal of Orthopsychiatry, 64*(2).

Salzman, C., & Nevis-Olesen, J. (1992). Psychopharmacologic treatment. In J. E. Birren, R. B. Sloane, & G. D. Cohen (Eds.), *Handbook of mental health and aging* (2nd ed.). New York: Academic Press.

SAMHSA. (l993a). *SAMHSA News, 1*(1). Washington, DC: U.S. Department of Health and Human Services.

SAMHSA. (1993b). *SAMHSA News 1*(2). Washington, DC: U.S. Department of Health and Human Services.

SAMHSA. (1993c). *SAMHSA News 1*(3). Washington, DC: U.S. Department of Health and Human Services.

SAMHSA. (1993d). *SAMHSA News 1*(4). Washington, DC: U.S. Department of Health and Human Services.

SAMHSA. (1994a). *SAMHSA News 2*(1). Washington, DC: U.S. Department of Health and Human Services.

SAMHSA. (1994b). *SAMHSA News 2*(2). Washington, DC: U.S. Department of Health and Human Services.

SAMHSA. (1994c). *SAMHSA News 2*(3). Washington, DC: U.S. Department of Health and Human Services.

SAMHSA. (1994d). *SAMHSA News 2*(4). Washington, DC: U.S. Department of Health and Human Services.

Sarafica, F. C., Schwebel, A. I., Russell, R. K., Isaac, P. D., & Myers, L. B. (1990). *Mental health of ethnic minorities.* New York: Praeger.

Sargent, M. (1989). Update on programs for the homeless mentally ill. *Hospital and Community Psychiatry, 40*(10).

Sartorius, N. (1992). Rehabilitation and quality of life. *Hospital and Community Psychiatry, 43*(12).

Savitz, S. A., Grace, J. D., & Brown, G. S. (1993). "Parity" for mental health: Can it be achieved? *Administration and Policy in Mental Health, 21*(1).

Sawyer, D. A., & Woodlock, D. J. (1994). Children's mental health services: Interactive planning and service provision. *Administration and Policy in Mental Health, 21*(4).

Schinnar, A. P., & Rothbard, A. B. (1989). Evaluation questions for Philadelphia's capitation plan for mental health services. *Hospital and Community Psychiatry, 40*(7).

Schneider, K. (1990, June 3). Feminist skewers psychiatry. *Detroit Free Press.*

Schowalter, J. E. (1989, December 8). The scapegoating of psychiatrists. *Wall Street Journal.*

Schulberg, H. C., & Manderscheid, R. W. (1989). The changing network of mental health service delivery. In C. A. Taube et al. (Eds.), *The future of mental health services research.* DHHS Pub. No. (ADM) 89-1600. Washington, DC: Supt. of Docs., U.S. Government Printing Office.

Schwartz, I. M. (1989). Hospitalization of adolescents for psychiatric and substance abuse treatment: Legal and ethical issues. *Journal of Adolescent Health Care, 10.*

Schwartz, M. S., Burns, B. J., Hiday, V. A., George, L. K., Swanson, J., & Wagner, H. R. (1995). New directions in research on involuntary outpatient commitment. *Psychiatric Services, 46*(4).

Schwartz, M. S., & Sibert, T. E. (1994). Should it be easier to commit people involuntarily to treatment? In S. A. Kirk & S. D. Einbinder (Eds.), *Controversial issues in mental health.* Boston: Allyn and Bacon.

Segal, S. P., & Kotler, P. (1989). Community residential care. In D. A. Rochefort (Ed.), *Handbook on mental health policy in the United States.* New York: Greenwood Press.

Segal, S. P., Silverman, C., & Temkin, T. (1993). Empowerment and self-help agency practice for people with mental disabilities. *Social Work, 38*(6).

Segal, S. P., Silverman, C., & Temkin, T. (1995). Characteristics and service use of long-term members of self-help agencies for mental health clients. *Psychiatric Services, 46*(3).

Segal, S. P., & VanderVoort, D. J. (1993). Daily hassles of persons with severe mental illness. *Hospital and Community Psychiatry, 44*(3).

Segal, S. P., Watson, M. A., Goldfinger, S. M., & Averbuck, D. S. (1988). Civil commitment in the psychiatric emergency room. *Archives of General Psychiatry, 45*(8).

Shah, S. A., & Sales, B. D. (1991). *Law and mental health: Major developments and research needs.* Washington, DC: U.S. Department of Health and Human Services Pub. No. (ADM) 91-1875.

Shapiro, S., Skinner, E. A., & Kessler, L. G. (1984). Utilization of health and mental health services. *Archives of General Psychiatry, 41*(10).

Shapiro, V. B., & Gisynski, M. (1989). Ghosts in the nursery revisited. *Child and Adolescent Social Work, 6*(1).

Sheehan, S. (1982). *Is there no place on earth for me?* New York: Vintage.

Sheehan, S. (1995, February 20–27). The last days of Sylvia Frumkin. *The New Yorker.*

Simon, R. I. (1992). *Psychiatry and law for clinicians.* Washington, DC: American Psychiatric Association.

Slaby, A. E. (1991). Dual diagnosis: Fact or fiction? In M. S. Gold & A. E. Slaby (Eds.), *Dual diagnosis in substance abuse.* New York: Marcel Dekker.

Slobogin, C. (1994). Involuntary community treatment of people who are violent and mentally ill: A legal analysis. *Hospital and Community Psychiatry, 45*(7).

Smith, S. R. (1994). Liability and mental health services. *American Journal of Orthopsychiatry, 64*(2).

Smith, S. R., & Meyer, R. C. (1987). *Law, behavior, and mental health: Policy and practice.* New York: New York University Press.

Smith-Bell, M., & Winslade, W. J. (1994). Privacy, confidentiality, and privilege in psychotherapeutic relationships. *American Journal of Orthopsychiatry, 64*(2).

Smyer, M. A. (Ed.). (1993). *Mental health and aging.* New York: Springer.

Snowden, L. R., & Cheung, F. K. (1990). Use of inpatient mental health services by members of ethnic minority groups. *American Psychologist, 45*(3).

Snowden, L. R., & Lieberman, M. A. (1994). African-American participation in self-help groups. In T. J. Powell (Ed.), *Understanding the self-help organization.* Thousand Oaks, CA: Sage Publications.

Sosin, M.R., Colson, P., Grossman, S. (1988). Homelessness in Chicago. Chicago: The Chicago Community Trust.

Spitzer, R. L., Gibbon, M., Skodol, A. E., Williams, J. B. W., & First, M. B. (Eds.). (1994). *DSM-IV case book.* Washington, DC: American Psychiatric Press.

State of Michigan. (1990). *Mission, values and principles.* Lansing, MI: Michigan Department of Mental Health.

State of Michigan. (1990a). *Michigan's Mental Health Code.* Lansing, MI: Michigan Department of Mental Health.

State of Michigan. (1991). *The promise of performance.* Lansing, MI: Michigan Department of Mental Health.

State of Michigan. (1992). *Delivering the promise.* Lansing, MI: Michigan Department of Mental Health.

Stefan, S. (1987). Preventive commitment: The concept and the pitfalls. *Mental and Physical Disability Law Review, 11*(4).

Stein, L. I., Test, M. A., & Marx, A. J. (1975). Alternative to the hospital: A controlled study. *American Journal of Psychiatry, 132*(5).

Steinberg, J. A., & Silverman, M. M. (Eds.). (1987). *Preventing mental disorders.* DHHS Pub. No. ADM 87-1492. Washington, DC: U.S. Government Printing Office.

Stiffman, A. R., & Davis, L. E. (1990). *Ethnic issues in adolescent mental health.* Newbury Park, CA: Sage Publications.

Stone, A. A. (1981). The right to refuse treatment. *Archives of General Psychiatry, 38*(3).

Stoner, M. R. (1995). *The civil rights of homeless people: Law, social policy, and social work practice.* New York: Aldine De Gruyter.

Stringer, D. M., & Welton, N. R. (1984). Female psychologists in policymaking positions. In L. E. Walker (Ed.), *Women and mental health policy.* Beverly Hills: Sage.

Stroul, B. A., Pires, S. A., Katz-Leavy, J. W., & Goldman, S. K. (1994). Implications of the health security act for mental health services for children and adolescents. *Hospital and Community Psychiatry, 45*(9).

Sue, S. (1977). Community mental health services to minority groups. *American Psychologist, 32*(8).

Sue, S. (1988). Psychotherapeutic services for ethnic minorities. *American Psychologist, 43*(4).

Sue, S., Fujino, D., Hu, L., Takeuchi, D., & Zane, N. (1991). Community mental health services for ethnic minority groups: A test of the cultural responsiveness hypothesis. *Journal of Consulting and Clinical Psychology, 59.*

Sue, S., & Morishima, J. K. (1982). *The mental health of Asian Americans.* San Francisco: Jossey-Bass.

Sue, S., & Zane, N. (1987). The role of culture and cultural techniques in psychotherapy. *American Psychologist, 42*(1).

Surles, R. C. (1994). Has deinstitutionalization failed? In S. A. Kirk & S. D. Einbinder (Eds.), *Controversial issues in mental health.* Boston: Allyn and Bacon.

Susser, E., Conover, S., & Struening, E. L. (1989). Problems of epidemiologic method in assessing the type and extent of mental illness among homeless adults. *Hospital and Community Psychiatry, 40*(3).

Swanson, J. W., Holzer, C. E., Ganju, V. K., & Jono, R. T. (1990). Violence and psychiatric disorder in the community: Evidence from the epidemiologic catchment area surveys. *Hospital and Community Psychiatry, 41*(7).

Swayze, F. V. (1992). Clinical case management with the homeless mentally ill. In H. R. Lamb et al., (Eds.), *Treating the homeless mentally ill.* Washington, DC: American Psychiatric Association.

Szapocznick, J., & Kurtines, W. (1980). Acculturation, biculturalism and adjustment among Cuban Americans. In A. Padilla (Ed.), *Acculturation: Theory, models, and some new findings.* Boulder, CO: Westview.

Szasz, T. (1960). The myth of mental illness. *The American Psychologist, 15*(2).

Szymanski, L. S. (1994). Mental retardation and mental health: Concepts, aetiology and incidence. In N. Bouras (Ed.), *Mental health in mental retardation.* Cambridge, England: University of Cambridge.

Szasz, T. (1974). *The myth of mental illness.* (rev. ed.). New York: Harper & Row.

Talbott, J. A. (1978). *The death of the asylum: A critical study of state hospital management services and care.* New York: Grune and Statton.

Talbott, J. A. (Ed.). (1980). *State mental hospitals: Problems and potentials.* New York: Human Services Press.

Talbott, J. A., & Sharfstein, S. S. (1986). A proposal for future funding of chronic and episodic mental illness. *Hospital and Community Psychiatry, 37*(11).

Taube, C. A. (1990). Funding and expenditures for mental illness. In R. W. Manderscheid & M. A. Sonnenschein (Eds.), *Mental health, U.S., 1990.* NIMH. DHHS Pub. No. (ADM) 90-1708. Washington, DC: Supt. of Docs., U.S. Government Printing Office.

Taube, C.A., Morlock, L., Burns, B. J., & Santos, A. B. (1990). New directions in research on Assertive Community Treatment. *Hospital and Community Psychiatry, 41*(6).

Tessler, R. C., & Dennis, D. L. (1989). *A synthesis of NIMH-funded research covering persons who are homeless and mentally ill.* Amherst, MA: University of Massachusetts.

Tessler, R. C., & Goldman, H. H. (1982). *The chronically mentally ill: Assessing community support programs.* Cambridge, MA: Ballinger.

Test, M. A. (1981). Effective community treatment of the chronically mentally ill: What is necessary? *Journal of Social Issues, 37*(3).

Thompson, J. W. (1994). Trends in the development of psychiatric services, 1944–1994. *Hospital and Community Psychiatry, 45*(10).

Thompson, J. W., Walker, R. D., & Silk-Walker, P. (1993). Psychiatric care of American Indians and Alaska natives. In A. C. Gaw (Ed.), *Culture, ethnicity, and mental illness.* Washington, DC: American Psychiatric Press.

Thompson, K. S., Griffith, E. E. H., & Leaf, P. J. (1990). A historical review of the Madison model of community care. *Hospital and Community Psychiatry, 41*(6).

Tien, L. (1992). Determinants of equality and equity for special populations served by public mental health systems. *Hospital and Community Psychiatry, 43*(11).

Toomey, G. G., First, R. J., Rife, J. C., & Belcher, J. R. (1989). Evaluating community care for homeless mentally ill people. *Social Work Research and Abstracts, 25*(4).

Torrey, E. F. (1990). *Care of the seriously mentally ill: A rating of state programs.* Washington, DC: Public Citizen Research Group and NAMI.

Torrey, E. F. (1994). Violent behavior by individuals with serious mental illness. *Hospital and Community Psychiatry, 45*(7).

Travis, C. B. (1988). *Women and health psychology: Mental health issues.* Hillsdale, N.J.: Lawrence Erlbaum Associates.

Tuma, J. M. (1989). Mental health services for children. *American Psychologist, 44*(2).

U.S. Department of Health and Human Services. (1987). *The surgeon general's workshop on self-help and public health.* DHHS, 224-250-88-2. Washington, DC: U.S. Government Printing Office.

U. S. Department of Health and Human Services. (1991). *Mental health research on homeless persons.* Program Announcement PA 91-60. Washington, DC: U.S. Government Printing Office.

U.S. Congress. (1946). P.L. 79-487. National Mental Health Act of 1946.

U.S. Congress. (1955). P.L. 84-182. Mental Health Study Act of 1955.

U.S.Congress. (1963). P.L. 88-164. Mental Retardation Facilities and Community Mental Health Centers Construction Act of 1963.

U.S. Congress. (1973). P.L. 93-222. Health Maintenance Organization Act of 1973.

U.S. Congress. (1975). P.L. 94-63. Community Mental Health Centers Act of 1975.

U.S. Congress. (1975a). P.L. 94-142. Individuals with Disabilities Act of 1975.

U.S. Congress. (1976). P.L. 94-437. Indian Health Care Improvement Act of 1976.

U.S. Congress. (1978). P.L. 95-602. Rehabilitation and Comprehensive Services and Developmental Disabilities Amendment of 1978.

U.S. Congress. (1980). P.L. 96-398. Mental Health Systems Act of 1980.

U.S. Congress. (1981). P.L. 97-35. Omnibus Reconciliation Act of 1981.

U.S. Congress. (1984). P.L. 98-509. Alcohol, Drug Abuse, and Mental Health Administration Act of 1984.

U.S. Congress. (1986). P.L. 99-319. Protection and Advocacy for Mentally Ill Individuals Act of 1986.

U.S. Congress. (1986a). P.L. 99-660. Mental Health Services Plan Act of 1986.

U.S. Congress. (1987). P.L. 100-77. Stewart B. McKinney Homeless Assistance Act of 1987.

U.S. Congress. (1987a). P.L. 100-203. Omnibus Budget Reconciliation Act of 1987: Nursing Home Reform Act.

U.S. Congress. (1990). P.L. 101-336. Americans with Disabilities Act of 1990.

U.S. Congress. (1990a). P.L. 101-625. National Affordable Housing Act of 1990.

U.S. Congress. (1992). P. L. 102-321. Alcohol, Drug Abuse, and Mental Health Administration Reorganization Act of 1992.

U.S. Congress. (1993). P.L. 103-3. Family and Medical Leave Act of 1993.

U.S. GAO. (1977). *Returning the mentally disabled to the community.* Washington, DC: U.S. Government Printing Office.

U.S. House of Representatives. (1963). Message from the President of the United States relative to mental illness and mental retardation. House of Rep. doc. 58. Washington, DC: U.S. Government Printing Office.

U.S. Public Health Service. (1990). Mental health and functional status of residents of nursing and personal care homes. *Research Findings, 7.*

Unzicker, R. E. (1994). Does NAMI represent the needs of all families with psychiatric patients? In S. A. Kirk & S. D. Einbinder (Eds.), *Controversial issues in mental health.* Boston: Allyn and Bacon.

Vega, W. A., & Murphy, J. W. (1990). Culture and the restructuring of community mental health. New York: Greenwood Press.

Wagenfeld, M. O. (Ed.). (1981). *Perspectives on rural mental health.* San Francisco: Jossey-Bass.

Wagenfeld, M. O., Murray, J. D., Mohatt, D. F., & DeBruyn, J. C. (1993). Mental health and rural America: 1980-1993. Washington, DC: Office of Rural Mental Health Research, NIMH, National Institutes of Health.

Wagner, J., & Gartner, C. (1994). Special Report: Highlights of the 45th Institute on Hospital and Community Psychiatry. *Hospital and Community Psychiatry, 45*(1).

Wakefield, J. C. (1992). The concept of mental disorder. *American Psychologist, 47*(3).

Wakefield, J. C. (1994). Is the concept of mental disorder culturally relative? In S. A. Kirk & S. D. Einbinder (Eds.), *Controversial issues in mental health*. Boston: Allyn and Bacon.

Walker, L. E. (1994). Are personality disorders gender biased? In S. A. Kirk & S. D. Einbinder, *Controversial issues in mental health*. Boston: Allyn and Bacon.

Wallace, C. J. (1993). Psychiatric rehabilitation. *Psychopharmacology Bulletin, 29*(4).

Ware, J. E., Jr. (1989). Measuring health and functional status in mental health services research. In C. A. Taube, D. Mechanic, & A. A. Hohmann (Eds.), *The future of mental health services research*. DHHS Pub. No. (ADM) 89-1600. Washington, DC: Supt. of Docs., U.S. Government Printing Office.

Waslow, M. (1993). The need for asylum revisited. *Hospital and Community Psychiatry, 44*(3).

Weiner, B. A., & Wettstein, R. M. (1993). *Legal issues in mental health care*. New York: Plenum Press.

Weiss, R. D., Mirin, S. M., & Frances, R. J. (1992). The myth of the dual diagnosis patient. *Hospital and Community Psychiatry, 43*(2).

Weisz, V. G. (1995). *Children and adolescents in need: A legal primer for the helping professional*. Thousand Oaks, CA: Sage.

Westermeyer, J. (1987). Clinical considerations in cross-cultural diagnosis. *Hospital and Community Psychiatry, 38*(2).

Wetzel, J. W. (1991). Universal mental health classification systems: Reclaiming women's experience. *Affilia, 6*(3).

Widiger, T. A., Corbitt, M. A., & Funtowicz, B. A. (1994). Are personality disorders gender biased? In S. A. Kirk & S. D. Einbinder (Eds.), *Controversial issues in mental health*. Boston: Allyn and Bacon.

Wiggins, J. G. (1994). Is primary prevention the best use of funds allocated for mental health intervention? In S. A. Kirk & S. D. Einbinder (Eds.), *Controversial issues in mental health*. Boston: Allyn and Bacon.

Wilcox, J. A., & Yates, W. R. (1993). Gender and psychiatric comorbidity in substance-abusing individuals. *The American Journal of Addictions, 2*(3).

Wilk, R. J. (1988). Involuntary outpatient commitment of the mentally ill. *Social Work, 33*(2).

Wilk, R. J. (1993). Federal legislation for rights of persons with mental illness: Obstacles to implementation. *American Journal of Orthopsychiatry, 63*(4).

Williams, J. B. W., & Spitzer, R. L. (1983). The issue of sex bias in DSM-III. *American Psychologist 38*(7).

Wilson, M. (1993). DSM-III and the transformation of American psychiatry: A history. *American Journal of Psychiatry, 150*(3).

Winslow, R. (1991, January 23). Rules will cut nursing homes' tranquilizer use. *Wall Street Journal.*

Witheridge, T. F. (1989). The assertive community treatment worker: An emerging role and its implications for professional training. *Hospital and Community Psychiatry, 40*(6).

Witkin, M .J., Atay, J. E., Fell, A. S., & Manderscheid, R. W. (1990). Specialty mental health system characteristics. In R. W. Manderscheid & M. A. Sonnenschein (Eds.), *Mental health, U.S., 1990.* NIMH. DHHS Pub. No. (ADM) 90-1708. Washington, DC: Supt. of Docs., U.S. Government Printing Office.

World Health Organization. (1948). *Constitution of the WHO Basic Documents.* Geneva: WHO.

Wright, R. (1995, March 13). The biology of violence. *New Yorker.*

Zeanah, C. H. (1993). *Handbook of infant mental health.* New York: Guilford Press.

Zigler, E. , Hopper, P., & Hall, N. W. (1993). Infant mental health and social policy. In C. H. Zeanah (Ed.), *Handbook of infant mental health.* New York: Guilford Press.

Zukerman, E. (1979). *Changing directions in the treatment of women: A mental health bibliography.* DHEW Pub. No. ADM 79-749. Washington, DC: ADAMHA.

Index

MENTAL HEALTH AND MENTAL ILLNESS
Edited by Janet Tilden
Production supervision by Kim Vander Steen
Cover design by Lesiak/Crampton Design, Inc., Park Ridge, Illinois
Composition by Point West, Inc., Carol Stream, Illinois
Paper, Finch Opaque
Printed and bound by McNaughton & Gunn, Saline, Michigan